The Skill and Courage of the
Elite 106th Rescue Wing—The True Story
of an Incredible Rescue at Sea and the Heroes
Who Pulled It Off

PARARESCUE

MICHAEL HIRSH

AVON BOOKS
An Imprint of HarperCollins*Publishers*

PARARESCUE is a journalistic account of the actual rescue at sea in December 1994 of the capsized ship, the *Salvador Allende*. The events identified in this book are true, although some of the names have been changed and identifying characteristics altered to safeguard the privacy of these individuals. The personalities, events, actions, and conversations portrayed in this book have been reconstructed using court documents, including trial transcripts, extensive interviews, letters, personal papers, research, and press accounts.

AVON BOOKS
An Imprint of HarperCollins*Publishers*
10 East 53rd Street
New York, New York 10022-5299

First Avon Books paperback printing: January 2001

Avon Trademark Reg. U.S. Pat. Off. and in Other Countries, Marca Registrada, Hecho en U.S.A.
HarperCollins® is a trademark of HarperCollins Publishers Inc.

Printed in the U.S.A.

10 9 8 7 6 5 4 3 2 1

*For Karen,
for always being there . . .*

ACKNOWLEDGMENTS

In December 1994 a group of New York Air National Guardsmen from the 106th Rescue Wing risked their lives to fly two air-refuelable helicopters more than 900 miles out to sea in the teeth of raging hurricane-force Atlantic storms in an attempt to rescue survivors of the merchant vessel *Salvador Allende*, a 450-foot cargo ship that had gone down after being knocked over by two giant rogue waves. The pilots were locked into the seats of the HH-60 for more than fifteen hours, six hours longer than any previous nonstop flight in that aircraft, and five hours past the time the Air Force wants this model of helicopter to undergo major maintenance. A feat like this had never before been attempted, and has not been duplicated since. Imagine driving your car nonstop from Boston to Chicago or Minneapolis to Dallas, with no breaks to get out of the seat and stretch or to use a bathroom, and you can begin to contemplate just the physical stress of the mission.

Before the Americans lifted off, the courageous crew of a Canadian Air Force Search and Rescue (SAR) plane flew into the same storm system, experiencing gut-busting turbulence for hours, in order to locate the ship and survivors, drop them supplies, and provide hope and encouragement just by their presence in conditions most aviators would never consider flying into, much less remain in for an extended period of time.

The motto of both the U.S. and Canadian rescue units is, "That Others May Live." Implicit is a willingness to sacrifice all to save someone they don't know, have never met, and will likely never see again. Their acknowledgment that they volunteered for SAR knowing that "big ships don't go down in good weather" is neither bravado nor false modesty, but merely their way of saying there's a humanitarian job to be done and they'll do it because they have the training, the skill, and a personal obligation to their fellow man.

The men who flew this mission could be your neighbors. They're husbands and fathers; they drive car pools, mow lawns, coach kids' soccer or hockey. Many are civilians. For them this is a part-time activity. All of them will tell you that they're ordinary men. However, when ordinary men perform extraordinary feats, knowingly risking their own lives in pursuit of neither fame nor fortune, they become heroes. *Pararescue* is the story of the *Salvador Allende* rescue mission and the selfless men who flew it. The world would be a better place with more people like them.

This narrative is based on extensive personal and telephone interviews with nearly all of the principal participants in the mission. With the passage of time, some quite specific details are remembered differently, even by crewmen who experienced them together, in the same aircraft. When conflicts of fact arose, I've chosen to report the scenario that seems most likely based on other supporting evidence, such as chronological logs or after-action situation reports. Failing that, the action is reported as remembered by the crewman most directly responsible for it.

Retelling their personal experiences often meant that the rescuers emotionally relived certain difficult moments. For their willingness to put themselves through it again, I'm most grateful.

My gratitude also goes to the former third engineer of the *Salvador Allende*, Alexander Taranov, for agreeing to tell me the story of his ordeal in minute detail, despite the emotional distress it would cause.

This book could not have been written without the assistance of several key military public affairs officers. They are: New York Air National Guard Major Jim Finkle, PIO of the 106th Rescue Wing; Canadian Air Force Captain Isabelle Robitaille, PAO of 14 Wing Greenwood; and Los Angeles–based U.S. Air Force media liaison Lieutenant Colonel Bruce Gillman. They provided access to key personnel and documentation, and Jim made it possible for me to experience aerial refueling from both ends—in one of the helicopters flown on this mission and in a C-130. (As an aside, from this nonaviator's perspective, the helicopter was bouncing all over trying to link up in twenty-knot winds; that they were able to do it in winds of sixty-plus knots several times is almost beyond comprehension.) U.S. Coast Guard Lieutenant Commander Bill Kelly was key to understanding what was happening in the Rescue Coordination Center on Governors Island, New York, during the mission, and generously took the time to help me understand both the ethos of the RCC and of the Coast Guard.

Canadian journalist Parker Barss Donham covered the story while it was still happening, and shared his taped interviews and documentation, which laid the foundation for nearly all of the subsequent interviews.

I'm grateful to all of them, as well as to many others whose names may or may not appear in the text, who provided specific information or fragments of detail that were essential for telling the story as accurately as possible.

To the individuals who read the manuscript while it was a work-in-progress and provided invaluable feedback and encouragement, a special thanks. These include my daughter Jennifer Hirsh, Roger Melton, Sam Sola, Jonathan Forrest, Graham Buschor, Mike Farrell, Patrick Creadon, Joan Parker, Adrian Wecer, and Kathy Kirkland, who typed all the interview transcripts and made certain I included all the good stuff.

I'd be remiss if I didn't thank my attorney, Thomas Patrick Rowan, and my friend and colleague, Marker Karahadian, for their generous assistance and support over the years.

Finally, my thanks go to three people at Avon Books: Bret Witter made my day with the most wonderful words a writer can hear from an editor, "I want to buy your book," and then proceeded to demonstrate what a great editor can do to help a writer tell his story better; Jennifer Sawyer Fisher, who took over after Bret's departure, proved that the School for the Care and Feeding of New Authors knew what it was doing when it granted her degree *magna cum laude*; and Jennifer's assistant, Clarissa Hutton, did a magnificent job of keeping track of all the bits and pieces, and never let an anxious e-mail go unanswered. Those who see the Internet as the place to publish in the future because there's no editor interposed between writer and reader will never know what they're missing.

Michael Hirsh
Los Angeles
January 2000

COURAGE
is resistance to fear,
mastery of fear
—not absence of fear.

MARK TWAIN

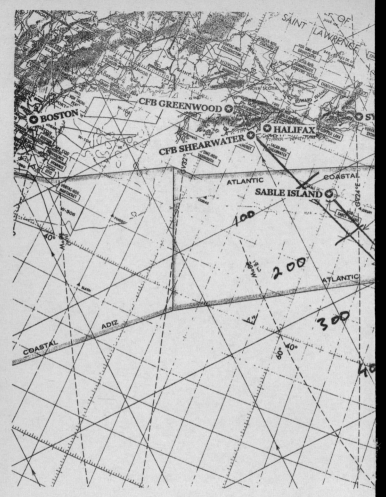

This chart was part of the briefing book given to crews on the helicopters and C-130s flying from Canadian Forces Base Shearwater to the search area southeast of where the M/V *Salvador Allende* went down. In addition to tracing the course to and from the search area, it indicates three shorter alternate routes back to land. One is to Sable Island, about 150 miles off the Nova Scotia coast. One is to the airport at Saint John's, NF, and a third is to the nearest landfall on Newfoundland. The nota-

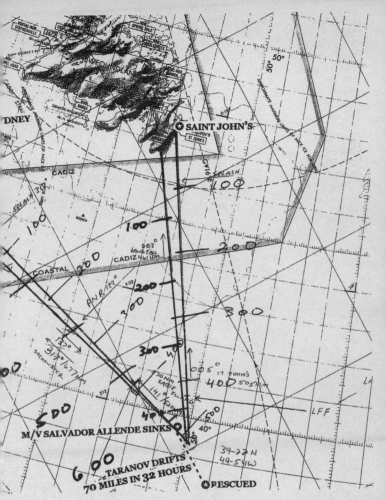

tion "splash" is an approximate point the helicopters would run out of fuel if they left the search area with tanks topped off and were unable to refuel again due to weather or other problems. "CADIZ" is Canadian Air Defense Identification Zone. Mileage from shore to the search area is indicated in nautical miles (see the Glossary for conversion to statute miles). Notations on the chart relating to the rescue of Alex Taranov were added by the author.

PARTICIPANTS IN THE
SALVADOR ALLENDE
RESCUE MISSION

106th Rescue Wing
Westhampton Beach, Long Island, New York
Jolly 14 (HH-60 Helicopter)
    Lieutenant Colonel Ed Fleming—pilot
    Captain Chris Bauer—copilot
    James "Doc" Dougherty—PJ
    Rich Davin—Flight Engineer

Jolly 08 (HH-60 Helicopter)
    Captain Graham Buschor—pilot
    Captain Eugene Sengstacken—copilot
    John Krulder—flight engineer
    Mike Moore—PJ

    Colonel David Hill, CO, 106th Rescue Wing
    Lieutenant Colonel Robert Landsiedel, CO, 102nd Rescue
      Squadron

Rescue 306 (Canadian Forces C-130 Hercules)
14 Wing Greenwood, Nova Scotia
    Captain Jonathan Forrest—pilot/aircraft commander

Captain Kevin Dort—copilot
Captain Gilles Bourgoin—navigator
Ron O'Reilly—SARtech team leader
Andre Hotton—SARtech
Marco Michaud—loadmaster

Yanky 03 (USMC KC-130T)
Marine Aircraft Group 49, Stewart Air Base
Newburgh, New York
Captain Jon Omey—pilot/aircraft commander
Captain Jim Hall—copilot
CWO4 Jack Guthrie—navigator
Bob Brought—loadmaster
Scott Blackman—first mech

RCC New York—United States Coast Guard
Lieutenant Bill Kelly—SAR Planner
Lieutenant Fred Mletzko
Petty Officer 1c Gary Parker
Lieutenant Commander Jay Topper, Sr. Controller
Commander Grant E. Leber, CO

CG 1503 (United States Coast Guard C-130)
CG Air Station, Elizabeth City, North Carolina

Air Force Rescue 852 C-130
71st Rescue Squadron, Patrick AFB, Florida

INTRODUCTION

**Aboard M/V *Salvador Allende* in the North Atlantic
10:00 P.M. local time (8:00 P.M. EST)**

As he strips to his shorts Alexander Taranov catches a glimpse of his less-than-svelte five-foot-six-inch body in the mirror hanging on the wall of the third engineer's cabin aboard the merchant vessel *Salvador Allende*. Not only is he paid better than the average Ukrainian, he eats better as well. And more often. Four meals a day are standard. The food, the sauna, gym, and swimming pool help make life at sea in the eight hours between four-hour shifts in the engine room bearable. Okay. A lot better than bearable. He loves being at sea, and now that the Cold War is over and the ship no longer carries a Communist Party-assigned First Officer to inflict weekly propaganda lectures on the crew, he has no complaints.

This is his first voyage on the 450-foot bulk cargo ship. The *Salvador Allende* is a step up in class for him. It's got automatic engine controls in an air-conditioned control room, which makes his working hours almost enjoyable.

Hanging onto a table to keep from getting upended

1

by the violent pitching and rolling caused by the storm
they're slogging through, Alex glances at the photo of
his wife and two daughters at home in the river town
of Kherson, Ukraine, then stubs out the Marlboro
from the carton he'd bought during their layover to
pick up 7,000 tons of rice in Freeport, Texas. He slides
into bed, fighting to wedge himself in place against the
bulkhead. It's ten P.M. in the middle of the North
Atlantic, somewhere between Bermuda and Newfoundland, not a happy place to be on the snowy winter night of December 8, 1994.

Alex had spent almost half his thirty-six years at
sea and couldn't remember experiencing conditions
this bad. They had begun to hit bad weather two days
earlier, and the captain ordered a course change.
Things eased up for several hours, but then the ship
returned to its original course, and the weather had
gotten progressively worse. The seas were running
thirty to fifty feet, occasionally higher. The wind was
screaming at more than sixty knots, well above the
threshold for the storm warnings that had been issued
by both the American and Canadian meteorological
services, and tossing the ship like a toy boat going
through heavy rapids. But he knew the *Salvador
Allende* was in good hands. He'd known Captain
Sergey Michailovich Chuluykov since they were in
Merchant Marine School together as teenagers. There
is nothing to be concerned about. So, wedged into his
bunk, Alex drops off to sleep. Four A.M., and his next
duty shift would be here too soon. He has no way of
knowing that he'll never see the *Salvador Allende*'s
engine room again.

Suddenly, he's shocked into consciousness by the
sounds of total chaos. Glass is breaking as dishes fly

from their shelves; furniture is crashing into walls. And there is noise. Noise from inside his cabin, from the cabin above him, from the cabin below him. At first he only senses something is not right with the ship. Long ago the mechanism deep in his inner ears that accounts for balance had adjusted to life at sea. But now, the fluid swirling past the hairs in the semicircular canals is telling his brain that something is wrong. It takes several long seconds for his brain to make the computations, to measure the forces being applied to the body and come to the inexorable conclusion that the ship is listing to port at an angle that feels like trouble. He'd been through storms before where his ship would heel over to one side and hang for what seemed like hours, but was in reality mere seconds, before rolling upright and over onto the other side. This time was different. She should have started back up by now. But she hadn't.

What Alex didn't know is that his ship had been hit by a rogue wave. Perhaps a hundred feet high, perhaps higher. This monster of the North Atlantic came rolling through the storm, slamming into the ship's starboard side, green water breaking around the bridge five stories above the open deck and knocking her over. *Knocking her over!*

The rogue wave phenomenon is always astounding, but not rare when compared with other unusual natural phenomena. Oceanographers believe that one wave in twenty-three is more than twice the height of the average wave at a given time and place. One in 1,175 is over three times the average height. And one in 300,000 is more than four times the average wave height. In a storm, that could easily be a 100-foot wall of water coming at you. When one of these monsters rolls against a fast-moving current like the Gulf Stream, in an area where the seabed topography funnels the current into oncoming waves, the face of the wave steepens precipitously and the waves break, even in deep water. What scientists and mathematicians have discovered more recently is that even in a relatively calm ocean, a rogue wave can rise up, seemingly out of nowhere, cause havoc with any boats in the immediate vicinity, and disappear, often taking the boats or ships down with them. The scientists believe this type of rogue or freak wave is created by the sea's swell interacting with not only currents, but random eddies which the oceans have in abundance. These eddies—large circular movements of water—are estimated to contain 95 percent of the kinetic energy of oceans, versus only five percent for main currents like the Gulf Stream. (For more information, see "rogue wave" in the Glossary.)

It's now believed that every year, several large vessels just disappear, victims of rogue waves. In 1966, 800 miles off New York, the Italian liner *Michelangelo* plunged into a gigantic trough that was followed by a huge wave. It crumpled the flare of the ship's bow and broke out the thick glass in the bridge windows some eighty feet above the waterline. Hundreds of passengers were injured; three were killed. Perhaps the most famous incident involving a rogue wave and a ship occurred in 1942, during World War II. The 1,000-foot-long, 81,000 ton *Queen Mary*, carrying 15,000 American troops to England, was about 700 miles from Scotland when it encountered a storm. Without warning a mountainous wave struck the ship broadside. The huge vessel rolled, listed enough for green water to wash onto her upper decks, came to within two degrees of her "point of no return," and for a moment it looked to the ship's crew as though she was going to broach. Fortunately, the ship righted itself and continued on its journey.

The *Salvador Allende* would not fare as well. Her 12,342 tons, 450 feet length, and 11,200 horsepower were insignificant to the wave that knocked her down, a momentary impediment in its journey through the storm.

Still jammed into his bunk, Alex senses the ship trying to fight her way back up, degree by degree. But another wave crashes into her starboard side and the list gets worse. Alex knows that his ship is still under power, but the list is bad—45 degrees to port, he estimates. He tries to get out of bed and stand on the deck, but quickly realizes he's actually standing on the wall, and this wall has a window. Hearing yet another strange noise, he bends down to look out the window and sees water rushing by. His cabin on the third deck of the superstructure seems to be underwater. Concerned but not panicked, he locks the window just as the ship's intercom comes to life, ordering everyone to the bridge—with life jackets.

As Alex reaches to pull the life vest from the jumble of furniture, broken glass, and clothing, another rogue wave materializes and delivers what proves to be the coup de grace. The small refrigerator in his cabin is launched across the room, barely missing his head. Suddenly it dawns on him: if he doesn't get out of the cabin now, he might never get out. Forcing open the door, Alex climbs out, then looks back, reaches in and grabs a sweater and orange thermal coveralls. Still clad only in shorts, he joins other crew members using the handrails to pull themselves up the crazily tilting stairs. There's no screaming. No yelling. Just shock at the realization that something is dreadfully wrong with their ship and they're in the middle of the ocean. At first Alex feels crazy; it's a surreal experience. As it becomes real to him, he feels sick inside.

The view from the bridge doesn't improve his condition. The *Salvador Allende* is about seventy feet wide on her open deck, and a third of that deck is underwater. As the waves crash over her, the angle of list incrementally increases.

Fighting to save his ship, Captain Sergey Michailovich Chuluykov orders the flooding of a small oil tank on the starboard side in the belief that the transfer of weight from left to right will help. "No, it's impossible," Alex tells him. "There's no connection between ballast tank and oil tank." With the chief engineer, second and fourth engineer heading to the engine room, Alex is the only one on the bridge who knows that the shipbuilders didn't allow for a way to pump ballast water or fuel oil from side to side, just bow to stern. As he's about to give the captain the bad news, another huge wave strikes the ship, knocking everyone on the bridge off their feet.

The waves in the storm are running in sets of nine. Most seem to be between thirty and forty feet high, breaking in furious whitecaps and crashing over the ship. But at least one wave in every other set is twice as high as the others, perhaps sixty or seventy feet.

Picking himself off the deck, the ship's master looks at the gauge showing engine rpm. It reads "zero." "Why did you stop the engine?" he shouts down to the chief engineer. No response. The voice of the chief radio operator breaks the silence.

"Sergey, maybe we need to send an SOS?"

It's 11:15 P.M., Thursday, December 8, 1994, on the dying M/V *Salvador Allende* in the mid-Atlantic.

Gabreski (Suffolk County) Airport
Long Island, N.Y.
9:22 P.M. EST

Early December in Suffolk County is a transitional season; temperatures are rarely lower than the mid-twenties at night, and often reach the low sixties during days characterized by rain, fog, and gusty winds.

At the home base of the New York Air National Guard's 106th Air Rescue Wing, Gabreski Airport in Westhampton Beach, just minutes from the edge of the North Atlantic, everything is quiet. Only one of the unit's four C-130 Hercules aircraft is up; the unit's commanding officer, Colonel David Hill, and Lieutenant Colonel Robert Landsiedel, the CO of the 102nd Air Rescue Squadron under Hill, are piloting the training mission, keeping their flight status current.

An hour earlier one of their five HH-60 PaveHawk helicopters, along with another C-130, had returned from a couple of hours practicing midair refueling in winds that were gusting to 32 mph. By now most of their flight crew members and Pararescuemen had already stashed their gear and headed home. There had been some excitement earlier in the day when a regular Air Force C-130, flying home to Patrick AFB, Florida, after ten days at the U.S. air base at Keflavic, Iceland, lost an engine, declared an emergency, and diverted to Gabreski. The huge Lockheed-built plane, outfitted for rescue work and air refueling, landed in the rain without incident, and was now in a hangar. Mechanics had stopped their scheduled maintenance work on one of the 106th's own Hercs in order to try and get the Patrick guys on their way home in the morning. In the operations office, the supervisor of flying, Major Mike Weiss, is completing his paperwork. Base Operations, the unit's nerve center, normally shuts down by ten o'clock. He has no reason to believe that things will be any different tonight.

Cutchogue, Long Island
9:30 P.M. EST

In the quaint, old, three-bedroom landmark house-by-the-barn at the corner of Leslie Road and Skunk Lane, Lieutenant Colonel Edward Fleming of the New York Air National Guard has just gone to bed. The ranking helicopter pilot for the 106th Rescue Wing is a charter member of the "early to bed, early to rise" fraternity. Even without a gunnery training mission to fly in the morning, the forty-seven-year-old Fleming would usually be in bed by nine.

For a couple of years now it's just been Ed and his wife, Jean, at home in Cutchogue, the center of an area of potato farms, wineries, and truck farms on the north fork of the eastern end of Long Island, just above Great Peconic Bay. Their sons, Keith and Cavan, both in their early twenties, are away at college.

Like the weather outside, Ed Fleming is in his own transitional period. Three weeks earlier he'd been removed from command of the 102nd Air Rescue Squadron, the upshot of antagonism between him and the bird colonel who commands the unit they'd both been part of for more than twenty years. Now he either must find another position with the New York Air National Guard, which would mean moving off Long Island, or retire from the service. Even though every twinge in his back tells him he's getting a little long in the tooth to be squeezing into the cockpit of a combat helicopter, retiring would not be his first choice. He still loves to fly, and he loves teaching the young pilots coming into the unit the nuances of rescue flying and aerial refueling under all sorts of circumstances.

Retirement would have one advantage: there'd be more time to make a concerted run at a doctorate. For some time he's been in the early stages of developing the concepts for a Ph.D. thesis about human decision making under stress while experiencing information overload. The topic grows naturally out of observations he's made in the cockpits of military helicopters during two dozen years of flying rescue in the regular Air Force and Air National Guard. The notion of "Doctor" Edward Fleming seems to fit right in with his serious public demeanor, a manner that is not belied by an examination of the eclectic collection of books on the nightstand next to his bed. Near the bottom of the pile are several technical flight manuals and a book or two on aviation. No novels. Nothing in any genre that might be considered pure recreational reading. On top of the pile are several volumes of Gaelic and Celtic stories which he's been studying for years. He's worked at mastering the languages with the same sort of intensity he brings to his job as a pilot and flight instructor, to the point where during occasional stressful moments of his own he's been known to let slip a Gaelic phrase or two in lieu of more traditional military expletives. It took a while, but his helicopter flight crews have gotten used to the eccentricity. They also learned that when the expletive *does* come in the King's English, the boss is *very* unhappy. To a man they like Fleming. Both officers and enlisted men call him friendly, a straight shooter, fair, a good commander, approachable. They were uniformly stupefied when he was fired.

The routine gunnery training flight in the morning was to have been Fleming's swan song as a helicopter pilot. He has no way of knowing that fate is about to intervene, refusing to let him go out with a whimper. His bang, heard 'round the world, would be a sinking ship called the *Salvador Allende* and a man named Alexander Taranov.

Centereach, Long Island
9:30 P.M. EST

Thirty-five miles west of Cutchogue, in the small suburban town of Centereach, New York Air National Guard Captain Graham Buschor, his wife Ann, and their two small children live in a very small home that's part of the original Long Island suburban development. Centereach is just far enough from the city to make the homes affordable and the rush hour commute nightmarish. Fortunately for Buschor, who will turn thirty-three in ten days, at about the same time he celebrates his ninth year with the 106th, he doesn't need to go anywhere near the Long Island Expressway on his way to the base.

For a boy who grew up wanting to fly—his father flew helicopters for an Army National Guard unit—it was a strange turn of events that led him to the Merchant Marine Academy and a commission in the Naval Reserve. But with seagoing jobs in short supply, he volunteered for the 106th, and served as a part-timer while waiting for a slot in flight school. Two years later, a freshly minted helicopter pilot, he took a full-time civilian job with Grumman Aerospace in flight test engineering while waiting for a full-time slot in the Guard. After another two years, he got the slot, and now flies rescue helicopters full-time, having been trained in the tricky business of midair refueling by Ed Fleming.

Ann Buschor is less than thrilled with her husband's passion for flying rescue missions that put him at risk in weather that would keep most pilots flying a bar stool in the officers' club. She copes with his assignments by knowing only as much as she needs to know. "Mrs. Buschor, this is the base. Captain Buschor's been sent on a mission. He asked if you could bring a bag to Operations with several changes of clothes for him. If you can have it here by noon, we'll be able to get it up to him." Where is he? When will he be back? Ann doesn't ask. She and their children, eight-year-old Alex and five-year-old Mary, are accustomed to these sudden absences, which would be easier to deal with if they'd already moved into the larger home they want, a home where Graham's told friends "there'll be more room for the kids to fight."

He'd gotten home early from the base, and the family ate dinner together—as usual, Graham did the cooking. The evening is spent in typical middle-American suburban fashion: making sure that homework gets finished, that the sibling revelry is kept to a low roar, that the usual answers to "Why do I have to go to bed now?" get the desired result, and that the kids are asleep before the parents finish wrapping and hiding all the Christmas presents that Annie has efficiently bought before the end of the first week of December.

Graham stays up a bit later than Ann, channel surfing between A&E, Discovery, and PBS. Finding nothing worth losing sleep over, he turns the TV off and heads to bed before the eleven o'clock news, missing the brief item about a ship in trouble in the North Atlantic.

Rocky Point, Long Island
9:35 P.M. EST

Twelve miles northeast of the Buschor home in Centereach is the town of Rocky Point. At the top of a gentle hill on Miller Road not far from Long Island Sound sits a cozy-looking, blue-painted house with a white sun room, the home of Tech Sergeant James "Doc" Dougherty, one of the Air Force's elite Pararescuemen—a PJ—his wife Barbara, and their four children.

The house is a Dougherty heirloom. Doc's grandfather began building it in 1926 as a summer place. He took seven years to finish it, hauling the lumber from the city on barely paved country roads, and camping nearby in a tent until it was habitable. Back then it wasn't even wired for electricity. Doc's mother was raised in the house, and Doc grew up in the little town of Shoreham, just a couple miles away. At seventeen, just out of high school, he enlisted in the Air National Guard in order to go to PJ school. When he turned twenty-two, he and Barbara made plans to be married. Doc moved into the Miller Road house and gutted it. He pulled out the original makeshift electrical wiring, brought it up to code, added insulation, and redid the plumbing, doing all the work by himself while still commuting to his day job as a New York City Housing Authority cop in Harlem. At the same time he held down a part-time slot in the PJ unit of the 106th.

Nine years and four children later, Doc is still excited about being a Pararescueman. Barbara says she expects him to grow up "any time now." It's wishful thinking.

He remains a part-timer in the Guard, working a full-time civilian job as a corrections officer in the Suffolk County Sheriff's Department. For both positions he needs to stay in shape, which is why, despite the cold on this Thursday evening, he went out to run down to the beach, along the Sound, and back home through the drizzle. The cold doesn't bother him as long as he's wearing his Gortex socks and his feet stay dry. It's a mental thing, a holdover from PJ school, where being wet and cold is de rigueur, and the rare occasions when he had warm, dry feet were moments to treasure.

As Doc peels off his running clothes he has no inkling there's a tragedy unfolding 1,200 miles to the east in which he's about to play a starring role. The last thing on his mind is the possibility of a rescue mission. He's scheduled to have a vasectomy in the morning.

ONE

The view from the Coast Guard station on Governors Island in New York harbor is world class. Two weeks before Christmas, lower Manhattan—only half a mile away—is bejeweled with colored lights that twinkle through the raindrops in the crisp night air. Up the stairs, through the security door, then up a ramp, and you're in the second-floor office that is RCC New York, also known as the Atlantic Command Center. The sixteen-by-sixteen room is all business. On one wall there's a huge map of the north Atlantic from the East Coast of the U.S. to mid-ocean, with the Rescue Coordination Center's area of responsibility (AOR)— the western Atlantic—delineated in black marker. The waters immediately north of New York's AOR are under the jurisdiction of the Canadian Forces controlled by RCC Halifax. At the moment, a few markers indicate the positions of patrolling Coast Guard cutters. Available for use are icons representing military vessels, civilian ships, and rescue aircraft.

On one side of the room are three doors: to the rest

14

room, a kitchen, and the commander's office. Three
desks covered with computers and telephones are
arranged perpendicular to the map wall. At one of the
desks is Lieutenant Fred Mletzko, the watch officer; at
another, Petty Officer First Class Gary Parker. They're
both in the second half of a twenty-four-hour shift, and
one of them is due to grab a nap on a cot in the locker
room just outside the RCC entrance. But there would
be no napping tonight. Until this moment—9:22 P.M.
EST—neither one of the men knows anything of the
drama unfolding 1,200 miles to the east.

All this changes with one ring of the phone.

Parker grabs it. "RCC New York."

Not a breath is wasted on pleasantries as a decidedly Canadian voice on the line says, "This is RCC
Halifax. We've received a mayday from the M/V *Salvador Allende*, call sign UWAG, in position 39-30
north 051-16 west. Vessel isn't a hundred percent sure
of their position. That's all the information we've got."

"Roger, we'll take it," Parker says. Hanging up, he
calls out the map coordinates, which tell them the latitude and longitude—the lat/long in rescue parlance—
to Lieutenant Mletzko, who's already starting to log
onto the AMVER data-link to Martinsburg, West Virginia. Before the Automated Mutual-assistance VEssel Rescue system comes on-line, the phone is ringing
again.

It's logged at 9:23 P.M. RCC Stavenger, Norway,
has the same mayday, with additional information.
"The vessel has a heavy list of fifty percent [sic] to
port. The thirty-one persons on board are preparing to
evacuate the ship. They will evacuate into four life
rafts. Weather: seas six meters, winds NE 37 knots.
They only have a 121.5 MHz beacon. The vessel is a

cargo ship en route from Freeport, Texas to Helsinki."
Stavenger also gives Parker the ship's marine satellite
telephone number.

The 121.5 beacon is the ship's EPIRB—Emergency
Position Indicating Radio Beacon—activated manually or by immersion in water. And the "only" in
Stavenger's message is significant: this is the least
expensive EPIRB made. Its signal is designed to be
detected by overflying commercial or military aircraft.
The signal can also be picked up by satellite, but for
detection and notification to occur, the satellite must
be within line of sight of both the EPIRB and a ground
terminal. What's worse, the radio frequency used by
these EPIRBs is congested, causing a satellite false
alert rate of 99.8 percent. And even if a real alert does
get through, two or more satellite passes are necessary
to determine if the signal really is from an EPIRB and
to determine its location, delaying rescue efforts by an
average of four to six hours.

Parker relays the information to Mletzko, who has
just called the senior controller of RCC New York,
Lieutenant Commander Jay Topper, at his home on the
island. Before Topper arrives, several more calls come
in from stations as far away as Puerto Rico and Hawaii
asking if they've heard the distress call on the 2182
frequency.

What's troubling is that the Coast Guard Greater
Antilles Section in Puerto Rico has reported the position of the ship to be 400 miles west of the location
they've received from Halifax and Stavenger. While an
airplane could quickly check out both, no aircraft are in
the area and it would be several hours before one would
arrive on-scene. When the boss arrives, he'll take the
time to play detective and sort out the discrepancy.

The computer monitor in front of Mletzko now has a text version of AMVER's surface picture on-screen, programmed to show him every participating vessel within a 200-mile radius. Twelve thousand vessels from 134 countries, ranging from tugboats to cruise ships, roughly forty percent of the world's civilian fleet belong to AMVER. On the night the *Salvador Allende* calls for help, 2,662 of them are "on plot." They are at sea, and before leaving port had filed a float plan detailing their destination, estimated time of arrival, course, and speed. Once every twenty-four hours, usually at noon, they would update the AMVER computer with their current position.

What Mletzko has on his screen is the result of the computer using the float plan data to calculate which ships should be in that 200-mile circle around the stricken vessel on the night of December 8. With a few keystrokes and clicks, he can pull up the Lloyd's of London registry information on each ship: type, size, speed, ownership, telex and satellite phone numbers. More clicks bring up float plan information indicating what radio frequencies the ship monitors, when the radio room is manned, and what type of medical personnel, if any, are on board.

By 9:36, fourteen minutes after receiving the first distress call, Parker is on the phone trying to reach the nearest AMVER vessel identified by Mlctzko, the M/V *Kansas Trader*. No luck.

A minute later he contacts the Marine Operator with a request to contact the first two AMVER ships, the *Kansas Trader* and M/V *Arabian Senator*, for a search and rescue (SAR) case. As Mletzko continues gathering data on the ships in the area of the disaster, Parker switches gears and calls the Coast Guard station at Elizabeth City, North Carolina. "How long would it take you to get *another* aircraft airborne?" He's aware that one of E-City's C-130 Hercules aircraft is being tasked by the fifth Coast Guard district in Portsmouth, Virginia. "About an hour and a half," comes the response he didn't want to hear. They also tell him that the Coast Guard District 5's C-130 is en route to Norfolk, Virginia, to take on fuel. The runway at E-City is under repair and too short at the moment for a C-130 carrying a full load of 63,000 pounds of fuel to take off. Playing the "my emergency is bigger than your emergency" card, Parker convinces E-City to give New York the aircraft that's already airborne en route to Naval Air Station Norfolk for fuel. The fact that it's still going to be a while before it's fueled for a lengthy overwater trip does not bring a smile to his face.

While Parker is on the phone to E-City, Topper comes in and Mletzko brings him up to speed. The senior controller is a "ship driver" by trade. This is his first assignment on dry land. Hearing that there are forty-foot seas with people in rafts, his only thought is "we have to get people there as fast as possible, no matter who." The quickest way to do that is launch a C-130. Parker's on the phone doing that. Since no one's had the time to actually try and call the *Salvador Allende*, Topper takes a shot. Using the emergency 800-number that gives them immediate access to the satellite phone system, he dials the stricken ship. In seconds the phone on the *Salvador Allende*'s bridge is ringing. And ringing. And ringing. He hangs up and dials again. More ringing. In his mind it's essential to get in voice contact with the ship because it's unclear whether the crew has actually abandoned ship. The first SOS said they were *planning* to get in the rafts. He's also hoping for an exact report on their position. On a stormy night, five miles off could be the difference between life and death.

The matter of whether the crew is still on the ship or in lifeboats or rafts is equally significant. Objects in the water drift at different speeds. Depending on the wind, a person actually in the water can move faster than a lifeboat or a raft. And all of them move faster than a drifting ship. Both the American and Canadian rescue units have developed computer programs that can calculate the different drifts. Using CASP—the Computer Assisted Search Program—they can program in the position of the shipwreck and calculate a reasonable estimate of how far people or rafts have drifted. If they know what the currents and wind are actually doing in the area of the wreck, their accuracy rate goes up significantly. But they won't have that information until the C-130 gets to the scene, drops a Self-Locating Datum Marker Buoy (SLDMB), and it begins sending that data by satellite link.

Unfortunately, Topper is not getting any quick answers. After dialing and redialing for nine minutes, he logs the attempt with the notation, "no joy," coastguardese for "I didn't learn anything that would make us happy."

Then Parker slams down his phone and adds another "no joy" to the log. "Marsat operator. Negative comms with *Kansas Trader* or *Arabian Senator.*"

Meanwhile, the pace of incoming calls hasn't abated. Mletzko takes two more 2182 calls in quick succession. District 5 relays that Saint John's, Newfoundland, passed a mayday signal in position 39-39N, 051-16W, which differs from the position called in by RCC Halifax at 9:22 P.M. Seconds later the Coast Guard's Greater Antilles station in Puerto Rico calls with the same position. Mletzko posts it on the wall map, scowling that they've got to deal with two different position reports based on the same mayday call.

Back at his desk, Mletzko grabs the secure red phone that will put him in immediate contact with CG Division 1 in Boston. A brief conversation, and Boston rogers that they'll divert the cutter *Seneca* to head immediately for the area of the wreck.

Pondering the new position plotted on the map, Commander Topper is getting more concerned. Which is it: 39-39 north or 39-30 north? The difference is only a bit more than ten nautical miles, but considering the weather in the area, that could translate to ten hours for ships trying to find the wreck and rescue the crew.

He picks up the phone and calls Puerto Rico. "What did you hear?"

"Mayday relay. Call sign UWAG. Position 39-39N, 051-16W and the words 'Saint John's radio.' No further information."

With a terse "roger," Topper sets the phone down.

Frustration with bad communications is part of the job. You're used to it, but that doesn't make it any easier to deal with, especially when you know thirty-one lives are on the line. You know what they're facing because you've driven cutters through forty-foot seas and spent way too much time walking on bulkheads as the vessels rolled sickeningly from side to side.

It's during that moment of introspection that a telex message arrives in the RCC. It was sent at 9:35, fourteen minutes ago by RCC Stavenger for relay through Coast Guard Atlantic Area Command in New York.

But it took fourteen minutes for COMLANTAREA to relay it to the RCC. That's a discussion to have another day. Meanwhile, it provides some definitive information.

```
FIRST POSITION GIVEN WAS 5139N [SIC], BUT WHEN
ASKED CONFIRMED 39-30N—51-16W TWICE. THE
DISTRESS CALL WAS RECEIVED VIA INMARSAT-A
FOR AOR-E REGION. THEY HAVE 121.5 EPIRB ON
BOARD AND ASKED TO ACTIVATE IT.
```

That's the best news Topper could hope for: confirmation of the sinking ship's position by voice over a telephone circuit, not code relayed through a chain of stations. The three men discuss their options and coordinate their efforts to throw as much as they can at that little spot in the North Atlantic, hoping the *search* part of the mission can be ended quickly, so they can get on with the *rescue*.

Two minutes later E-City is given a revised position and formally ordered to launch its C-130 and "proceed to the position of the mayday at best speed."

The reality of rescue in the middle of the ocean is that even if the RCC could put an entire squadron of C-130s over the survivors, tossing rafts and survival gear at them as though it were rice at a wedding, it's going to take a ship to get them out of the water. So they augment the targeted approach of singling out nearby AMVER ships with a shotgun approach: the Urgent Marine Information Bulletin—UMIB. By 10:26 the *Salvador Allende*'s mayday call has been relayed to the North Atlantic on all radio frequencies monitored by ships at sea, and would continue to be broadcast every hour for at least two days, unless modified or canceled by the RCC.

> A MAYDAY CALL WAS RECEIVED FROM THE M/V *SALVADOR ALLENDE*. THE M/V HAS 31 PEOPLE ONBOARD AND IS ABANDONING SHIP INTO FOUR LIFERAFTS IN POSITION 39-39N, 051-16W. VESSELS WITHIN THE AREA ARE REQUESTED TO DIVERT AND ASSIST. VESSELS WITHIN 40 NAUTICAL MILES THAT WOULD BE ABLE TO DIVERT ARE REQUESTED TO CONTACT RCC NEW YORK.

Forty-five minutes later the UMIB was updated, giving the position of the sinking ship as 39-29.5N, 050-06W.

Aboard the *Salvador Allende*
11:30 P.M. mid-Atlantic time

Captain Sergey Michailovich Chulyukov had been master of the *Salvador Allende* for less than six months. When he took command of the vessel after a refitting at Rostok, the sight that confronts him now would have been unimaginable. The vessel is almost lying on its port side. Its three huge cargo cranes and nearly half of the open deck are awash. He cannot deny the awful truth: he had stayed the planned course to Helsinki and sailed his ship to her death. Burial would be 16,000 feet beneath the surface of the Atlantic, roughly 148 miles northeast of where the wreck of the *Titanic* lay.

His only thought now is to save his crew. With the engine dead, he realizes there's nothing to be gained by keeping the chief engineer, second and fourth engineers, and the motorman below any longer. He dispatches a messenger with orders for them to abandon the engine room. Looking around, the captain sees twenty-three men and two women on the bridge, hanging onto anything that offers support as giant waves continue to batter the ship. They are all depending on him to save their lives. With the ship at more than a 45-degree list from which it can't possibly recover, in the worst part of a ferocious storm in the middle of the North Atlantic, he finds it difficult to voice reassurance.

The only one who can tell them if they have a chance at all is the chief radio officer, but he's left the bridge, climbing along the wall to the door that takes him to the radio room. The first SOS sent from an emergency radio on the bridge had received an almost immediate response, but the ship's name and position weren't picked up. He knows they have a better chance if he can get to the more powerful radio, and to the EPIRB.

Without waiting for confirmation from the radio officer, the captain orders everyone off the bridge and to the boat deck. It's a horrible moment, a moment of ultimate truth for the crew. The ship is going down, and any chance they have for survival lies with the two lifeboats and four survival rafts they carry. Each of the motorized lifeboats could easily take all thirty-one people off the ship. Each of the four inflatable life rafts can carry twenty people. The redundancy is planned in the event a boat or rafts on one side of the ship can't be launched. Unspoken is the obvious question: if a 450-foot-long ship can be knocked over by the storm, what chance does a thirty-foot wooden lifeboat have?

Nevertheless, there is no panic. Once every five years the Black Sea Shipping Company puts each of its seagoing employees through a survival and emergency course at a special training center aboard a retired ship in the Odessa harbor. They're taught how to deal with damage to the hull, how to put out fires, and how to survive if they have to abandon ship. Everyone is supposed to learn how to operate the life rafts and boats, how to make repairs at sea, how to collect rainwater. They are convinced that they can learn to survive almost any disaster. Now those lessons are being tested.

Despite having to crawl on the crazily canted deck and walls to avoid being injured as waves continue to assault the ship, the crew is in relative physical comfort on the bridge. They're out of the elements, communication is not difficult, and the ship's generator is continuing to provide power for lights. With each large wave slamming into the starboard side and washing over the vessel, however, they're forced to confront the fact that they can't stay on the bridge. There's no way of knowing how long she'll remain afloat. Or how fast she'll go down. The ship's officers are confident that the cargo holds filled with plastic totes or superbags of rice have not been breached. Had the hatches popped and allowed the ocean to enter, the ship would have gone down bow first, like a rock. And while they speculate that the cargo may have shifted to port from the impact of the two giant waves, they know that at least up until a few hours earlier, there had been no water in the holds. Wells are provided to check regularly for water in each of the five holds, and every test in this voyage thus far had come up dry.

The first person to the door at the rear of the bridge

struggles to open it and tie it open. With the ship almost on its side, the door is functioning more like a hatch that has to be lifted up rather than pulled open. Slowly they move off the bridge and down a stairwell past the crew's gym. This is the lifeboat deck.

Opening the door, the crew is confronted with the full force of the storm, which is showing no signs of abating. Although the air temperature is in the low forties, they're being pelted with wind-driven rain and salt spray, and tormented by the awful roar of the storm tearing at them as they cling to whatever handhold can be found. Beyond the range of the lights on the superstructure there is nothing but blackness. Survival training in Odessa harbor was never like this.

The last person to emerge through the door is the radio officer. "Don't worry, guys," he shouts in Russian, trying to be heard above the storm. "People on shore heard our SOS. They got it all. They're going to help us, so everything is going to be okay." He had either found the captain's supply of vodka or was a born optimist who refused to let the reality of their plight dampen his spirits.

For a moment everyone is heartened, and they turn to the task of releasing the portside lifeboat from its davits. With the ship almost on its left side, they believe gravity will help them free the boat and launch it. Had the wind and waves abated, that would have been a good theory. Instead, as they free the ropes holding the boat in its davits, it begins swinging crazily. As the ship rocks with the impact of another fifty-foot wave, the stern of the lifeboat smashes into the superstructure. Pieces of wood fly off in the wind, and the boat drops to the water, useless. Another wave picks the *Salvador Allende* up, then drops her back down, and the lifeboat is torn loose of the ship and drifts out of reach, and with it goes the optimism of the radio officer. They've got one boat, which will be difficult to launch from the high side of the listing ship; four rafts, which have to be inflated in a seventy-mile-an-hour wind; and no idea how much longer the ship will stay afloat.

RCC New York
10:14 P.M. EST

```
090314Z DEC 94
FM: COMLANTAREA COGARD NEW YORK
TO: EASYLINK
KANSAS TRADER
ARABIAN SENATOR
SIBOELF
OBOELIF
NEBRASKA
BRAVO SUCCESS
BENNY QUEEN
SUBJ: 31 POB ABANDON SHIP
1. YOU ARE REQUESTED TO DIVERT AS SOON AS
POSSIBLE TO POSITION 39-39N, 051-16W. 31 POB
ARE ABANDONING SHIP INTO FOUR LIFE RAFTS.
2. REQUEST YOU CONTACT RCC NEW YORK VIA
VOICE UPON RECEIPT OF THIS MESSAGE (212) 668-
7055.
3. REGARDS. RCC NEW YORK TELEX 12775
```

The four phone lines into the Governors Island facility are smoking. In rapid succession: RCC Halifax calls and tells Fred Mletzko that two vessels, prob-

ably Russian fishing trawlers, are diverting to help.
Gary Parker contacts New York Ocean Control, where
all transatlantic flights are monitored, and asks for
"high-flyer reports"—contacts from airliners that may
pick up the EPIRB signal from the *Salvador Allende*.
RCC Halifax calls again at 10:25. Their Hercules will
be airborne in ninety minutes, and should be on scene
in four hours. At 10:17, Coast Guard District 1 in
Boston tells Lieutenant Commander Topper that the
106th Rescue Wing of the New York Air National
Guard has a C-130 with pararescue jumpers in the air
on a training mission. Can he use them? At 10:19,
Topper is on the phone to Captain Chris Baur at the
106th's home base, Gabreski Field in Westhampton
Beach, Long Island. Baur says the crew aboard that
aircraft is "bagged." By the time they return they'll
have limited out on their duty day. But he offers them
a C-130 with air-droppable life rafts in the morning.
Topper says he'll call back.

HQ 106th Rescue Wing
Long Island
10:28 P.M. EST

Helicopter pilot Chris Baur and flight engineer Dennis
Richardson were putting away gear following a training flight when the call came from RCC New York.
When he hangs up the phone, Baur plots the location
of the *Salvador Allende* on a map so the two of them
can try and figure out if it's a doable mission for the
HH-60 helicopters. While the ship is sinking approximately 1,200 miles due east of Westhampton Beach,
they immediately see that by hugging the coast and

flying first to Halifax and then out to sea, they cut several hundred miles off the overwater portion of the mission. Would it be easy? No. The HH-60 carries enough fuel for four hours of flight; however, they're air refuelable off the unit's C-130 tankers, and with multiple refuelings, it's doable. They recognize that crew fatigue would be a major factor, but when they weigh that against the possibility of saving thirty lives, it still comes up doable.

Knowing that they themselves can't fly because they won't have adequate crew rest, they figure they can "cock" the helicopters—get them ready to go, so crews coming in at two or three in the morning can take off immediately after getting briefed. Cocking the aircraft means running through the entire preflight checklist, which includes checking power settings while hovering at ten feet over the tarmac and turning all the switches on so that when the flight crew hits the battery switch, they're ready to go. All they need to do then is run the scramble checklist, and in less than ten minutes they're in the air.

They'd also plan to check the hoists on each of the aircraft, and run the ⅜-inch braided steel cables out to their full 300-foot length, then run it through their hands while bringing it back in slowly to make sure none of the strands are broken.

While they're concerned solely with the helicopters, both men know that maintenance crews for the C-130 tankers work all night, and these aircraft too could be prepped in order to relocate to Halifax first thing in the morning carrying fresh crews, who would then fly the refueling mission.

With thirty people in the water and the knowledge that their unit is the only one in the western Atlantic equipped to pull it off—neither the U.S. Coast Guard nor the Canadians have air-refuelable helicopters— they go down to the base operations office to lay out their plan for the supervisor of flying, Major Mike Weiss. Weiss immediately contacts the 106th Air Rescue Wing's commanding officer, Colonel David Hill, Jr., who along with the 102nd Rescue Squadron's commanding officer, Lieutenant Colonel Robert Landsiedel, are flying a C-130 back to base from a training mission over southern New England.

Telling Weiss they'll get back to him quickly, the fixed-wing pilots immediately do the same thing Baur and Richardson did: plot the location of the sinking on a map. It's instantly apparent that this will be a long and difficult mission. Because they've been on duty since early in the day, it's not one they can fly. Heading out to sea immediately is out of the question.

A few minutes later they contact Weiss to say they're returning to base to begin the necessary planning so a C-130 crew can be ready to go first thing in the morning. Asking about Baur and Richardson's notion of cocking the helicopters, Weiss is told that because of the distance "the helicopters are not a player in this mission."

Hill has been with the 106th for twenty-seven years, twenty-two of them flying rescue C-130s, the last three as commanding officer. The year he took over, the unit lost a helicopter during a night search in stormy weather sixty miles out to sea. One of the five crewmen onboard was never found, and the impact of the loss on Hill was profound. Losing men in combat is to be expected; losing them on a civilian rescue mission that they don't have to undertake is something else. The scheme to send helicopters 800 miles out to sea in weather bad enough to sink a ship brings back nothing but bad memories. Yes, this time there are thirty-one people in the water, but it still doesn't sway him. Clearly this is a mission for surface ships, not for helicopters configured to fly relatively short missions for the purpose of plucking a downed pilot out of enemy territory.

The dismissal of their plan enrages Baur, but there's nothing he and Richardson can do about it. Logic is on the side of the brass. The distance to the sinking ship is daunting for a helicopter that can't venture more than 200 miles offshore without air refueling. The low altitude weather between Long Island and the *Salvador Allende* is terrible, and at the wreck site it's worse. They'd have to allow at least six hours for the outbound trip in the HH-60 PaveHawk helicopters and six hours back. Add the time it would take to locate and hoist thirty-one people off the ship or out of lifeboats, and you'd be seriously stretching the physical limits of crew endurance. Now consider the need for eight to ten midair refuelings from C-130 tankers for each of the two helicopters, a maneuver that requires absolute precision in the unnatural mating of two distinctly different type of aircraft—one of which has to fly as slow as it can, the other almost as fast as it can. Factor in extreme pilot fatigue and physical debilitation caused by a dozen hours or more of intense vibration while strapped into a seat the Air Force says shouldn't be continuously occupied for more than four, add the hard-learned lesson that Murphy never rests—if it can go wrong, it will, at the worst possible time—and remember the loss three years earlier when they couldn't refuel in a horrific Atlantic winter storm, and to the logical mind there's only one conclusion possible: sending the helicopters is a fool's errand.

Hill knows there's never been an HH-60 helicopter mission that even approaches the length of nonstop flight time that this one would require. The issue is not how long the pilots would have to stay in the air; it's how long they'd have to stay in their seats.

The HH-60 was originally designed by Sikorsky as a utility helicopter for the Army to fly missions lasting no longer than two hours. When the Air Force bought it, the craft was modified with internal fuel tanks, increasing flight time to four hours, but nothing was done to make the seats more comfortable. In fact, where the pilot and copilot's seats in the original Army model were designed to dump over backward so a wounded flier could be pulled out of the chair and treated by someone in the rear cabin, the addition of numerous radios directly behind the seats eliminated even that option in the Air Force model. When air refueling capability was added, the range of the HH-60 technically became "unlimited," even though the aircraft was supposed to undergo major maintenance after ten hours of flight. But "unlimited" in an HH-60 is not the same as "unlimited" in the older, larger H-3, the famed Jolly Green Giant of the Vietnam War. In that aircraft, the flight crew can leave their seats and move around, even grab a nap in the back. It's what made possible a 1967 record-setting, nonstop New York to Paris flight in two HH-3Es of the 48th ARR Squadron, closely paralleling Charles Lindbergh's route forty years earlier. The 4,270-mile flight took 30 hours 46 minutes.

Colonel Hill is acutely aware of the fatigue factor in the constantly vibrating HH-60 seats. He's cognizant of the horrible flying conditions and the unprecedented distance from shore to sinking ship. He's not looking to have his pilots set endurance records . . . or die trying. That's why he believes the best chance for the rescue of the *Salvador Allende* crew rests with AMVER ships being redirected to the scene. What the 106th can and will do is to send a C-130 to help locate the survivors and lead ships to them.

The helicopter crewmen and the Pararescuemen, however, are prone to disagree. After all, they're in the air rescue business by choice. They chose it knowing it's the most dangerous job in the Air Force. And they chose the 106th Air Rescue Wing. It's no secret that the loss of Jolly 110 during a civilian rescue attempt three years earlier, and the death of an extremely popular and highly skilled PJ, Rick Smith, had changed the command's attitude toward volunteering for non-military missions. Yet the helicopter crews and PJs all think that had Rick Smith been around on the night of December 8, 1994, he'd have his gear packed and ready to go; it didn't matter to him whether it was twelve miles or 1,200—this is what they had signed up to do.

TWO

It is my duty as Pararescueman to save life and aid the injured. I will be prepared at all times to perform my assigned duties quickly and efficiently, placing these duties before personal desires and comforts. These things I do, "That others may live."

THE PARARESCUEMAN'S CODE

Despite numerous instances of heroic courage, no PJ has ever won the Medal of Honor. That's a fact.

No PJ ever will. That's folklore, but thus far it's stood the test of time. The basic measuring stick for the nation's highest military honor is heroism above and beyond the call of duty. As PJs explain it to the properly awed who've read chronicles of their exploits, there is no assignment, no action, they can take that is above and beyond *their* call of duty.

It's a standard of performance that makes them unique among the nation's special operations forces. Neither the vaunted Navy SEALs, the Army Special Forces, nor the Marine Corps Force Recon are expected to rise to that level of performance.

Because the standard is so high, relatively few are able to attain it. The PJs are the most elite combat unit in the American Armed Forces; there are slots for only 316 on active duty, another 110 in the Air National Guard, and 108 more in the Reserves, with roughly ten percent of the slots unfilled. The numbers vary, usually in relation to the number of available rescue aircraft. (By way of contrast, there are more than 3,100 Navy SEALs on active duty, 604 officers and 2,555 enlisted.) The Air Force would like to increase the number of PJs available for assignment, but not at the cost of lowering their standards. It's not that there aren't a lot of candidates for the job, rather, that even after they pass the rigorous physical tests to get into the indoctrination course, the dropout rate is high.

What's it take to get into the ten-week course at Lackland Air Force Base near San Antonio? Applicants for both pararescue and combat controller specialties are required to swim 25 meters underwater without surfacing, swim 1,000 meters in twenty-six minutes or less, run 1.5 miles in less than 10:30, and, with only three minutes of rest between exercises, do eight chin-ups in a minute, fifty sit-ups in two minutes, continuous push-ups until either muscle failure or three minutes—whichever comes first—followed by flutter kicks to muscle failure or three minutes. And the entire test must be completed within a three hour time limit.

In 1998, 201 candidates began the class; only 45 graduated. In 1999, 159 candidates started the program, only 39 graduated. On average, only one in four who start training will make it through the indoctrination course and begin the fifteen-month-long journey that leads to the designation "Pararescueman."

The first two weeks of the indoctrination course

are spent learning the basic exercises and classroom lessons in order to make sure everyone is on the same page when training begins in earnest. All of this is accompanied by the orchestrated kind of verbal harassment that military drill sergeants have refined to an art form. Candidates may also be required to retake the physical fitness test that was required to get them into PJ school. The instructors have discovered that occasionally an overeager recruiting sergeant has helped a candidate "pencil-whip" the test, so they use the retest to flush the system of people who are not physically prepared for the rigors of the course. (In some cases highly motivated recruits will be given a chance to get in shape, pass the test, and get assigned to the next group going through the course.) The process of "self-elimination" begins in the first week. The *Indoctrination Course Handbook* says:

> The majority of those who select themselves out do so in the first week of training. They lose the focus of why they are here, having difficulty seeing past training elements that exist in this phase, and lose sight of their long-term goals. Phase I is made up of three skills demonstrations areas. It is the most difficult and intense phase in the program.

Those who stick it out through those first two weeks next get to discover the special joys of "Motivation Week." Seven "nonstandard duty days" of up to twenty-one hours each, all under the watchful eyes of two shifts of instructors who, rumor has it, were valedictorians of their class at the de Sade Charm School. But the physical and mental abuse plays a legitimate role in the making of a PJ. Once again, the *Indoctrination Course Handbook*:

> Motivation week is your gut check. By that we mean, do you really want to be here and eventually wear the beret of a Pararescueman or Combat Controller? If you do, you will graduate motivation week and move on to Phase II.
>
> You will be challenged to the limit of your ability to overcome physical as well as mental stresses during a non-standard training day. The words "Never Quit" have not had as much meaning up to this point as they will during this week. Throughout the week you will be given the opportunity to function as a team. You will learn how even the simplest team tasks can be adversely affected by high physical and mental stress when you have moved out of your comfort zone. More important, you will learn, hopefully, how to overcome such adversity. Do not think for a minute that you are tough enough to get through this alone. Rely on your team and never quit!

Harassment doesn't stop with the conclusion of "Motivation Week." One veteran PJ is sure that over the course of his ten weeks, he did more than 10,000 push-ups, the punishment-of-choice for infractions real and imagined.

Master Sergeant Tim Malloy, who's been a PJ at the 106th since 1976, still remembers how tough they made it for him as a twenty-one-year-old who joined the Air Force just to be a Pararescueman. He'd lettered in ten sports at Islip High School on Long Island, and thought he was in great shape before entering indoctrination. Even the fact that he'd never been a swimmer didn't daunt him. Nevertheless, the mental and physical stress finally got to him. "I had decided that I'd had enough. I went to the office, went up to the sergeant and said, 'I want to quit.' He said, 'Oh, good, I knew you were going to quit.' He handed me this piece of paper and said, 'Sign it.' The piece of paper basically read, 'I am a loser. I am a waste of life. I can't handle a little stress.' Then he said, 'Sign at the bottom.'

"I picked up a pen and looked at it. Then said, 'Aaaarrrgggghhh. I can't sign this.' So I put it down and walked away. And the sergeant said, 'By the way . . . ' I said 'Yes, sergeant?' 'Drop down and give me three hundred push-ups.' I was in a leaning rest doing push-ups for the next three hours."

The harassment doesn't stop at the water's edge. It follows the candidates into the pool, where the goal is to "drownproof" them. It's essential that they are fully confident in the water, irrespective of the conditions. In order to pass the indoctrination phase, they have to do five minutes of bobbing, two of floating, followed by 100 meters of travel with hands and feet tied. Candidates also have to do seven minutes of swimming wearing a sixteen-pound weight belt. Additionally, they must survive two minutes of buddy breathing, remaining completely submerged while sharing a snorkel with a fellow trainee. As their proficiency at this exercise increased during the past weeks, so did the level of harassment, to the point where, in their final test, the training sergeant in the nine-foot-deep pool with them is allowed to deliberately block the snorkel's air intake for two consecutive breaths while subjecting the trainees to "gator rolls" and other physical irritations.

By the time they're evaluated during the eighth

week of indoctrination, candidates are expected to do 70 push-ups, 75 sit-ups, 14 chin-ups, and 84 flutter kicks, within the same time constraints as on the entry exam. They have to be able to swim 4,000 meters in eighty minutes, 50 meters underwater, and run six miles in 45 minutes, followed immediately by a 35-foot-rope climb. All of these exercises are done while they're sleep deprived and constantly harassed.

The commandant of the school, Master Sergeant Craig Showers, says the sole purpose of the indoctrination course is to prepare candidates for the mental and physical stress of the real job, and get them through the pipeline—the fifteen months of specialized training leading to the coveted PJ's maroon beret. Proof that their methods work is the 96 percent graduation rate at the end of the pipeline.

Pipeline training begins with four weeks at the Army's combat diving school in Key West, three weeks of parachute training at Fort Benning, Georgia, followed by five weeks of instruction in free-fall HALO—High Altitude, Low Opening—parachuting at Fort Bragg, North Carolina, or Yuma, Arizona. Next comes two and a half weeks of basic survival training at Fairchild, Washington, followed by a day at the Navy's Pensacola underwater egress course, which teaches them how to exit a submerged aircraft. (Helicopters are top heavy; in water they quickly flip upside down, often disorienting crew members trapped inside.) After that comes twenty-two weeks at Fort Bragg for the Special Operations Combat Medical Course, where they learn minor field surgery, combat trauma management, and other relevant procedures. Completion of the medic course earns them EMT-Paramedic Certification. Then it's on to twenty weeks at Kirtland, New Mexico, for qualification as pararescue recovery specialists capable of being assigned to any PJ unit worldwide. Here they're trained in mountaineering, combat tactics, advanced parachuting, and helicopter insertion and extraction. At some point in the training, scuba diving and parachuting are combined, and they bail out for an underwater mission, carrying 170 pounds of gear.

Only when he successfully completes the entire fifteen-month curriculum and has proven he can be trusted to perform the mission no matter what the difficulty or personal risk, is a trainee awarded the maroon beret, which symbolizes the blood sacrificed by Pararescuemen, and their devotion to duty by aiding others in distress.

Seeing a group of PJs together, it's apparent there is no one personality type that chooses the profession. Look at a major league baseball team. Twenty-five distinct individuals who really only share one trait: the ability to excel at the game. The trait that PJs share is much less visible. It's a deep-seated need to help others, to experience the gratification that comes from risking your life to save someone else's and bringing them back to their loved ones.

The compulsion is strong enough to overcome fear and, to a degree, reason. After twenty-two years in pararescue, Tim Malloy still looks off the ramp of a C-130 at 13,000 feet and remembers that he doesn't care all that much for jumping out of airplanes; he still experiences an instant when he looks at the waves and how huge they are, or at the mountain and how cold and foreboding it is, or remembers how Larry Arnott, a PJ he'd known since their high school days together, died in his arms when wind slammed his parachute into rocks, breaking his back. Deep inside his mind, Malloy withdraws. But then he goes ahead and jumps, because his overwhelming need is to save a life.

Pararescue's origins can be traced back to August 1943 in uncharted jungle near the China-Burma border. Twenty-one people had bailed out of a disabled C-46 into a site so remote that the only means to get them help was by parachute. Three soldiers, two of them medical corpsmen, volunteered for the assignment, parachuted in, and for a month cared for the injured until the entire party could be brought to safety. One of the survivors was CBS Newsman Eric Sevareid, who later wrote of the men who risked their lives to save his: "Gallant is a precious word; they deserve it."

Since then Pararescuemen—the term "jumpers" is no longer used even though the acronym "PJs" remains—have performed feats of heroism all over the world, both in combat and during peacetime.

During the Vietnam War, PJs routinely volunteered to ride a hoist cable from a chopper down into the jungle to extract wounded soldiers and downed pilots, often while they and the helicopter were under enemy fire. Of the nineteen Air Force Crosses awarded to enlisted personnel during the war, ten went to PJs.

PJs were among the first U.S. combatants to parachute into Panama during Operation Just Cause in 1989. That same year, Pararescuemen came to the aid of motorists trapped by a collapsed section of freeway following the San Francisco earthquake. The PJs were the only people who volunteered to crawl between sections of the collapsed roadway to reach victims and bring them out.

In 1992, working with Army Rangers, PJs flew in
Army helicopters during the operation in Somalia, and
found themselves in the middle of a battle zone assisting the survivors and treating the wounded when two
choppers were shot down.

During Operation Desert Storm, PJs were on
standby to rescue downed fliers, a job characterized by
weeks upon weeks of absolute boredom, punctuated
by occasional flurries of life-threatening action. When
an F-14 went down in hostile territory, PJs rescued the
plane's navigator in an operation that the Air Force
coyly says "involved the destruction of enemy forces
in very close proximity to the survivor."

Currently, PJs are stationed at fourteen bases in the
states, including Alaska, and overseas in Okinawa,
England, and Iceland. Six of the stateside units,
including the 106th, are part of the Air National
Guard, which means that many of its PJs are part-
timers, civilians who hold down regular jobs. The
Westhampton Beach unit has had PJs who are cops,
firemen, EMTs, and correctional officers. Some of its
pilots fly for the commercial airlines; one flies helicopters for a nearby police department. Working as a
part-timer in a rescue unit usually means you have a
civilian employer who's willing to put up with last
minute calls saying "they need so-and-so at the base."
Longer deployments are more problematic for em-
ployers who can't plan on the certainty of a two week
"summer camp" plus a weekend a month for Guard
employees. The downsizing of the regular military has
meant an end to the "weekend warrior" concept for the
Reserve and National Guard. At the same time, it often
means that those who stay in the program may get
activated for six week stints several times a year, often

to be sent overseas to places like Turkey and Iceland to plug holes for which no regular Air Force personnel are available.

The 106th wasn't always a rescue unit. The group traces its lineage back to 1916, when it was a detachment of the 1st Battalion Signal Corps of the New York National Guard. It didn't get into the rescue business until June 14, 1975, when it swapped its designation as the 106th Fighter Interceptor Group and their supersonic F-102A Delta Daggers for the Lockheed C-130H/P and the Sikorsky HH-3E Jolly Green Giant helicopter, becoming the 106th Aerospace Rescue and Recovery Group, of which the 102nd ARR Squadron is a part. The designation was later shortened to Air Rescue Squadron and Air Rescue Group, and in 1995 it became simply the 106th Rescue Wing with the 102nd Rescue Group. The unit's base of operations has also been through a few changes of name and ownership. In 1969 what had been Suffolk County Air Force Base since WWII was closed. The county took title, renaming it Suffolk County Airport, and later Francis S. Gabreski Airport, leasing half the facility to the New York Air National Guard.

The 106th's first mission that captured headlines was on December 27, 1979, when the *John F. Leavitt*, the first U.S. commercial sailing vessel built in forty years, was knocked to pieces in heavy seas 280 miles east of Long Island. The *Leavitt* was on her maiden voyage, carrying a load of lumber to Haiti, when she ran into trouble. A Jolly Green Giant located the vessel and put two Pararescuemen into the water near the ship. They boarded her and safely got all nine sailors hoisted to the helicopter before the ship went down.

Despite the publicity that comes from spectacular rescues like the *Leavitt*, and the fact that the unit is credited with saving nearly three hundred civilian lives, the 106th is not in business for the purpose of civilian rescue. Their entire raison d'etre is combat search and rescue. But the Air National Guard and the Pentagon recognize that taking the civilian missions provides an excellent opportunity for relevant training under real emergency conditions. Knowing that they have the green light to accept these assignments, their biggest frustration at the Long Island base is that they're not tasked often enough.

The problem is primarily one of jurisdiction. The Coast Guard is responsible for civilian rescues at sea, and has aircraft capable of handling missions as far as 200 miles out to sea. What's more, the Coast Guard *wants* to handle those rescues, since its funding comes not from the Department of Defense, but from the Department of Transportation, and is directly related to the number of rescue missions they undertake.

When help is needed beyond the 200-mile range, the 106th often gets the call. In May 1998 the RCC in Lisbon, Portugal, received a distress call from the fishing vessel *Cam Civet*. A crewman was hemorrhaging internally and had been drifting in and out of consciousness for several hours. The boat was 1,000 miles east of Bermuda, 800 miles southwest of the Azores.

The U.S. Coast Guard responded by sending a C-130 from Elizabeth City, North Carolina, to Suffolk, where it picked up four PJs and a flight surgeon before heading out to sea. At ten P.M., after a five hour flight, they located the *Cam Civet*. Pushing a RAMZ (Rigged Alternate Method Zodiacs) kit ahead of them, the PJs jumped, using their highly controllable parachutes to maneuver into the water next to their equipment. In ten minutes they had the Zodiac inflated and were motoring to the vessel. Climbing aboard, they immediately assessed the patient's condition, established radio contact with the flight surgeon on the orbiting C-130, and by three A.M. had controlled the bleeding.

The next morning, the patient and PJs were transferred to a Miami-bound cargo ship, and several days later they arrived back home on Long Island.

While water rescues are few and far between, it's not at all unusual for the 106th to get involved in mountain search and rescue in the northeastern United States. In 1982, PJs Kevin Carrick and Scott Simpson were aboard a C-130 participating in a search for a private plane that had gone down in the Blue Ridge Mountains of West Virginia. After several hours of searching, the radio operator picked up a signal from an Emergency Locator Transmitter (ELT), a device designed to be triggered on impact in a plane crash. Homing in on the signal, they spotted a swath cut through the forest leading to wreckage on the top of a mountain. The PJs parachuted from the C-130, using the old-style round military chutes which, unlike the modern rectangular parachutes they use today, are not steerable. Their target was a clear area at the bottom of the mountain. Both of them got hung up in trees and had to cut themselves loose. Then they hiked up the mountain to the wreckage, which contained the bodies of four adults and a child.

The first thing they did was radio the tail number of the airplane to search headquarters. To everyone's shock, this was not the missing plane they were searching for. This aircraft was apparently flown by an Arkansas pilot who had taken family or friends to an

Arkansas–Penn State football game. When the time came for the return flight, the weather at the tiny, uncontrolled airport they were using was bad enough to require the pilot to have an instrument rating. This pilot didn't, but took off anyway, and flew the aircraft right into the top of the mountain. Since no flight plan had been filed, the FAA had no way of knowing that the plane was missing, and no search for it had been launched.

In June 1994, six months before the *Salvador Allende* mission, a helicopter crew from the 106th had flown Jolly 08, one of their HH-60s, to New Hampshire to do a SAR demonstration for a group of civilian instructors who teach wilderness medicine and survival courses. The exercise was being observed by the lieutenant in charge of the region's state fish and game officers, who routinely get involved in search and rescue cases. To test the helicopter's capabilities, a "victim" was hidden in a ten-square-mile heavily wooded area. The expectation of the civilians was that the search would take a while, but on the first pass over the area, the PaveHawk's infrared radar spotted the "victim." The PJs exited the hovering helicopter by sliding down a fast rope, then prepared their injured patient to be flown to a nearby hospital in the helicopter, which had landed in a nearby clearing.

Before the helicopter could lift off, a real rescue call came in. Although it was summer and the weather in the woods was warm, on nearby Mount Washington winter sports enthusiasts knew that good snow can be found in Tuckerman's Ravine well into June. A twenty-one-year-old skier had hiked up the mountain and started his run down, when he fell and severely fractured both bones in his left leg just above the ankle. It was already late in the afternoon, and a ground-based rescue unit wouldn't be able to find the man before dark. The man's companion, who had hiked down to a lodge near the base of the mountain to call for help, reported that the victim was also suffering from mild hypothermia.

With Captain Mike Noyes as pilot, copilot Major Anthony Mola, Rich Davin as flight engineer, PJ Mike Hewson, and Shaun Brady—on his very first mission as a newly minted PJ—the helicopter took off, bringing the fish and game lieutenant along to guide them into Tuckerman, a very steep, rocky ravine on the northeast side of Mount Washington. About halfway up they ran into a snowstorm that cut visibility to between a quarter and a half mile, and the ceiling—the bottom of the cloud layer—began dropping lower and lower, to the point where they were hovering their way up the mountain at a speed of five knots, no more than sixty feet above the ground. But the larger problem was that heavy, wet snow was sticking to the helicopter. If it got much worse, the aircraft could be in jeopardy.

They found the victim at the 4,500 foot level. With Davin talking the pilots into a five-foot hover over a rocky outcropping surrounded by fir trees, they used the hoist to lower the PJs, their gear, and a litter basket. The plan was for the helicopter to fly down to warmer air in order to melt the accumulated snow and ice, and wait for the PJs to radio that the victim was ready to be picked up. In the meantime, the PJs, who were only wearing lightweight flight suits, since they had no expectation of a winter mission under blizzard conditions in the middle of the summer, administered first aid, splinted the badly broken leg, and prepared the skier to be evacuated. When they were ready, they radioed for the HH-60 to come back. In the interim the weather had gotten worse—heavier snow and gusty winds, with visibility still hampered in blowing snow. Once they got back up the ravine it quickly became apparent there would be no time to do a routine extraction—a high hover using the hoist to lift the victim and PJs out of there safely.

It took four tries, but finally Davin was able to talk the pilots down between the treetops into a three-foot hover over the rocky outcropping. As the PJs began to hand the litter up to Davin, Noyes ever so gently brought the HH-60 down even lower, till its right wheel was resting on the rocky ledge, the left wheel still hanging in space about twenty feet above the steeply sloping mountainside. As the fish and game officer's eyes widened to the size of silver dollars, Noyes held the hover for the five minutes it took to get the patient and PJs safely aboard, then carefully lifted straight up till they were clear of the trees, backed away from the slope, turned and made the quick seventeen minute flight down the mountain to the nearest hospital. Total time from start to finish was less than an hour.

Not long after that mission, Ed Fleming flew an HH-60 out to sea to evacuate a woman from a 100-foot commercial fishing boat. She had been stung by a bee and was suffering a potentially fatal allergic reaction. When they found the vessel, it was in moderately heavy seas and presented the usual obstacles to a hovering helicopter—masts, antennas, and booms. With Rich Davin operating the hoist, they lowered a PJ to the deck with a Stokes litter for the patient. Somehow, the woman had gotten the notion that the helicopter would just land on the boat and she'd climb aboard. A ride in a basket dangling on a cable from a hovering helicopter was not in her travel plans. Finally, they convinced her to get in the basket, covered completely—face and all—with a blanket, and hoisted her off the boat. When Davin pulled the litter into the cabin, he removed the blanket to find their patient more terrified by the hoist than by the reaction to the bee sting.

Elements of the 106th have been regularly rotated to bases in Turkey to be on standby in the event allied personnel or aircraft flying over Iraq get into trouble. They logged combat sortie time on one occasion in 1996 when a peace delegation deep inside Iraq was threatened with death. A bomb exploded close to where the delegation was staying, and the military command ordered two of the 106th's helicopters to fly in and evacuate the delegation, which they were able to do without firing a shot. In April 1999 elements of the unit were sent to Turkey again, to provide helicopter rescue cover for planes enforcing the northern no-fly zone in Iraq. From there a number of the PJs were sent on to Kuwait, standing alert with a C-130 unit.

Aside from combat assignments and the occasional civilian rescue, the 106th gets tasked for stateside paramilitary duties from time to time. They keep a C-130 on standby whenever *Air Force One* is crossing the Atlantic; and whenever NASA is launching a space shuttle mission, one of their C-130s orbits approximately 175 miles downrange from Cape Canaveral, in case an emergency is declared and the astronauts have to use the bailout system that was installed after the Challenger tragedy. It's an assignment the 106th

Pararescuemen won after NASA held a timed competition between several rescue units.

If the astronauts were to bail out, the PRC-112 personal radio carried by each of them would transmit a signal on a discrete frequency, allowing the radio operator in the orbiting C-130 to locate them individually. Once located, the PJs aboard the Hercules would parachute in groups of three as close as possible to the astronauts. Each group would push a RAMZ kit—motorized inflatable Zodiac boats—rigged to a cargo parachute off the ramp, and then follow it down. Within ten minutes the Zodiacs would be inflated and running, picking up astronauts and any other PJs who may have deployed from the plane with MA-1 seven-person life rafts. If things went as planned, the Zodiacs would meet at a midway point, where they'd wait for two HH-60 helicopters accompanied by a C-130 refueler that would have lifted off from Patrick Air Force Base and headed to the recovery area as soon as the emergency was declared. Once on-scene, the helicopters would use their hoists to pull astronauts and PJs out of the water.

Much of a Pararescueman's early training is aimed at making him so comfortable in the water, despite the conditions, that he seems to believe he can't drown. What else could account for intelligent men leaping from airplanes and helicopters into sea conditions bad enough to sink a ship?

Consider Senior Master Sergeant Tim Malloy, who along with newly minted PJ Craig Johnson went to the aid of four Portuguese fishermen whose boat had gone down in rough seas. It was around four in the afternoon on a wintry February day when the helicopter carrying the PJs and its accompanying C-130 began searching the ocean a hundred miles off Long Island. Just as it began to get dark they spotted a tiny two-man life raft with the survivors clinging to it.

The pilot put the PaveHawk into a low-and-slow, and as they got upcurrent of the raft, Malloy and Johnson jumped. They swam over to the raft, where one of the survivors immediately grabbed Malloy, almost drowning him. Breaking loose from his grasp, Malloy saw that one of the fishermen, apparently hypothermic, had succumbed to the numbing cold, given up, and slipped beneath the surface of the water.

Malloy immediately let go of the raft and dove down—he doesn't know if it was ten feet or forty—till he could grab the man by his shirt collar and haul him back up to the surface. Then it was a matter of muscling the inert fisherman out of the freezing water and into the life raft. The situation was very bad. He had to revive him with mouth-to-mouth resuscitation, while at the same time Johnson was trying to convince the other three men, who were also hypothermic, that they were going to be saved, that they had to fight to stay alive. Meanwhile, giant waves continued to break over them.

The shipwreck survivors got an emotional jolt when the huge C-130 did a pass directly over them. Moments later the helicopter came to a hover, the hoist came down, and over the next half hour all four fishermen and the two PJs were hauled aboard. Now the problem was warming them sufficiently to prevent a shutdown of their vital functions. Quickly, Malloy and Johnson stripped the four survivors and stuffed them into sleeping bags they had prepped with chemical heating pads.

Once the situation appeared to be under control, Malloy ordered Johnson, the newbie on his first rescue mission, to strip off his wet suit and get into a sleeping bag with one of the victims. When Johnson hesitated, Malloy claimed to have recently read that it was the newest emergency technique for warming a hypothermic victim while still in the field.

Too new to argue with the head of the PJ unit, Johnson did as he was told, not noticing that Malloy had turned around and was shaking uncontrollably with laughter. They radioed ahead to the Stony Brook University Hospital, and when the rescue helicopter landed, they were greeted by reporters, photographers, and TV cameras, all of whom duly recorded that *five* victims were transferred to litters and immediately rushed into the E.R.

A few moments later the HH-60 crew followed them inside, where they heard nothing but yelling and screaming, as Johnson fought the doctors and nurses who wanted him to stay in the bag until they could assess his condition. "Get your fuckin' hands off me! I'm one of the PJs!" he screamed. "This is the patient!" When the docs realized that only four of the "patients" were hypothermic, they let the PJ out of the bag and turned to treating the fishermen, all of whom survived.

Pranks aside, missions like these are both physically and emotionally draining in a way only those who've done them can comprehend. Many PJs say that even their families don't really understand what they go through, and that may explain why their divorce rate is higher than average. Most of the men were already PJs before they got married. The women knew what their fiancés did, and for most it was a turn-on. But years later, with children in the picture and several of the unit's PJs well into their forties, many of their wives are more than ready for them to quit this ready-to-go-on-a-moment's-notice foolishness.

The toughest time for a PJ is right after a mission. Tim Malloy says it's virtually impossible to convey, even to a spouse, what you've just experienced. "They don't understand what it's like to dive out of an airplane into the ocean at three o'clock in the morning to go to a ship and stop someone from bleeding to death. When you get home, you collapse, you're exhausted." And the one question you can't answer is: "Why do you do it?"

Malloy's long-held point of view was rattled when at the age of twenty-one his son came to him and said, "Dad, you know, I've always admired what you do. And I want to be a PJ." It was a moment he could never have anticipated, but he has no trouble explaining that the glow he felt in his heart was so bright, it could have lit up the neighborhood on the night of a new moon.

When the shock wore off, Malloy tried to dissuade his son, telling him how difficult PJ school would be. But the kid was determined. He passed the entrance tests and was accepted into training. Every night, an exhausted Tim, Jr., called home to get a motivational pep talk from his dad, whose twenty-two years as a PJ have helped him understand the purpose behind the rigors of PJ school.

"On life-or-death rescue missions, you become mentally drained. Physically, I think anybody can do it. But it's the mental part, and the heart, that comes into play. You have to learn how to deal with a great deal of stress, fatigue, and emotional trauma. I've lost six Pararescuemen, one who died in my arms."

There is one lesson PJs have to learn that may even be more difficult than how to cope with the death of a comrade, and that is the recognition that they can't save everyone who calls for their help. All their heart, courage, strength, desire, and training goes for naught if they can't reach the victims. That would prove to be the frustration of the *Salvador Allende* rescue mission. The would-be rescuers could monitor the cries for help, they could drop supplies from an airplane to the crewmen in the ocean, but without a way to get them out of the water, the seamen were doomed. A ship could do it, but none could crash through the mountainous seas quickly enough. That left only one possibility: the tandem team of Pararescuemen and HH-60 helicopters. And they were tied down to the tarmac of Gabreski Field by cables . . . and the commanding officer.

THREE

At 10:38 the first responses to the UMIB come in. The Halifax Marine Operator reports two Russian fishing trawlers offering to divert. One is identified only by call sign CGKTF; the other is the 34-meter-long *Slepyashchiy*, call sign LYDY. The operator gives Parker the position of both vessels, and he logs them into the computer.

At 10:45 the first of the AMVER ships checks in by INMARSAT phone. "If we divert we can make about nine knots. ETA on-scene is sixteen hours," says the master of the M/V *Benny Queen*, a 730-foot, Japanese-owned gas tanker.

At 11:15, RCC Halifax calls to tell them that the call sign of the Canadian C-130 Hercules is Rescue 306. They also provide an update on one of the two trawlers that volunteered to divert. "On scene time for *Slepyashchiy* is 0900 Zulu." Under the circumstances, that's almost cause for celebration. It means a rescue vessel will reach the location where the *Salvador Allende* crew reported they were abandoning ship by four A.M. New York time, six A.M. in the middle of the North Atlantic.

A few moments later Lloyd's of London calls to confirm the name and ownership of the *Salvador Allende*. While Parker is talking with London, Mletzko takes a radio call on a phone patch from Rescue 1503. The Coast Guard C-130 is en route, and will be on scene in four and a half hours.

Seconds after hanging up with Lloyd's, Gary Parker is back on the phone, calling the offices of BLASCO, the Black Sea Shipping Company in Odessa, the Ukraine. The connection is lousy and the language barrier makes the conversation rudimentary.

"Verify the name of the vessel." The *Salvador Allende*, 450 feet. "How many life rafts are on board?" Six, with a capacity of sixty POB. "Do they have a drogue? Do they have canopies?" (A drogue is a funnel or parachute-shaped device that works like a sea anchor to help the raft remain stable.) Roger to both. "What type of EPIRB is on board?" A 121.5 should be in one of the rafts. "What type of cargo?" Rice. "If we get further information we'll give you a call."

The significance of the "How many life rafts?" question has more to do with deciding when to call off a rescue mission than initiating one. If they know how many life rafts a ship carries, and search planes can account for all of them, they can deduce that they've either found everyone who can be found or know they're now looking for PIW—people in water.

While Parker is shouting his way through the conversation with the Ukraine, Topper takes a call from the FAA at New York Ocean. An eastbound commercial jet at 31,000 feet has picked up a 121.5 EPIRB signal. The signal died at 38-34N, 48-21W. This is one of those good news/bad news calls. The good news is that they've got a signal from an EPIRB in the *general* area of the *Salvador Allende*. The bad news is that the location reported by the high flier is several hundred miles from the position reported by the ship. They make a quick assumption, based on experience: it's the EPIRB from the *Salvador Allende*, but the coordinates provided by the pilot are where he was when he heard and then lost the signal, not necessarily where the signal was coming from. At 31,000 feet the plane could have been receiving a signal from a transmitter several hundred miles away from them, in any direction. The new coordinates are logged, but ignored.

At 11:50 P.M. the operations officer at the 106th Rescue Squadron at Westhampton Beach calls. "Our C-130 call sign King 52 can be on-scene at 1500 Zulu [ten A.M. New York time] with rafts, Zodiacs, and PJs. King 46 can be on-scene similarly equipped by 1700 Zulu." Topper is told to call Lieutenant Colonel Robert Landsiedel at 3:45, with a go/no go. In the meantime, the RCC needs to initiate contact with the Air Force Rescue Coordination Center at Langley Air Force Base, to start the procedure that will give the 106th authorization to participate in the mission.

With a vessel in distress so far out to sea, the initial concern for the RCC is to get an aircraft into the area and have it locate the ship if it's still afloat. If it's already gone down and they're now looking for people, rafts, or lifeboats, they need to flood the area with aircraft, giving each one a specific starting point for its search, and a specific pattern to fly. Their preference is to have a Coast Guard ship serve as OSC—on-scene commander. In this case, there'll be no CG ship. The nearest cutter available, the *Seneca*, was dispatched from Boston when the distress call came in, but her tasking was canceled when she reported that the trip to the scene would take forty-eight hours, putting her there at about ten P.M. EST on December 11.

This means that one of the aircraft will be designated OSC and be responsible for assigning altitudes and search areas to other planes in order to ensure that in the heat of the search no mishaps occur. It's a work-intensive job, much more easily handled on a ship than in the cockpit of a rescue plane, where the pilot, copilot, navigator, flight engineer and radio operator—if they have one—are already tasked to the max. The RCC's next concern is to *keep* an aircraft on-scene at all times. This means coordinating schedules for all of the planes on this mission, regardless of what agency or country is providing them. And this necessarily means keeping track of constantly changing "bingo" times for every aircraft involved in the mission. "Bingo" is what they call the moment when the aircraft has to begin its return flight. It's calculated by the navigator, who takes fuel consumption, flight time to primary and secondary airports, and weather into consideration, and it's constantly being recalculated during the flight to allow for redesignation of recovery airports due to changing weather.

Their need is to keep the aircraft on-scene for as long as possible. Under normal flight conditions, they'd do this by returning—recovering—to the nearest airport. In this case, the closest is Saint John's, Newfoundland. But a monstrous snowstorm has now paralyzed that city. Next choice is Sydney, Nova Scotia, followed by Halifax (either the civilian airport or the nearby military field at Shearwater), and then Greenwood, home base for the Canadian Herc. CG

1503, flying out of Norfolk, doesn't even consider returning nonstop to its home base. They tell New York they can spend three hours on-scene if they recover to Nova Scotia, two hours if they recover to Hamilton, Bermuda.

**Aboard the *Salvador Allende*
1:40 A.M. local time**

Meanwhile, the thirty-one people onboard the *Salvador Allende* are struggling with the task of abandoning ship. Sounds easy, but how do you accomplish it when the ship is getting slammed by thirty- and forty-foot waves, when the wind is roaring with gusts up to eighty mph, and when you still haven't come to grips with the fact that you're safer out *there* than you are right here?

One lifeboat is gone; the attempt to launch it was sobering. It's one thing to train for emergencies at sea in Odessa harbor. It's another to deal with them in the middle of a North Atlantic storm. But they have no choice. They believe they can survive if they can launch the two life rafts stored astern of where the lifeboat had been. Tying the rope that will hold the first raft to the ship, one of the deckhands trips the mechanism that releases high pressure air, watching the raft pop its plastic cover and inflate. As the raft gets larger it drops to the surface of the water, riding up and down while the *Salvador Allende* is lifted then dropped by the waves. Finally it's ready, but the ship rises up over a huge breaker, and the rope holding the raft is stretched so tight it snaps, allowing the raft to break free. The rope is designed to hold the raft to a sinking ship but to automatically break as the ship goes down, releasing the inflated raft and allowing it to float to the surface. It's good planning, but didn't take into account the stress that a ship *rising* out of the water would put on it as it lifted the raft up into the wind.

They try again, to no avail, with the second life raft, then move to the starboard side to attempt to launch rafts three and four. But the wind and the movement of the sea conspire against them. All four rafts are ripped away from the ship, leaving lifeboat number one, high out of the water on the starboard side of the superstructure, as their last hope.

When the ship stopped in Baltimore en route to Freeport, it underwent a full Coast Guard inspection, which included lowering one of the motorized lifeboats. Everything worked as it was supposed to. The lifeboats were Alex Taranov's charge, and he made certain that things were in perfect condition even before the inspection. Now he has every reason to believe that the mechanism for lowering the boat should still work perfectly.

Under the leadership of second officer Igor Skiba, the crew pulls the lifeboat from its davits, leaving the cables from the winch attached to the boat. By sheer force of muscle they drag the thirty-foot wooden boat up the side of the superstructure, away from the breaking waves, knocking out several windows in the process. The plan is to load everyone in the boat, and then as the ship continues its slow roll to port, let it slide off into the ocean. The two women who work in the ship's galley are helped aboard first. Skiba gets in and assists several more crewmen into the boat. As the eleventh person scrambles in, the lifeboat starts to slide, pulling cable from the winch. Someone tries setting the brake, but with the ship rolling from side to side and the additional weight of the people aboard, the brake can't hold it. Bumping and scraping the bottom of its wooden hull, the lifeboat slides torturously down the side of the superstructure. Seventeen or eighteen people watch helplessly as the boat they should have been on hits the water and is torn away from the ship.

Taranov's hope is that they'll start the engine and come close to the ship, allowing the remaining crew to jump into the water and swim to the boat. But the captain sees that the waves will force the little boat toward the stern, with the possibility that it will get chewed apart by the giant propeller. He shouts over the storm, ordering the second officer to start the engine and get away from the ship. As Alex watches helplessly, the lifeboat moves off, disappearing into the darkness beyond the dim circle of light surrounding the stricken vessel.

It's a chilling moment for him. The realization sets in that it's two or three in the morning, they're on a sinking ship in a driving storm in the middle of the North Atlantic, with no lifeboats and no life rafts. Just life jackets and a walkie-talkie radio. And he's still wearing only shorts and a sweater.

As Alex is sitting there, the notion of what's about to happen starts to sink in. One of the engine room officers calls to him. "Look, they have a dressing room for the sailors. Let's go in and get you some clothes. I'll go with you. I have two bottles of vodka in my cabin."

Easier said than done. With the ship now listing more than fifty degrees, they have to walk the side of the superstructure, then three of them muscle the steel door almost straight up, opening it as though it were a trapdoor down to a cellar. They tie the door open. Then Alex finds a longer rope, ties it to the deck railing and drops it through the door. If the ship rolls, they can use the rope to climb out. As carefully as possible the three men climb down and raid the sailors' lockers. Alex takes one more sweater, then dons his orange thermal coverall. He finishes it off by slipping his life jacket over his head and tying the ropes as tightly as he can. Still in stocking feet, he looks for a pair of shoes, but can't find any that fit.

Then Alex and one of the men half walk, half crawl down the corridor. They manage to open the door to the officer's cabin, and grab Cokes and cigarettes. To their extreme disappointment, the cabinet holding the two bottles of Smirnoff vodka purchased just before they sailed from Texas is blocked by a jumble of furniture and they can't get to it. They leave, beginning the climb out, when Alex hears the ship's cat crying. He climbs upstairs, following the sound until he sees the animal. But when the cat takes one look at Alex coming at him in an orange-colored suit, it goes nuts. Realizing the cat doesn't recognize him dressed like that, Alex unties the straps of the life jacket, takes it off, then removes the suit. Calming down, the cat comes to him. Alex then redresses, stuffs the animal down the front of the coverall, and zips it up. Retracing his steps, he links up with his friend, climbs out of the doorway, closes the steel door, and makes his way down the starboard side, where the crew is huddled together, sitting on the wall of the superstructure.

The wind is still howling, rain mixed with salt spray pelting them, when the cat begins clawing at Alex inside the coverall. He unzips it, and the cat leaps out and disappears. Alex figures the cat knows how bad things are. They have no boats, no rafts. It's one of those situations where you don't know whether to laugh or to cry. And members of the crew do both.

Chief radioman A. V. Lagno asks, "What's the temperature of the water?"

"Eighteen to twenty degrees, Celsius." That's mid-to high sixties Fahrenheit.

"Then we can go swimming," he laughs.

Electrician Vitaly Plotnichenko served in the Russian Navy on a submarine that had to be abandoned at sea because of an accident. "Nothing will happen to us. I've been on a sinking ship once before. We will be rescued."

But senior motorman Igor Kulbida wasn't having any of it. "People," he cries, "this is the end." Ignoring him, Alex sits down, passes out cigarettes, then shields his face from the wind so he can light up. Finishing the smoke, he tucks his face inside the zippered coverall and tries to sleep. Sunrise will be at about 7:45, still more than three hours away. He can't help but wonder if he'll live to see it.

Aboard Rescue 306
4:20 A.M. In the North Atlantic (2:20 A.M. EST)

Less than two hours after receiving the first call, Canadian Air Force Captain Jonathan Forrest put the power to Rescue 306's four engines, and the C-130 Hercules lifted off the runway at Canadian Forces Base Greenwood, about 85 miles northwest of Halifax.

This C-130 is an early 1960s model of the workhorse cargo plane built by Lockheed. While the aircraft is well-maintained, much of the electronics, including the weather radar, is vintage sixties technology. It has a black and white picture, and is operated by the navigator, who sits behind and to the right of the flight engineer, facing the starboard side of the aircraft. To see the radar scope, he has to put his eyes to a rubber-gasketed viewfinder, much the same way a submarine captain uses a periscope, while adjusting knobs on the control head. Between the two pilots is a repeater scope on an extending arm that either can pull toward them in order to see the same picture the nav is seeing. The system is archaic; it'll pick up intense precipitation like a thunderstorm, but it won't show them other aircraft in the area, nor can they count on it to pick up a ship in the water below.

In the rear of the aircraft SARtech team leader Ron O'Reilly is directing preparations for the search. The Canadian SAR technicians are the equivalent of U.S. Air Force PJs, with one exception: they have no combat training. Their reason for being is strictly search and rescue in any of the vast Canadian territory that ranges from the Arctic to the U.S. border.

O'Reilly needs to be certain that anyone who plans to be moving around when the ramp is opened is wearing a harness with a long tether hooked to it, tying them to the plane. The huge Plexiglas scanning doors are in mounts that allow them to be pushed forward and snapped into place flush with the side of the aircraft once the loading doors are slid up. But that operation can't take place until the plane is below 10,000 feet and no longer needs to be pressurized. For everyone on board Rescue 306, this is quite literally the calm before the storm.

The flight out above the weather has been routine. Leaving his copilot, Kevin Dort, at the controls,

Jonathan Forrest has time to take a break, grab a sandwich, and wash it down with hot chocolate. Coffee's just not his drink of choice. Walking back into the cockpit, climbing the steps, he scoots past the bunk, squeezes by the flight engineer, and straps himself back into the left-hand seat.

The sky outside is black. The pilots can see a few stars and a sliver of a moon that helps them make out towering cumulus clouds, the thunderheads that they've seen on radar and have been detouring around. Every so often a lightning bolt flashes across the sky, lighting up the clouds like a klieg light at a Hollywood premiere.

It's navigator Gilles Bourgoin's job to calculate the distance to the coordinates they've been given, and get them there as expeditiously as possible. As they close in on the area, he fine-tunes his numbers, factoring in the C-130's normal rate of descent of 2,000 feet per minute, and then tells Forrest when it's time to take the Herc down to search altitude.

With the aircraft commander at the controls, the plane heads down from 17,000 feet. The object is to try and avoid flying into the weather until it's no longer avoidable. They cross that threshold in less than five minutes. In the cockpit it suddenly sounds as if somebody's throwing rocks at the windshield. Actually, a whole lot of somebodies. Imagine driving behind a gravel truck on a bumpy road. Times a hundred. It's a mixture of heavy rain and sleet. Accompanied by turbulence. Gut-wrenching, neck-snapping, vomit-inducing turbulence. In seconds Bourgoin is losing his postmidnight snack and quickly working his way back to yesterday's breakfast. It's apparent that whomever designed the cockpit seating had (a) never researched the physiological consequences of seating anyone perpendicular to the direction the aircraft is attempting to head through turbulence, (b) never flew through turbulence seated at the navigator's position, (c) had a long-standing grudge against navigators as a class, or (d) all of the above.

In the rear of the plane the two SARtechs and the loadmaster are coping with a three-person Canadian Broadcasting Company documentary crew that's puking its collective guts out while entertaining random thoughts of the Herc slamming into the ocean. Making matters worse for the civilians, they're literally sitting in the dark, because in anticipation of using night vision goggles (NVGs), *every* light in the cargo compartment—even tiny LED indicators—has been taped over. Any light leakage would hamper attempts to look through the Plexi while trying to spot lights from either people or rafts in the water. Without any horizon to look at and without any warning that they're about to pull positive g's going up or negative g's dropping down, their bodies are beginning to rebel. O'Reilly, loadmaster Marco Michaud, and SARtech Andre Hotton have been through it enough that after an initial bout of nausea they're able to adjust to the constant, sickening movement of the plane. The camera crew, however, doesn't have the luxury of experience.

Forrest, meantime, is not at all concerned about his ability to keep the thirty-four-year-old C-130 in the air; what worries him is how the turbulence is going to affect their efforts. Dropping rafts to people in the water as you fly by at 130 knots is a tricky business in decent weather. Doing it in winds that are absolutely unpredictable will take not only all the skill he can muster, but a good bit of luck.

The plan had been to slow the plane from its cruising speed of 295 knots (340 mph) to about 140 knots (160 mph), bringing it level at an altitude of 1,000 feet to do an electronic search of the area, scanning the emergency marine frequencies, listening for a mayday, and calling for the vessel in distress. On this same pass the crew normally expects a briefing over headsets by the pilot, who will lay out his plans for the search. Then the flaps are extended to give the wings extra lift at slower speeds, and the SARtechs open both side doors and install the clear Plexiglas doors they'll sit or crouch behind in twenty-minute shifts over the next five or six hours.

The situation they're suddenly in, however, is far from normal. The turbulence is so bad that Forrest is having a hard time keeping the plane level. Neither he nor Dort can read the instruments because their eyes can't move fast enough to compensate for the bouncing they're doing in their seats and the erratic movements of the plane. And it isn't helped by the fact that the cockpit lighting had been dialed down so as not to interfere with their night vision—or what's left of it after continuous exposure to irregular, blinding flashes of lightning around the plane. (Earlier, they had drawn the curtain behind them, so the lights from the navigation area wouldn't cause problems. The curtain did little, however, to muffle the retching sounds coming from behind it.)

Trying to focus on the altitude and airspeed indicators is impossible. Altitude is not that much of a concern. While the 100-foot fluctuations are causing major motion sickness, at an altitude over a thousand feet it's nothing they need to worry about. The big problem is airspeed. Once they've got the rear door open and the SARtechs looking out the windows calling drops to the loadmaster hanging on the ramp, they've got to maintain a relatively constant speed, fluctuating by no more than ten knots up or down.

The plan is to fly low and slow, try to spot any survivors, drop life support to them, and if possible vector a ship directly to the PIWs so they can be picked up. Forrest decides to take the plane back up to 5,000 feet, where the air is smoother, to run the presearch checklists and give the SARtechs an opportunity to get their observation doors in place. As soon as he levels out he looks at his copilot and says over the intercom, "You have control." Dort puts his right hand on the yoke, his left on the engine throttles and responds, "I have control." It's a ritual that will be repeated dozens of times in the flight, a standard by-the-book way for one pilot to turn responsibility for flying the plane over to the other, leaving no room for doubt, no ambiguity, no confusion over who's handling the aircraft at that moment.

Forrest's m.o. on search missions is not to be, as he puts it, "the proud pilot," but to sit back and do the guidance. While Kevin Dort is hands on, watching the instruments, the aircraft commander is doing the presearch checks. During the remainder of the mission, Forrest'll be giving him headings, calling turns, talking to the navigator, who's keeping track of where targets they've spotted in the water are relative to their current position, and to the flight engineer, who's monitoring fuel consumption, air-conditioning, pressurization, the electrical panels, and other engine performance indicators. He's also listening to Ron O'Reilly, who's actually spotting targets and, in effect, flying the plane by remote control. It's the SARtechs in back who will call for turns, and who expect an immediate response from the cockpit. Years of experience have convinced Forrest that he's more effective watching, listening, and thinking, than he would be if he had to put all his effort into flying the plane—especially in weather like this, when it's a physically demanding job.

What Dort will be coping with as he brings the plane down from 5,000 to 1,000 feet is turbulence that rolls the aircraft from side to side. Pitch—nose up and down—isn't the problem, because the plane is being bumped either straight up or straight down. But a gust on one wing and not the other will roll the C-130, requiring a lot of back and forth cranking, often lock-to-lock. And it's all done with his right hand, because his left has to stay on the engine throttles to respond to sudden changes in speed. The task is extremely critical early in the flight, when the plane is heavy with twenty-five tons of fuel. To stay safely above stall speed, they can't fly slower than 135 to 137 knots. The calculation is based on a 45-degree bank, flap fifty percent, power off, stall speed, and then they add a twenty-knot safety margin to account for turbulence, bank angles, and fluctuations in airspeed. But low speed is only half the problem. In order for the crew in back to do their job with the door open, they can't fly faster than 150 knots. His technique is to pick a speed in the middle of that thirteen-knot range, say 142 knots, and stay on it, reacting instantaneously as the turbulence affects their airspeed. In his year flying C-130s, Dort has gotten used to muscling the yoke with one hand, and as he's gained confidence in the aircraft, it's gotten easier. In the beginning, new pilots try to fight every gust of wind that rolls them left or right. Now he'll roll with it to some degree, knowing that the

C-130 is a fairly stable, forgiving airplane, and it'll usually come back level of its own accord.

Just as they're completing the presearch check, both Bourgoin and Dort hear something in their headsets that stops them in their tracks. Dort busts in, "Hey, wait a sec. There's something on FM!" At any given moment the pilots can be monitoring a combination of two VHF radios, a UHF radio, a marine band FM radio, and the onboard intercom with SARtechs, loadmaster, navigator, and flight engineer. They can also add in two high-frequency radios, but they typically only do that when they're actively calling on the HF, usually to try and reach CAMSLANT—the Communications Area Master Station Atlantic in Alexandria, Virginia—for a phone patch to RCC New York. When a checklist is being run, there's a lot of talking going on. What Dort's ears pick out, however, brings all the chatter to a halt. The call is on FM Channel 16. In heavily accented English they hear: "Mayday, mayday, mayday, *Salvador Allende*, mayday."

Dort answers, "Ship in distress declaring mayday, this is Rescue 306."

No response.

"This is Rescue 306 calling *Salvador Allende*, call sign U-W-A-G. Rescue 306 calling *Salvador Allende* Uniform Whiskey Alpha Golf. Is this the *Salvador Allende* declaring mayday?"

They all know that FM radio transmission is line of sight. If there's a thirty-foot wave or the steel superstructure of the ship between the transmitter and the receiver, no one's going to hear the call or the response.

Moments pass. Then, "Yes, it is."

From that moment on they can't think of the crew of

the *Salvador Allende* as POBs or PIWs. In an instant the thirty-one became very real to the crew onboard Rescue 306. Now the crew on the sinking ship knows *who* is out here to try and save their lives. They don't know these seven men; they don't know—and might not even understand—why these men would choose to climb out of warm beds, to leave wives and children and friends, to fly into the teeth of a hurricane-force storm in order to try and save complete strangers. For the crew of Rescue 306, hearing that one mayday call raises the stakes exponentially. Now it's personal. Now they *know* there are real people counting on them, real people they have spoken to, real people whose only hope of survival depended at that moment on how well the seven of them could do their job.

With difficulty, Kevin continues the conversation with one man on the ship, while another in the background is obviously trying to help decipher what is being asked. They're standing awkwardly because the ship is listing to at least 50 degrees, and they're getting bounced around quite a bit. The copilot imagines he's talking to the radio room of the *Salvador Allende*. He has no way of knowing the men are using a handheld transceiver while hanging onto the storm-tossed ship. There's no panic in the anonymous voices, but a definite sense of urgency. And then comms are lost.

The Canadians make immediate contact with the U.S. Coast Guard's C-130, CG 1503, which is approaching the area and heading for the latest position given them by RCC New York, and advise them of the radio contact.

It's 0720Z, 2:20 A.M. in New York, 4:20 A.M. in the mid-Atlantic. Within minutes the Coast Guard plane's side-looking aperture radar (SLAR) picks up a target

in the water at 39-29.1N, 050-06.8W. It can only be
the ship. First order of business: make sure the two aircraft stay out of each other's way. The weather's
awful, it's dark out, and they're both concentrating on
locating the same needle in the North Atlantic
haystack. Each selects a TACAN (Tactical Air Navigation) channel and dials it in. Now they've got a digital
readout indicating the miles of separation between
them. With the target's position fixed, 306 says they'll
stay a minimum of five miles away, and move above
3,000 feet; 1503 agrees to take the airspace below
3,000.

The expectation in the cockpit of Rescue 306 is that
the Coast Guard plane is going to move in, actually
see the ship, and drop a datum marker buoy so that the
drift in the immediate area can be tracked. CG 1503
left Norfolk carrying two of the self-locating buoys
and three life-raft kits.

At 0725Z the commander of 1503 notes in his official
written log of the mission a conversation with one of the
survivors on VHF-FM Channel 16. A minute later they
record diverting Rescue 306 to the coordinates where
the SLAR fixed the ship, noting that the Canadian Herc
is NVG (night vision goggle) capable. At 0735Z, 1503
logs that 306 has reported an undetermined number of
life rafts in the vicinity of the subject vessel, concluding
the entry, "Comms with survivor lost."

RCC New York
2:55 A.M. EST (0755Z)

CAMSLANT calls and passes along a message from
Coast Guard 1503. "Rescue 306 located subject vessel

with multiple rafts in the water in the vicinity of the vessel. Updated position is 39-29N, 050-06W."

Six minutes later, at 3:01 A.M., Gary Parker gets a call patched through directly from Coast Guard 1503. He notes in the RCC's contemporaneous chronological log, "Vessel located. We have vectored Rescue 306 to the position. They have NVGs and is reporting they believe all POB are aboard rafts and they are tied together. They have talked to the master via VHF Comms. Comms are very bad due to interpretation. We have two and a half hours on-scene. Rescue 306 has three hours." It's 0801Z, which means that 1503 should be on-scene until at least 1031Z. Parker rogers the information, and tells 1503 that a Canadian CP-140 Aurora will be airborne in two hours, heading toward the scene to maintain coverage over the survivors when 306 is bingo and has to return to base. The position of the vessel is marked at 39-29.5N, 050-06.1W.

Aboard Rescue 306
Near the *Salvador Allende*
4:25 A.M. local time (2:25 A.M. EST)

While the presearch check is under way up front, the three crew members in the back are positioning the SKADs (survival kit air droppable) near the ramp so there's no delay when the time comes for a drop. A SKAD is a ten-man life raft attached to 280 feet of floating polypropylene rope, at the end of which is a survival bundle that carries clothing, radios, desalination kits, flares, food and water. The SARtechs configure the kits two ways: one raft and one bundle, or

raft-bundle-bundle-raft, with 280 feet of line from
piece to piece. The rafts are rigged to open during the
drop, and are made with pockets on the bottom
designed to fill with water, stabilizing them.

With everything and everyone in place, copilot
Kevin Dort begins the descent. Rather than the usual
250 knots, he doesn't want to exceed 180, because he
knows that the slower you fly in turbulence, the easier
it is on the airplane, not to mention the people in it.
Nevertheless, it's a bumpy ride down to a thousand
feet, and maintaining 180 proves to be difficult because the airspeed indicator is bouncing all over the
place. Fortunately, speed on the descent isn't critical.
Now, however, they're moving into search mode,
where precise speed is essential, and they're still fighting the same turbulence.

The instrument he's watching has a rotating drum
in a window that shows airspeed. There are two indicators, one that shows an approximate speed and
another that lets the pilot see knot by knot, precisely
what the plane is doing. Turbulence is causing both to
roll back and forth like a thimble on the end of a pen.
With the plane rigged for searches, Plexi doors in
place and the ramp at the rear about to open, he's got
to keep the speed between 130 and 150 knots. Trouble
is, the cockpit is shaking so much he can't distinguish
between a 3 and a 5. Reading the hash marks that indicate speed knot by knot is out of the question. Fine-
tuning their speed is just not going to be possible.

The other critical instrument adversely affected by
the turbulence is the A-I, the attitude indicator. It tells
the pilot at night and in clouds which way is up and
which is down. It's showing Dort an artificial horizon,
and he knows that if it's a choice between believing

his internal gyro or the A-I, go with the instrument. All the bouncing around is affecting the semicircular canals in his inner ear, where the body's set of gyros is located. It's a bit like the game little children play where they spin around as fast as they can, then stop and laugh and giggle as they stagger around, trying to overcome the dizziness.

But when you're at the controls of seventy tons of metal, kerosene, and assorted other natural and artificial ingredients hurtling seaward through a storm at around 200 miles an hour, there's not much to laugh and giggle about. The danger is that vertigo sets in and the pilot feels as though he's rolling sideways when he's actually flying straight and level. If he believes his instruments rather than his instinct at that moment— assuming he can read them—he won't make any serious mistakes. While Kevin Dort isn't getting sick to his stomach, there's no question that he's not operating at peak efficiency. He tells Forrest that this reminds him of driving a four-by-four down a washboard dirt road at sixty mph, with the whole dashboard shaking.

As if speed and attitude aren't enough to worry about, there's a significant problem determining your altitude over the ocean. Particularly a storm-tossed ocean. When Herc crews practice dropping SKADs, they generally do it from an altitude of 300 feet. So in theory Jonnie Forrest should bring his plane down to 300 feet above the water. But does that mean 300 feet above the crest of a sixty-foot wave? Or above the trough? The polite term of reference used on land, "sea level," has little meaning out here. They can't even count on their altimeter to tell them how high up they are. That far out over the ocean, there's no control tower to call and determine barometric pressure, which then allows a pilot to calibrate his altimeter before takeoff, and again prior to landing. To solve this problem, rescue planes and helicopters also have a radar altimeter, but while it's an accurate instrument, in rough weather its value is questionable because in a fraction of a second the plane can be plus or minus fifty feet. Now add plus or minus forty feet—depending on whether the aircraft is over a wave peak or trough—and the notion of blithely saying "take her to 300 feet" holds less allure.

Forrest is already mentally calculating how he's going to deal with another wind-caused complication when they get ready to make their drops. When they do a drop to people in the water, they do it crosswind, so that the raft and packages will be blown in the direction of the PIW. With the turbulence they're encountering, he's going to have to fly the plane crabbed, with the nose pointing 45 degrees off to the right of the direction the plane is moving, actually quartering into the wind. If he doesn't make that adjustment, the wind will blow the aircraft downwind, and before he knows it, he'll be past the drop point.

It may seem that a much easier solution is to start the crosswind track much farther upwind of the target, fly straight across, and let the wind blow the plane toward the target. Sounds logical, but it wouldn't allow them to drop the four bundles in a line perpendicular to the wind direction. By the time they hit the water they'd be angling away from the PIW, minimizing the chance that it'll drift in a perfect U shape around the survivor, enabling him to come in contact with the floating rope.

This is the sort of thinking Jonnie Forrest is able to

do while Kevin Dort has control of the plane. In the heavy turbulence they're experiencing, it would be a Herculean task to be hands-on flying and figuring the next five moves that will get a raft from the cargo bay of the plane into the ocean within reach of people whose lives may depend on that one drop being executed perfectly.

Leveling off at something less than a thousand feet, they begin executing an expanding square search pattern, starting at a position relayed to them from RCC New York. At the same time, CG 1503 is heading to the position that New York received from an EPIRB believed to be off the *Salvador Allende*.

The Coast Guard's C-130 is a much more technically up-to-date model of this venerable aircraft, which first saw service just after the Korean War. The American plane is equipped with a state-of-the-art radar—designed to pick up objects that may be in the water. The weather radar aboard Rescue 306 *might* see something as large as a ship, if it were tweaked properly, if the operator was top-notch, and if the weather was fairly decent.

In what seems mere seconds after beginning their search pattern, they get a call from 1503. They've found the ship on radar precisely where the EPIRB said it would be. The Coast Guard plane offers to move out of the area so 306 can make a low pass, scanning the water for indications of rafts, boats, or people on their approach to the *Salvador Allende*. Since the storm hasn't abated, the sea state is still big and ugly, and with heavy cloud cover, there's no moonlight to help them. With the exception of occasional flashes of lightning, and the glow from their landing lights reflecting off the salt spray, they're flying through a pitch-black sky. The *only* thing they would expect to have a chance of spotting in the water is a light. Life rafts carry one mounted on the dome, and its battery activates as soon as it comes in contact with saltwater. If the PIWs are wearing proper life vests, they'll also have a single cell light showing. And a lifeboat is likely to be equipped with at least one, possibly more, of these same lights. Even though they're not much more powerful than an ordinary flashlight, the SARtechs know they could see them with the NVGs at a distance of at least ten miles on a pitch-black night.

Night vision goggles, a linear descendant of the starlight scopes used in Vietnam, are such a powerful SAR tool it's surprising that the U.S. Coast Guard didn't have them as regular equipment on its C-130 SAR planes by late 1994. The stories of the lives that have been saved just because of this one relatively small and inexpensive technological device are legion. Ron O'Reilly tells of a case in the Canadian Rockies where they were searching for a missing climber. He was spotted by NVG-equipped SARtechs in an aircraft who, quite literally, saw the lost man flicking his Bic. The lighter had run out of fuel, so the man just kept flicking it until he was spotted. O'Reilly says that watching him through NVGs, the sparks from the flint looked as bright as a survival strobe light.

NVGs are not being used in the cockpit of Rescue 306, which is why no one believed Jonnie Forrest when he insisted that he had just seen several lights in the water at their eleven o'clock, near the horizon.

From his position in the right-hand seat, Kevin Dort can't confirm the sighting. He does suggest without a trace of ridicule that maybe Jonnie is seeing stars close to the horizon.

The skepticism is set aside seconds later when, from the scanning seat on the left side of the plane, Ron O'Reilly also reports seeing lights. At first there are two, close together. Moments later Andre Hotton reports another one, and then a fourth. They have to be life rafts. What else could be out in the middle of the ocean with a light? As the plane gets closer, Ron believes he can see that one of the lights is atop a raft, and he thinks there's a second raft tied to the first. That accounts for the two lights together.

It's a moment where shivers go simultaneously up and down several spines. This is what they're out here for. This is why they've been willing to endure the pounding. It's what they train for. It's why they commit to being part of a SAR unit. By collectively using the skills they've developed, they've found what they've been looking for, and the search has brought them to what is absolutely the most hellish spot in the North Atlantic this night. Even the CBC cameraman has gotten caught up in the excitement, which has moved him, as the SARtechs so delicately and considerately described it, from puke mode to shoot mode.

Marine weather forecasting has come a long way from the days when "red sky at morning, sailors take warning" was state of the art. With permanent deep water buoys, satellite photography, reports from hundreds of ships and airplanes, the U.S. National Weather Service is capable of sending mariners accurate predictions of relatively large-scale storms in a

time frame that gives them an opportunity to do something about it—like get the hell out of there. In the
case of the *Salvador Allende*, there was fair warning
early on of what was to come. This is the high seas
forecast issued at eleven P.M. EST on the night of
December 7:

```
HIGH SEAS FORECAST
0400 UTC DEC 08 1994 (UTC-Z OR ZULU=GREEN-
WICH MEAN TIME)
PAN PAN
NORTH ATLANTIC NORTH OF 32N TO 65N AND
WEST OF 35W
FORECAST VALID 1200 UTC DEC 10 1994

WARNINGS
STORM 46N 52W 971 MB AT 0000 UTC MOVING SE
20 KTS. WINDS 45 TO 70 KTS SEAS 18 TO 36 FT
WITHIN 480 NM OVER SW QUADRANT.
```

"Pan pan" is an extreme warning. When used by an
aircraft or ship, it indicates that the safety of the craft
or person is in jeopardy. "Pan pan, pan pan, pan pan,"
is the message Swissair Flight 111 sent moments
before crashing into the ocean near Peggy's Cove.
("Mayday" would indicate an escalation of the danger. It indicates the sender is threatened by grave and
imminent danger and requests immediate assistance.
Swissair 111 never issued a mayday.) When the U.S.
Weather Service issues a "pan pan" warning, it's notifying mariners of an *extratropical storm of hurricane
strength*, a storm that should be avoided at all costs.

Six hours later, at 1000 UTC, which converts to five
A.M. in New York, six A.M. in Halifax, and seven A.M.

at the point where the *Salvador Allende* would sink—
39-22N, 49-54W—the warning was intensified.

```
PAN PAN
NORTH ATLANTIC NORTH OF 32N TO 65N
AND WEST OF 35W
FORECAST VALID 1800 UTC DEC 10 1994

WARNINGS.
COMPLEX STORM 46N 45W 962 MB AT 0600 UTC
WILL MOVE NE 25 KT. WINDS 45 TO 65 KT SEAS 18
TO 38 FT WITHIN 600 NM OVER SW AND W QUAD-
RANTS EXCEPT WINDS TO 70 KT AND SEAS TO
50 FT IN THE VICINITY OF THE GULF STREAM
NEAR 40N 50W.
[EMPHASIS ADDED]
```

"Complex storm" is a low pressure center with a
warm or cold front coming out of it, a low off to one
side of it, with another one or two lows within it. It's
storms within a storm. Average sea level barometric
pressure is 1013 millibars. A "normal low" runs about
990 Mb; 980 is very low. The Weather Service predic-
tion is that atmospheric pressure in this storm will fall
to 962 millibars of mercury. Seventy knot winds translate to just over eighty mph. On the Beaufort Scale of
1 to 12, that's a 12. Hurricane force.

The position of the *Salvador Allende* when it's
found on radar by CG 1503 is 39-29.5N, 050-06.1W,
barely 36 miles from the precise spot at 40N 50W the
Weather Service forecast said would be the most dangerous. If John Elway had been on her bridge, he
could have almost tossed a Hail Mary pass to the 40N

50W bull's-eye. With luck and a tailwind, he would have made it for sure. And he had the tailwind. Eighty miles an hour worth.

It was as though Captain Sergey Michailovich Chuluykov of the M/V *Salvador Allende* had called Canadian Air Force Captain Jonathan Forrest and said, "What do you say we pick the worst spot in the entire North Atlantic and meet there Thursday night?"

The absence of potential rescue vessels anywhere near 40N 50W is mute testimony to the fact that most ship's masters who could act on the weather warning did so. Not only did Captain Chuluykov put his ship in harm's way by setting this course, his action virtually assured that no help would be available to save his crew. From RCC New York to RCC Halifax, from 14 Wing Greenwood to the 106th Air Rescue Squadron on Long Island, and on every AMVER vessel whose assistance was being sought, one look at the weather charts brought the same question to the minds of the would-be rescuers: why would a master—especially one with seventeen years experience on the high seas—go there? There had to be a reason.

FOUR

In mid-October the *Salvador Allende*, heavy with a cargo of construction material and aluminum, sailed out of the harbor at Tallinn, Estonia, into the Gulf of Finland, bound for Baltimore. Four hundred miles to the east was Saint Petersburg, Russia. Less than fifty miles across the narrow neck of the gulf is Helsinki, the ship's ultimate destination. Her route took her southeast into the Baltic Sea, past the Polish port of Gdansk, then north past Copenhagen, through the narrow strait between Sweden and Denmark, past Stavenger on the southern tip of Norway, where the RCC is located, and out into the North Atlantic. The ship was routed to take advantage of favorable following winds and seas and to avoid as much adverse weather as possible.

Upon her arrival in the Port of Baltimore on November 1, a U.S. Coast Guard safety inspection team boarded the twenty-one-year-old vessel, which was due for its annual safety examination. She came through with flying colors. The only deficiency noted by the boarding party was that volume two of a required USCG light list had not been updated. Two days later, after unloading a portion of her cargo, the

Salvador Allende left Baltimore and sailed south, came around Florida and headed northwest toward New Orleans. Entering the Mississippi River, she slowly steamed upriver about sixty miles past the city, where she docked and discharged the remainder of her cargo. Reversing her course, she threaded her way south through heavy river traffic until she finally returned to the Gulf of Mexico, where she turned almost due west, toward Galveston. In the Gulf, the crew used saltwater to clean the huge cargo holds to ensure that they'd pass the required sanitation inspection before the cargo of rice could be loaded. Going past the entrance to the Houston Ship Canal, the vessel continued southwest, paralleling twenty-five-mile-long Galveston Island on her starboard beam. Once past the long barrier island, she followed the marked ship channel the final twenty miles into Brazos Harbor at Freeport, tying up on November 25 at the concrete dock owned by the American Rice Company. The process of loading the ship with 7,000 tons of rice bound for Helsinki, Finland, took about four days.

The rice was packaged for ease of handling in heavy white plastic totes—sometimes called "superbags"—four-foot cubes with a capacity of 2,000 pounds—which were lifted off the dock and into the holds with the ship's cranes, then maneuvered into position by a forklift. Once the port and starboard sides of the holds were filled, the cranes lifted the forklifts out and set them on the dock. Then the center of each hold was filled, using the cranes to lower the totes, which were guided into position by stevedores. The loading plan was worked out by the company that employed the stevedores, and approved by the master and second officer. The 7,000 tons of rice was to be packed in the five holds forward of the superstructure. The sixth cargo hold in the stern would not be used. When loading was complete, the holds were filled with totes to within three feet of the top. Ropes would be used to secure the upper layers.

On the afternoon of November 30 preparations were made by all the ship's departments for a departure around midnight. For Alex Taranov, it meant running a complete check on lifeboats one and two. It's a set routine. Remove the canvas cover from the open center section, climb in, start the motor, check the prop in both forward and reverse. There is no need to lower the boats. During the Coast Guard safety inspection in Baltimore a few days earlier, they had lowered one of them and everything was working fine. Finishing with the boats, he checked the emergency diesel generator on deck to make sure it had fuel and was operating properly.

Just after midnight the *Salvador Allende* sailed out of Freeport, Texas, beginning what would turn out to be her final voyage. Alex was off duty, asleep in his cabin. His regular duty shifts are four to eight, night and day, and they were scheduled to stay that way during the entire eighteen- to-twenty-day voyage to Helsinki. If a problem developed in the engine room, he'd put in extra hours to fix it, but for now everything was running just the way it was supposed to.

Sometime late on the third or early on the fourth of December, the ship came around Florida, entered the Atlantic Ocean, and set a northerly course, hitching a free ride in the three-knot current of the Gulf Stream.

The earliest historical reference to the Gulf Stream was made by Ponce de Leon in 1513, when he experienced great difficulty crossing the massive current north of what is now Cape Canaveral, Florida. Within six years its existence was widely known and accepted by sailors plying the seas between Spain and America. Two hundred fifty years later, in 1769, the postmaster general of the colonies, Benjamin Franklin, became vexed, the story goes, that British mail ships taking a northerly route from England were running two weeks late. American postal ships, which usually took a more southerly route, made the journey from England days, if not weeks, faster than the Brits.

In response to a request for help from British postal authorities, Franklin consulted his cousin, Timothy Folger, a whaling ship captain from Nantucket, for an explanation. Folger told Franklin about the Gulf Stream and created a chart illustrating its effect on ships. At this time most of the American and Spanish ship captains were well aware of the current and knew to sail in it while en route to Europe and to stay out of it when returning to the colonies. Whalers told him the current was so strong it could significantly slow the progress of westbound ships from England, even to the point of pushing them backward in light winds. Franklin recorded this discovery and his subsequent action in his journals. "We have informed [the British captains] that they were stemming a current that was against them to the value of three miles an hour and advised them to cross it, but they were too wise to be counseled by American fishermen."

It's doubtful even Franklin could have comprehended the immensity and complexity of the Gulf Stream. Its origin is in the North Equatorial Current, which moves parallel to the Equator, where it's joined by a portion of the South Equatorial Current, which is shunted northward along the South American coast. This northerly flow then splits in two; the Antilles Current, which flows along the Atlantic side of the West Indies, and the Caribbean Current, which passes through the Yucatan Channel into the Gulf of Mexico. These reconverge as the Florida Current, which flows close to shore over the continental shelf. It becomes the Gulf Stream where it moves offshore near Cape Hatteras, North Carolina, flowing across the deep ocean in a northeasterly direction. It's the western edge of the Gulf Stream that usually has a very defined boundary—the so-called "north wall."

The Gulf Stream is, without question, the largest of the globe's ocean currents. Oceanographers measure currents the same way rivers are measured: by the amount of water flowing past a given point per second. But the volume in the oceans is so great, they've come up with a unique unit of measure to try and make the numbers comprehensible. The unit is the Sverdrup; one sv equals one million cubic meters per second. The average flow of the Gulf Stream is 55 Sverdrups. That's 14.5 billion gallons a second, all moving northward, then eastward, in a "river" with an average width of 43 miles extending to 1,500 feet beneath the surface, and in places to as deep as a mile. That's equivalent to 300 Amazons, the largest river in the world in terms of water volume. Or 3,200 Mississippi Rivers. And that's on an average day. Where it flows past the Chesapeake Bay outflow, it can increase to ninety sv, greater than the size of all the Earth's freshwater rivers combined. The flow is smaller on the Gulf Stream's eastward leg where it passes Newfoundland, but it's still a sizable forty sv.

The average speed of this river is about three miles

an hour; but it's been measured as slow as two mph and as fast as six mph. Oceanographers and meteorologists keep track of the direction and speed of the current by using data from permanently moored deep water buoys, from floating buoys with radio transmitters, and by satellite observation. It's this tracking data that the RCC staff inputs into their Computer Aided Search Program, so they can more accurately estimate how far a survivor, a lifeboat, or a raft has drifted from its last known position.

For some reason Alex Taranov didn't entirely understand, the *Salvador Allende*'s engine ran more efficiently when the ship was sailed with a one-degree list to port, which was hardly enough to be noticed in a constantly moving sea. They were not in the Atlantic very long when the instruments in the control room told him the ship was listing 1.5 degrees. Yes, there was a wind from starboard which might account for it, but it just didn't seem right. Alex gradually corrected the list by burning more fuel oil from the portside tanks, but he still wasn't happy. He took the problem to the chief engineer, who ordered him to continue taking oil from one side in order to keep the ship in trim. But Alex felt it was a problem that the ship's captain needed to know about. "You know the master is my friend," he said to the chief engineer, "but I can't go and tell him. You can go, 'cause it's not really a good idea for me to go to the master. It's the chief engineer's responsibility, not mine."

The ship continued northward in three- or four-foot seas near the western edge of the Gulf Stream, at a speed of sixteen or seventeen knots. They were budgeted to burn no more than twenty-four tons of fuel oil a day, and by controlling which tanks it came from,

Alex was able to keep her properly trimmed. Sailing in the Gulf Stream gave them an extra three knots, increasing speed and fuel efficiency.

Sometime early on December 8, when they were north of Bermuda, the captain spread the word that there was a big storm ahead, and he ordered a change of course to avoid it. For several hours they sailed on this new course, and then, inexplicably, the ship returned to its original heading. Alex and the other crewmen soon noticed that the seas were getting higher and the wind was picking up. During his morning shift he also noticed that once again the ship was listing beyond the allotted one degree. Throughout the day the weather continued to deteriorate. Around five P.M., when the sun went down, it turned even worse, the wind screaming out of the northwest, and the *Salvador Allende* began rolling heavily from side to side. Alex went up to take a look and saw that the waves were "really bad."

"That's when the waves are really high. The ship not just—how you call it?—ship move from side to side. Ship not list slow; ship go to one side, go up, then suddenly go down so you can't understand which way it go the next time." And then he returned to his cabin and climbed into bed for what would prove to be the last time.

The north wall of the Gulf Stream as it turns east to curve around the Maritime Provinces is where the warm waters from the south collide with the cold waters of the Labrador Current. More significantly, the cold air moving southward *above* the Labrador Current slams into the tropical air above the Gulf Stream, creating a localized storm effect that in both myth and truth has sent many a ship to the bottom. This effect is dramatically magnified when winds from the north-west are in opposition to the Gulf Stream's three-knot current. On this hellish night, the master of the *Salvador Allende* had received warnings that a major storm system was rapidly moving to the southeast, packing winds up to seventy knots. Monstrous waves were building up near the north wall.

Alex had no way of knowing that his friend Sergey had been ordered to resume the original, planned course, taking them directly into the teeth of the storm. The master routinely reported his position to the company at least once every twenty-four hours, usually at noon. When he called in on December 8, the company official noted that the *Salvador Allende* was not on course. Sergey explained that he was altering course to avoid the worst of the storm. No, he was told. If you change course, you'll be late arriving in Helsinki and jeopardize our bonus. He was ordered to return to the original course.

He broke the connection and, poring over his charts and the faxes showing him the immense storm he had just been ordered to sail into, ordered the helmsman to resume their original heading. Turning, Captain Sergey Michailovich Chuluykov looked directly at his second officer, Igor Skiba, and muttered the Russian equivalent of "They've fucked us!"

FIVE

Aboard Rescue 306
Near the *Salvador Allende*
Approximately 5:00 A.M. local time (3:00 A.M. EST)

On the flight deck of Rescue 306, Jonathan Forrest and Kevin Dort react instinctively to the lights they've spotted. Without night vision goggles, they shouldn't be seeing *anything* out there. It has to be associated with the ship. Rescue 306 is already in a tight turn toward the lights when, over the headsets, they hear Ron O'Reilly's voice again. "At the 7:30 position," he says, which means it's not quite behind them on their left side, "I see lights. A lot of lights. It looks like a boat."

And then he begins giving instructions that will help get the aircraft pointed toward the vessel. "Okay, left turn. It's at seven o'clock, coming around eight o'clock, nine o'clock, ten, eleven o'clock, on the nose." Instructions from the guys in the rear are responded to instantaneously, if not faster. It's very easy to catch sight of a man in the water and lose him seconds later. Therefore, it's imperative when Ron or Andre call for a course change, they get it immediately. In this case it didn't take long for the cockpit to see what the SARtechs were taking them to. In the distance they could see the *Salvador Allende*, her bridge near the top of the superstructure still lit up like a Christmas tree.

They make one more pass over the two rafts that appeared to be tied together, giving loadmaster Marco Michaud an opportunity to drop a datum marker buoy. Later they'll be able to home in on its signal, and since it should drift at close to the same rate and in the same direction as the life rafts, it'll help find them again, even in the dark.

Everyone on 306 by now assumes that the crew has already abandoned ship and are in those four life rafts. That's what an early version of the distress call had said: "We are abandoning ship in four life rafts." No confirmation has ever been received that the crew had actually taken to the rafts, but considering the state of the ship, still being savaged by giant waves, it's not a stretch to make that assumption.

That assumption is given more credence as Rescue 306 flies past the *Salvador Allende*. The ship is at more than a 45-degree list. Water covers half her main deck and is breaking at least halfway up the superstructure. She's low enough in the water that the huge waves regularly slamming into her are rolling all the way across the seventy-foot width of the deck. And there is no sign of life on the vessel, at least none that anyone aboard 306 can see. The combination of heavy salt spray, extreme turbulence, shadows cast by the superstructure, and the speed at which the plane, pushed by eighty mph winds, is rocketed past the starboard side of the ship, conspire to prevent the observers on the plane from seeing the twenty crew members who are strung out in a line from the super-structure to the stern. Not even NVGs help.

O'Reilly is frustrated. Ordinarily it's difficult enough to spot targets at night. All the bouncing around is making it even more difficult. On top of that, the wind is so strong the pilots can't fly a decent circle pattern around the ship. Every time they turn down-wind, they're forced away from the *Salvador Allende*, turning their pattern into a mile-long oval. Under the circumstances, they can't see any life aboard the stricken ship.

Looking at the ship lying almost on its side in the water does confirm for O'Reilly how huge the seas are, and he reports this to the flight deck, where both pilots have their hands full. Kevin Dort is experiencing the first signs of vertigo, and Forrest is concerned both about his copilot's condition and what the airplane is doing. Flying in this weather at an altitude of only 500 feet doesn't offer a comfortable margin of safety, especially with bumps that take them up and down as much as fifty feet in seconds. Things are so bad that neither one of them can take a moment to look at the *Salvador Allende*. Keeping Rescue 306 in the air is their first priority.

Not discovering anyone on the ship, Forrest's plan is to backtrack, locate the rafts, and go into the flare-dropping procedure they'd practiced hundreds of times. He wants that two million candlepower of off-white light shining down on the rafts when he brings the plane in low and slow to make the SKAD drop. It's going to be hard enough putting the SKAD within reach of the survivors in the turbulence; trying to do it in total darkness would be plain silly.

The other reason for dropping a flare is to wake up

the neighborhood. O'Reilly says it's not only possible, but likely, that people in the water can't hear the C-130's four jet-prop engines over the noise of the storm. They may have no idea they've been found. On a dark and stormy night, a two-million-candlepower light is a surefire way of delivering that message.

The recommended procedure for the drop is to get up to altitude, usually between 4,000 and 4,500 feet, drop the flare out the back, then crank and bank the aircraft around as fast and hard as they can in order to be near the flare when it drifts over the target. That would be the ideal situation. Unfortunately, there's nothing about this mission that is falling neatly in the category of "ideal."

The problem is the low ceiling. At 4,500 feet, they'll have four and a half minutes of burn time, with the flare sputtering out around 1,000 feet. Dropping it from 3,000 feet gives them no more than three minutes of light before it plummets into the sea, still burning, giving off a spectacular but useless underwater glow. A low drop also increases the chances of dripping hot magnesium onto a rubber life raft filled with people who already have enough problems.

Then there's the matter of wind velocity. The first mayday from the *Salvador Allende* indicated wind speed at 37 knots. Either the ship's instrumentation was wrong, it was wishful thinking, or the situation has gotten even more desperate since the initial call, because Forrest knows he was fighting a lot more than a 37-knot wind when he passed over the ship at about 500 feet. The C-130 was down to sixty knots ground speed, which means he was flying into a sixty- or seventy-knot wind.

Flying rescue is like five card stud poker. You've

got to make the best of the cards you're dealt. So Forrest makes the adjustments, runs the calculations in his head, and gets everyone ready for the first drop. This maneuver calls for a lot to happen in the space of very little time, and everyone needs to be prepared. In the back, SARtech O'Reilly stays in the left window scanning through his NVGs. His team member, Andre Hotton, and the loadmaster, Marco Michaud, have slipped their NVGs up on top of their flight helmets. Since the goggles virtually eliminate all depth perception and peripheral vision, they're not used by crew working on the open ramp. When Rescue 306 left Greenwood, it was carrying thirty Styrofoam boxes, each containing two three-foot-long flares. Now the two men begin unpacking several of the boxes, in preparation for the drop.

Unlike when dropping SKADs, it's the navigator's job to make the call here. He's the one who's done the final calculations to determine how many miles upwind the drop point should be. With everyone ready and copilot Dort at the controls, they fight their way upwind. Bourgoin, battling his continuing nausea, uses the Doppler navigation system to determine when they've reached the drop point, passing the information to the aircraft commander.

"Ready . . . drop!" says Forrest.

On the ramp, Hotton tosses the canister. As it goes sailing out, Michaud hits his intercom switch. "Flare's away and clear." Even before the word "clear" has reached the cockpit, Dort cranks the plane into a flaps-down, 45-degree, left-bank-angle level turn to chase the cylinder downwind. Initially they need to make a U-turn, but despite an immediate need to dive down to 300 to 500 feet for the SKAD drop, they have to hold their altitude until they can be sure where the flare is. A level turn assures they'll be above it and not have to worry about smacking into a five-inch-diameter tube packed with twenty-one pounds of magnesium sodium nitrate on a short fuse.

In the dark, the canister free-falls the preset 500 feet, then pops its eighteen-foot parachute. All three crew members in back are hanging on and watching for the first sign of light, which should come about ten seconds after the drop. They wait. Seven, eight, nine, ten . . . "Flare ignition!" The instant he knows the flare is visible, Dort puts the power to flight idle, the nose goes over, and the plane hits its maximum flap speed of 150 knots. In back, Michaud is assisting Hotton in preparing the raft bundles on the ramp. They need to go out in a precise order, carefully timed. It won't do to have one of the ropes get caught up in something or someone at a critical moment.

Up front, reality confronts the pilots. There's not going to be a SKAD drop. They're shocked to see the flare go screaming downwind so fast they have no hope of catching up and getting into the cone of light underneath it. The book says that a flare under a parachute, even one being pushed along by seventy-knot winds, should drift slower than an airplane flying at twice that speed in those same winds. Another rescue theory shot to hell by reality.

Forrest calls for a second attempt to light up the rafts with a flare, this time, having learned a lesson the first time, dropping it even farther upwind. Same result. This is getting frustrating. All the bouncing around makes it difficult to concentrate on the calculations he needs to make. Navigator Bourgoin says the turbulence is like riding your bicycle down a railroad track. But you can't stop because there's a train on your tail. What it boils down to is that you have to function because you don't have a choice, and because you know there are people down below who are counting on you.

A strong ego is a requirement for an aircraft commander. He—or she—has to believe they have the ability to take the plane up, perform their assigned mission regardless of the conditions, and bring it back down safely. A pilot filled with self-doubt is not likely to inspire confidence in his crew, and perhaps is less likely to push his own personal envelope to get the job done under difficult circumstances. At five in the morning over the mid-Atlantic in the heart of what the U.S. Weather Service benignly calls an "extratropical storm," Jonnie Forrest is most definitely pushing his envelope. He and his crew have flown in turbulence like this before, but it would last only a minute or two. This is constant; it's taking a mental and physical toll on everyone, and the only way to stop it would be to get above the weather and return home, an option that's not in their playbook.

While possessed of a healthy ego, Forrest is not a captive of it. He learned a long time ago that seven minds working on a solution are almost always better than just one. So he asks his crew for feedback. "Here's what I'm figuring. . . . This should work if we go . . . but it's not working. What's wrong?"

Gilles and Kevin, the nav and the copilot, don't have a better solution. In the back, SARtech team leader O'Reilly, who's used to making quick, instinctive decisions, says what they've been doing sounds right to him. Let's give it one more shot.

So they try a third flare. No improvement. It's clearly

time to punt. After a brief discussion, they all agree to try dropping a SKAD to the life rafts in the dark. This means that the SARtechs are back on NVGs and will have to call the drop; without a flare, the pilots haven't got a prayer of seeing the target they're aiming for.

That puts the pressure on Ron O'Reilly. He has to spot the raft, guide the pilot into the proper upwind/crosswind pattern, and calculate how far upwind of the target they should drop the SKAD. The navigator tells him the wind speed and direction. The drop point is fifty feet upwind of the target for every ten knots of wind above the first fifteen knots. It's not calculus, but consider: he's concentrating on looking through NVGs to keep the target in sight, it's noisy as hell with the ramp open (the C-130 isn't exactly whisper quiet with the ramp closed, which is why everyone is issued earplugs), they're being bounced all over the sky by the storm, the wind speed is constantly changing, he's monitoring conversation on the intercom, giving the pilot course adjustments to keep the aircraft on track, and he knows that someone's life may depend on him getting it right.

O'Reilly keys his mic switch. "This will be a standard four-bundle SKAD drop. The target is the life raft in the water. First pass will be fifty feet downwind, and two seconds past abeam of target I'll drop a timer smoke. Second pass we'll do a crosswind upwind pattern 300 feet upwind of target."

They set up and drop a timing smoke. It's a flare that O'Reilly can drop through a port in his scanning door. On the way down it generates white smoke and helps them calculate wind direction. When it hits the water, it burns with a bright flame for a short time, giving them another reference point.

Now it's time for the real thing. The ramp is open and Hotton has positioned all four bundles of the SKAD across it. Michaud's role at this point is to keep his weight on the final three bundles so they're not accidentally launched. Lanyards from each of the rafts are attached to the ramp. The SARtech team leader guides the plane around. In the front, they're trying to keep things low and slow, flying the C-130 just above stall speed.

"Left . . . steady . . . steady . . . right . . . steady . . . on my word command 'Now' drop SKAD. . . ." They approach the drop point, "Prepare to drop SKAD . . . drop SKAD *Now*!"

Hotton shoves the raft out, watching the accordion-folded rope bundles attached to the package pay out. When there are only three rope bundles left attached to the raft, he shoves the second package off the ramp and again monitors the rope breaking free of the bundle. The same with the third package, and the fourth, another ten-man raft. The object is to make certain that the floating rope between the packages is stretched to its full 800-foot-length by the time it hits the water. At the same time, he's keeping an eye on the lanyards that pull out of the raft packages, triggering large CO_2 bottles. By the time the rafts hit the water, they're fully inflated.

What they want to do is have all four bundles land upwind of the target. Since the rafts on either end have more freeboard than the supply packages, the wind should push them faster, creating a U shape around the life raft in the water. If any point on the rope comes in contact with people in the water, they can haul all four packages to them. That's the theory. Now add the "extratropical storm" force winds.

"Did you see that SKAD?" O'Reilly shouts, disheartened. What he's watching is their rafts hitting the crest of a wave where the wind grabs them and spirals them away like pinwheeling kites on 300 feet of line anchored to the water by the supply packages. The rafts come to the end of their tethers, drop back into the water, ride to the crest of the next wave, and repeat the cycle, cartwheeling off into the distance. They all know that the chances of somebody getting hold of either raft or the rope in these conditions are pretty slim.

Everyone had been aware that the odds of a successful drop weren't great, but knowing that the pounding they've been taking has been for naught is sobering. Forrest assesses the situation, and it's not pretty. "We're getting bounced around. People are having trouble keeping their cookies down. Feeling ill, sick, everything. It's hard to move, hard to see. We're all tired. It's in the middle of the night, everyone's had maybe one, two hours of sleep. So what are we doing, throwing all our gear out if, in half an hour to an hour, we're going to be able to do it under daylight. Is it going to save anybody? Not really. In that half hour? Is it worthwhile getting rid of everything to be sitting there with nothing later on? No."

Sharing his decision with the crew, he tells his copilot to take it up and find some clear air so they can clean up the plane, move around a bit, get their act together and come up with an action plan for daylight operations. There are no objections. On the way up they contact Coast Guard 1503. It would be a good time for them to go in and drop a self-locating datum marker buoy, which would also let the survivors know they haven't been forsaken. Assuming that's 1503's plan, they take the unpressurized plane up to just below 10,000 feet. While the air may be thin, at least it's not blowing them all over the sky. This truly is the pause that refreshes.

RCC New York
4:17 A.M. EST
Near the wreck site, 6:17 A.M.

Coast Guard 1503 reports that they've just dropped a self-locating datum marker buoy at position 39-27.6N, 050-08.8W. The aircraft also says they've been unable to establish communications with the survivors, and that the ship's life rafts are separated from the sinking vessel by two nautical miles. In response to a question, 1503 says it's also been unable to make contact with any of the merchant vessels responding to the SOS. Before breaking contact, the Elizabeth City–based plane relays that the Canadian Herc will be able to remain on-scene no later than nine A.M. local time.

What the pilot of Coast Guard 1503 apparently *doesn't* tell RCC New York is that they've already departed the area of the shipwreck. The Coast Guard plane does contact Rescue 306, surprising them with the news that they're "bingo fuel" and are headed back to base.

Just under three hours later, CG 1503 is on the ground at Shearwater. It's 8:10 A.M. local time. The postmission situation report they file indicates total flight time of 8.3 hours, significantly less than the twelve-plus hours of potential time the C-130 could fly with the full load of fuel they took on at Norfolk. The three life-raft kits and one of the two SLDMBs they left Norfolk with are still onboard the aircraft.

SIX

Using data from satellites and buoys, oceanographers tracking water temperatures in the Gulf Stream on the morning the *Salvador Allende* is sinking report that it ranges from 66 degrees Fahrenheit southeast of Newfoundland, to 79 degrees F off Cape Hatteras, North Carolina. At the precise spot the *Salvador Allende* reported being knocked over, she was almost straddling the so-called "north wall" of the Gulf Stream, and was most likely in the slightly cooler water of the continental slope, where the temperature is 63 degrees. But the data available to the Coast Guardsmen manning the RCC tells them that the hurricane-force northwest winds should very quickly push any survivors in the water, or in rafts or lifeboats, southeast into the Gulf Stream, where the water temperature jumps to 72 degrees, providing a significant increase in survivability over a longer period of immersion time.

In the case of the *Salvador Allende*, there's an irony at work that the captain may even have thought about as he contemplated the fate of his ship. The vessel was sailing in the Gulf Stream to increase its speed across the Atlantic, but just as there's no free lunch, there's also no free ride. The price paid for riding the current, especially near the north wall, is that the vessel will traverse the area where the Gulf Stream collides with the cold, southward-flowing Labrador Current resulting in magnification of the intensity of any storm coming through, as well as increasing the size of the seas. Had the *Salvador Allende* stayed on her altered course, taking her east and out of the Gulf Stream, the ship may not have experienced the extreme sea conditions that were her undoing. But here's where the ironic twist turns back on itself: sinking in the Gulf Stream's waters gives the crew a significantly better chance of survival than if the *Salvador Allende* had gone down outside the warm current. Consider that just a bit more than two degrees—about 150 miles— farther north, the temperature in the continental shelf water is only 43 degrees Fahrenheit, which would be fatal in less than an hour.

Hampton Bays, Long Island
4:00 A.M. EST

Four in the morning comes much too soon for Lieutenant Colonel Robert Landsiedel, but he promised RCC New York they'd have a C-130 airborne by 7:30, and as mission commander, it's his job to wake up the troops. It would have been easier to call them before he went to bed at midnight, but that would have broken their required twelve hours of "crew rest," and shortened the amount of time they'd have to participate in the search. It may be the Air National Guard and not regular Air Force, but rules are rules.

RCC New York
4:15 A.M. EST

Message traffic from AMVER ships responding to the mayday, as well as traffic from ships answering the widely broadcast SOS, is beginning to stack up. The veteran Coast Guardsmen manning the RCC aren't surprised at receiving some negative responses. When weather is bad for one ship, it's usually bad for all of them. Less than an hour after the general SOS went out, a telex arrives from an Indian flag bulk carrier, the M/V *Chennai Veeram*.

> From Master MV Chennai Veeram bound for
> Belladune Canada from Singang China
> speed 5 knots
> Indian flag bulk carrier
> we are 505 NM from reported posn of mv sa.
> Presently we are facing severe storm. BF 10
> winds, very rough seas. Vessel rolling and
> pitching violently. Manoevering with difficulty.
> In view above conditions and over 505 nm dis-
> tant from vsl in distress, we are proceeding on
> cours to Belladune (New Brunswick, Canada)

"B.F. 10" is shorthand for "Beaufort Scale Force 10." What it means is that the ship is caught in a "whole gale" with winds from 55 to 63 mph, and a high-churning white sea. While international law requires vessels to come to the aid of a ship in distress, it leaves it up to the master to determine whether doing so would present too great a risk to his own ship. It quickly became apparent to the trio of Coast Guardsmen manning the Rescue Coordination Center that finding ships willing *and able* to divert to the wreck site was not going to be easy.

```
09 0956Z telex
from  Master of Brandenburg  relayed to
Stavanger rcc to NY via amver easylink
psn 41-30.7n  044-55.3w
course 100 degre sped 11.8 knots with 560
tons iron pipes ondeck  have difficulties with
lashing, some pipes rolling between the dck
container. Pls advie if necwessaryto preceed to
distress position with 12 knots. I can't give no
more speed due to deck cargo and heavy swell.
Brgds
```

For rescue professionals, just about the only thing worse than bad news is good news that turns into bad news. When the first mayday was sent, RCC Halifax reported that several fishing trawlers—probably Russian—were within fifty miles of the *Salvador Allende* and thought they could be on-scene in eight or nine hours. At nine P.M., Lieutenant Commander Jay Topper thinks, "We're going to have four fishing vessels there at four in the morning. This is outstanding." They kept sending estimated times of arrival: "Okay, now we'll be there in three hours." And Topper is looking at a satellite picture, seeing nothing, and thinking, "They must be within three miles. What's goin' on?"

The trawlers never materialize. One eventually sends a message saying, "We're turning around; we're heading to port 'cause this is just too bad." It wasn't hard to believe. These are 100-foot boats in forty-foot seas.

Topper's boss, Commander Grant E. Leber, had

worked enough missions to have developed a realistic perspective on the rescue business: "One of the things that I think is very difficult to convey to anybody who's not been down to the sea in ships is the sheer power of forty-foot seas. You know, we live in a high-tech world where you can do marvelous things with computers and life support systems, the things you can do with medical science. And everybody thinks that you can save everybody from everything. And the truth is that there are some times that all the technology in the world isn't going to save you from the elements.

"And if you've got forty-foot seas and . . . what were the winds out there? Sixty knots? Fifty? And the initial reports that we had from the [*Salvador Allende*] that they were basically knocked down by rogue waves. You're talking about a 450-foot cargo vessel getting knocked over by rogue waves. Who's going to go poke their nose into that? People were trying to do that, and were getting turned around by the weather."

Of the men in the RCC during the rescue effort, all but Commander Leber are "boat drivers." Leber, as he puts it, is "an airplane driver by trade, and from previous missions that I've been involved with, I can tell you that there's a great sense of frustration being in a fixed-wing aircraft on the scene of a major search case like this, because there's really not much more that you can do other than circle and look at them, talk to them in some cases, and drop survival equipment. And there's so many times that you drop survival equipment, you do your very best, and it winds up not being of any use to them. I've been on missions where the sole thing that we were able to say was, 'Yeah, this is the last place on earth that these people were seen alive.' And there's a great sense of frustration. You wish you could do more. But you can't."

Lt. Col. Robert Landsiedel's home
Hampton Bays, Long Island
4:45 A.M. EST

It took about forty-five minutes for Robert Landsiedel to complete all the phone calls necessary to ensure that a full C-130 crew would be at the base and ready to take off by 7:30. The aircraft commander would be Colonel Bill Stratemeier, vice wing commander of the 106th. He joined the unit twenty years earlier, after separating from the Air Force, and was an experienced search and rescue pilot. In the brief phone conversation, use of the unit's helicopters is not discussed.

Aboard the *Salvador Allende*
5:00 A.M. (3:00 A.M. EST)

The twenty crew members still onboard the *Salvador Allende* receive a rude wake-up call just after five o'clock. The ship begins to change position, from a more than fifty-degree list it rolls onto its port side, a full ninety-degree list. Alex Taranov hears something big drop in the engine room, and then a new sound. The rushing sound of a waterfall as the sea begins to pour into every available opening—funnel, broken windows, ventilator shafts. Until this moment the diesel generators he had carefully maintained for the past month had been running, supplying power to keep

the lights on the bridge lit. But now they've stopped.
For a couple of seconds the lights just barely glow,
then the ship goes dark.

Alex waits, knowing what should come next. And it
does. The emergency diesel generator on the main
deck, which was also his responsibility, detects the
drop in voltage and kicks in, turning the lights back
on. Taranov knows the ship is going to go down; yet
the question that interests him is whether his generator
would start.

He quickly comes back to the problem at hand, as
the false board they'd all been resting on—the strip
between the deck railing and the top of the steel hull—
slips underwater. "Everybody, try to move to the stern
to go overboard. I don't want you guys hitting your
heads on the propeller blades," the captain says. With
each passing wave, the blades are being lifted out of
the water, then dropped down. Sliding off the over-
hanging fantail of the ship would put them down-cur-
rent from the prop.

Looking around, Alex sees eighteen people beginning to crawl along the false board toward the stern,
which is now being regularly swept by the waves. The
youngest, one of the motormen, is twenty-four. The
oldest, a doctor and the chief engineer, are in their sixties. Wearing bulky life jackets, it's tough going, especially when they have to hang on to keep from being
washed overboard by each passing wave. It doesn't
make things any easier when water finally gets to the
emergency generator and all the lights go out, leaving
them in pitch-black darkness. Alex jams his stocking
feet into the space between the false board and the
board that normally allows water to drain from the
deck of an upright ship. Big mistake. A huge breaker

rolls over him and he discovers his feet are caught. All he can do is hold his breath and wait, hoping this isn't the moment the ship begins to slide under. Seconds pass slowly. Then the wave rushes on and his head is out of the water. He catches his breath, takes a moment to calm down, and extracts his feet from their trap just as the next wave slams into the ship, knocking three people into the water.

Looking into the darkness, Alex sees lights on the water. "Look. Those two planes dropped us something."

"No," someone near him says, "it's people in the water." It's a moment of realization. Taranov's response is involuntary. "Oh my God." After that, no one speaks. It's not a time for talking. It's a crazy moment. A time to confront personal demons. One man makes the sign of the cross as the waves continue to rip his coworkers from the ship, two and three at a time. When there are only ten of the crew still on the vessel another large breaker comes in, tearing Alex away from the others and throwing him into the maelstrom.

It's like a surreal storm sequence in a Disney cartoon. He feels himself rolling over and over and over and has no idea where he is or what's going on. The noise of the storm is gone, the wind in his face is gone. Up is down and down is up. And then his life jacket pulls him to the surface. He has enough time to count four or five people still on the ship and see the others nearby before he's forced under once more. He gasps, trying to grab some air, but all he can get is saltwater. He needs to find a position where the buoyancy of the life jacket can keep his head clear of the water. At first he tries resting on his stomach, with the vest beneath him, but it's not designed to work that way. The vest has three sections; his head is through the top one, creating a buoyant collar that cradles it from behind; the two larger sections are in front of him, held in place by the ropes he put around his back and then tied into knots while on the ship. What he needs to do is relax and lay *back* in the water, allowing the sections in front of his body to float on top and the one behind him to push his head out of the water. After fighting it for a while, he gets it properly oriented. Now, the shock of being in the water slowly fades, the terror of not being able to breathe abates. He adjusts to the cycles of the waves and tries to get used to the constant swallowing and regurgitating of saltwater. And then he's able to look around. Not far away he spots a small group of people and begins swimming toward them. It's sort of a one-handed crawl, the other being used to push the life jacket to his side. Reaching the group, he discovers it's two of the motormen and the chief engineer clinging to a pair of wooden pallets. All four have lost all sense of time (Alex is wearing a watch but it's covered by the survival suit and he can't get to it). The only indication that they've been in the water for a while is the first hint of twilight. Looking around, they can actually see other people, or the lights on their life jackets. What he wants to see is the ship.

And then he does. The *Salvador Allende* is vertical in the water, her bow pointing skyward. The engine room has filled with water, but the four cargo holds forward of the superstructure are still hermetically sealed, providing buoyancy. Slowly, battered by hurricane force winds, driving rain and occasional snow, she sinks silently beneath the surface. If she makes any sounds as she goes under, they're drowned out by the raging wind and roiling water. What they can't drown out are the thoughts in Alex Taranov's head. Strangely, they're all positive. No lifeboat, no raft, no ships in sight. It doesn't seem to matter. He knows he's going to live.

RCC New York
5:36 A.M. EST

By Fax

```
MSC Giovanna psn 3926N 5157 w course
086 spd 19 kts  eta psn now 5 hours  will
contact Halifax radio by voice in 2 hours with
new eta distress psn
master
```

The frustration of sitting in an office on an island in New York harbor knowing that a ship is sinking and lives are at stake is that you really can't *do* anything. You don't actually *control* anything, which is probably why what used to be casually referred to as the Rescue Control Center was now called a Rescue Coordination Center. They've already done as much coordinating as could possibly be done with surface vessels. All they can do now is wait and see who makes it to the scene. Then they can begin assigning search sectors, primarily downwind of the place where the *Salvador Allende* went down.

What they're struggling to do right now is make sure there's always an aircraft on-station above the survivors. It means finding out who has planes available and crews to fly them. The two don't necessarily go hand in hand.

An hour earlier Canadian Forces Base Greenwood called to tell them that the Aurora that was due to replace Rescue 306 was down for repairs. They were scrambling to find another aircraft and crew. A half hour later Greenwood calls back and tells Gary Parker that the replacement, Rescue 111, should be off the deck in fifteen minutes. En route time will be just under two hours, but once there, they'll be able to stay for six-plus hours. Again, it's good news and bad news. That's a six-hour time slot plugged with a C-130 operated by trained rescue pilots and SARtechs who'll show up with every SKAD they can find. The bad news: Rescue 306 will bingo at least ninety minutes before Rescue 111 shows up. And there's no other aircraft available to fill that hole.

At 6:36 A.M., the M/V *Obo Elif*, one of the first AMVER ships tasked for the rescue, sends a telex message to New York. It's more bad news.

```
I RCVD SUBJ MSG FRM NAVTEX SAME TIME AND
TRY TO PROSIDE TOWORD SUBJECT VSL BUT DUE
TO STRONG WIND AND WAVE ABT BFRS 11/11 I
UNABLE TO MOVE AGAINS WIND AND WAVE. MY
PRSNT POS IS 41-30.6N / 049 00.1W COURSE 270
AND SPEED ZERO ALTHOUGH MY ALL EFFORT
UNFORTUNITLY AT THIS WATHER CONDITION MY
VSL NEVER MOVE ANY POINT.
REGRDS/MASTER
```

At this point there's nothing more the RCC can do to send ships to the area, so they continue to concentrate on air coverage. Gary Parker calls Elizabeth City, North Carolina, with a request that they stage a Coast Guard C-130 at Norfolk, fueled and ready for a ten

A.M. launch. That should put them on-scene shortly before the second Canadian aircraft bingos. What's next? Another call to E-City. They've got CG 1530, another C-130, en route to Shearwater. When will it be available? The crew will be bagged when they land at the Canadian base. The earliest it can go operational is seven P.M. They'll take it. What choice do they have?

By this time a little good news would be nice, and it comes with the next phone call. It's Radio Halifax relaying a message from the container ship MSC *Giovanna*. "Vessel is five miles from the distress site. ETA approximately three hours. No medical personnel on-board. Position 39-28N, 051-12W. Proceeding to site. Will standby on four MHz radio frequency. No satellite communications available."

In decent weather, that would be cause for elation. But when the master of the *Giovanna* says it's going to take three hours to travel five miles, the yellow caution flag is run up in the RCC. When it happens, they'll believe it.

Home of Captain Graham Buschor
Centereach, Long Island
5:45 A.M. EST

Graham Buschor slaps at the alarm clock, trying to silence it before it wakes his wife, Ann. He's got a seven A.M. call at the base to fly a low-level gunnery mission in an HH-60 PaveHawk helicopter, but there's no need for Ann or either of their two kids to be up this early. To keep the noise level down and buy him a few more minutes in bed, he'd showered the night before.

As he comes into the tiny kitchen the thought

crosses his mind that he's about due for his annual
night-long struggle to make the Christmas tree that
they'll buy together from the volunteer fire department
stand up straight. It's the only thing about the Christmas holiday the normally jovial dad dislikes.
Installing the tree tends to bring out the vernacular he
learned in the Merchant Marine. Not even the dreaded
"some assembly required" on a couple of the kids'
presents causes as much consternation. The tradeoff,
of course, is the joy he knows the kids get from every
ritual related to the holiday. Annie has wrapped and
Graham has hidden dozens of presents for them in the
basement, and they'll appear, as if by magic, under the
tree on Christmas morning. The kids still believe in
Santa Claus, still believe that anything is possible if
you wish hard enough, and he wants them to hold on
to that innocence for as long as possible.

Wearing his dark gray flight suit with a jacket over
it, he steps outdoors and subconsciously assesses the
weather. Still no snow, and it's unseasonably warm for
December 9. A tropical storm from the south has
pushed warm air north, bringing with it gusty winds
that'll make flying interesting, especially if they're
scheduled to practice aerial refueling after machine-
gunning phantom targets in the Atlantic just offshore.

He points the '87 Isuzu pickup truck toward the
nearby 7-Eleven, where he grabs a twenty-ounce
coffee with low fat milk—no sugar—and a roll—no
butter—and begins the thirty-five minute drive to the
base. Food is his enemy, or at least the good stuff is.
He tries to save calories wherever he can because he
knows that sooner rather than later he'll give into
temptation and it'll be steak and potatoes, hamburgers,
hot dogs, fries, eggs, cheese, pizza, calzones, and

pasta with a sauce that hasn't won the American Heart
Association's seal of approval and isn't likely to in his
lifetime.

He's left early enough to drive the flat Long Island
roads at a leisurely pace. It gives him time to enjoy a
few salacious minutes with Howard Stern before
switching over to one of an eclectic group of stations
on the preset buttons. Buschor's taste ranges across
the entire musical spectrum, from classical (no
opera) to rock, with stops along the way for everything from reggae to technopop. At ten minutes to
seven he's saluted by the air policeman in the guard
shack and waved through the gate of the small Air
National Guard base eighty miles east of New York
City.

Gabreski Field
Westhampton Beach, Long Island
6:50 A.M. EST

The Operations building of the 102nd Air Rescue
Squadron of the 106th Air Rescue Wing is a long, low
concrete block structure with direct access to the aircraft parked on the tarmac. Every frill was spared in its
construction. Ambling down the corridor, Buschor
sees enough activity to know that something's up, and
as soon as he can get a refill on his coffee, he'll check
it out.

Meantime, in the briefing room, Colonel Bill
Stratemeier is bringing his C-130 crew up to speed on
the SAR mission that had been planned for them the
night before by Colonel Hill and Lieutenant Colonel

Landsiedel. The aircraft they'll be flying is rigged strictly for search and rescue; it's not set up to refuel helicopters. Even though Stratemeier will be taking three PJs with him, he makes it clear that the weather in the mid-Atlantic precludes their parachuting in with inflatable Zodiac motorboats to aid the survivors.

As the C-130 crew heads for its aircraft, Graham Buschor tracks down the mission commander for their morning training flight, Lieutenant Colonel Ed Fleming. "Hey, did you hear about this ship that went down?" Fleming has no idea what he's talking about, so Buschor fills him in, concluding with, "Whaddaya think, boss, about getting helicopters out there?"

Fleming asks, "Are we tasked?"

"No."

"How many people are we talking about?"

"Well, there was a crew of twenty-eight or thirty, and we have a 130 going out there right now."

With that many people in the water, and the certain knowledge that unless a ship can get to them, their only hope is a helicopter, Fleming decides to go down to the operations center and have Buschor use his engineering training to grind out the numbers. How many tankers would they need? Could they get them in time? Considering the winds, could they get to the scene in time to do some good? At what risk?

There's no discussion as to whether Fleming can authorize the mission. That authority is vested in the wing commander, Colonel Hill, and Fleming realizes that Hill could have ordered the helicopters to make an early morning departure for the scene, but didn't. Nevertheless, Fleming believes that if in his judgment it can be done safely, he's authorized to launch the HH-60s. After all, Hill regularly preaches use of individual initiative. Looming over that logic, of course, is the knowledge that three weeks earlier Hill had removed Fleming from command of the 102nd and gave the job to Landsiedel.

After learning all he can in base operations, Ed Fleming decides that helicopters can safely partici-pate in the *Salvador Allende* rescue, and he gives the go-ahead to scrub the gunnery training mission and suit up for a major rescue at sea. What drives his decision to go for it is the entry made in the base ops log at seven A.M. "Vessel sunk. 11 people in life boat. 3 people clinging to wreckage. 'Few' people in deflated life raft. Other people in water. Water temp 63 degrees air 50 degrees wind 40-50 kts sea state 20–25 ft."

There's no question in his mind that there's an ele-ment of risk involved, but he deems it a reasonable risk. At age forty-seven, Fleming is not a daredevil. The men he commands have confidence in him as a pilot and as a decision maker. He's been flying rescue helicopters since he was twenty-one years old and stationed at Clark Air Force Base in the Philippines, where he flew Charles Lindbergh back to civilization after he'd been lost in the jungles, and also brought out the last remain-ing Japanese Army World War II combatant after a shootout that left the man's partner dead. That was 1970. If Fleming says they can do it, then they can.

Now that he's made the decision Buschor was hop-ing for, Fleming begins to work his way through the logistics. He doesn't want any lengthy delays round-ing up pilots, flight engineers, and PJs for two helicopters, all qualified for overwater hoist rescue missions. Every passing minute means that much less daylight once they get to the scene of the sinking. He delegates Buschor to round up the crews and PJ Mike Moore to locate a second Pararescueman.

Fleming figures this mission is going to require at least three C-130 tankers operating in rotation. It could possibly be done with two, but that means everything would have to work perfectly, and the world of military aviation is an imperfect one. They've already experienced the consequences of a C-130 losing an engine in the middle of a mission in bad weather; they won't ignore the lessons learned. That said, Fleming has every confidence the problem can be dealt with—unit ops will find a third tanker.

"I learned this in the Air Force. I want to get the slower aircraft moving down the road." So Fleming tells base operations, "We're going to get going. We've got to coordinate the tankers. Call Colonel Hill, call Landsiedel. We think we might be able to do this." He's aware that an HH-60 flight of twelve-plus hours has never before been attempted, but his motivation is the number of people whose lives are at risk.

Looking at the roster of qualified pilots, Buschor quickly calls the Suffolk County Police Department, locates their helicopter pilot, Gene Sengstacken, and tells him they've got a rescue mission to fly, there's no time to go home and get his Guard uniform, just get to the base right now. Sengstacken borrows a pair of pants from one cop, a shirt from another, then realizes he's only got five bucks in his wallet, and hits up the owner of the shirt for twenty bucks before hopping into his car.

PJ "Doc" Dougherty's home
Rocky Point, Long Island
7:20 A.M. EST

James "Doc" Dougherty is in the shower when the
phone rings in his home on the north side of Long
Island. His wife Barbara, in the midst of getting
the kids ready to catch the school bus, grabs it. She listens for a moment, incredulous at what she's hearing.
Not that it's unusual for her husband of ten years to
be called in on a day off. Just not on *this* day. The
Doughertys have four children—seven-year-old Jimmy,
five-year-old Dianna, four-year-old Bobby, and two-
year-old Christie—and they've decided four kids in
five years is plenty, so today is the day Jim is going to
have a vasectomy. What makes the call suspect is that
the last time he had the procedure scheduled, he got
called for an emergency mission. And the time before
that, a trip came up that he had to take. Now he's going
to be three for three? She's thinking, It has to be
baloney. It's something the PJs would do as a gag. The
only thing that gives her pause is that the PJ on the
phone is Mike Moore. This just doesn't sound like his
kind of joke. Barbara's thinking, "Tough tooties on
this guy. Whatever it is, I have more important stuff to
take care of. But what am I gonna do? He'll be out the
door in five minutes."

Standing there wrapped in a towel, Doc doesn't
look like the kind of guy who would be one of the Air
Force's elite pararescue jumpers. At a muscular but
not-pumped-up five-eight, and with his glasses, sandy-
colored hair, and quiet-spoken manner, he seems more
like a high school teacher than a guy who's been
jumping out of planes and helicopters into all sorts of

strange situations for the past seventeen years. In other words, he's a lot more Clark Kent than Superman. Doc's been based at Westhampton Beach since he earned the maroon beret at the age of eighteen, having joined the service right out of high school. At age twenty-one he got fixed up with one of his sister's girlfriends, and married Barbara four years later. As a part-time Guardsman—he's a full-time civilian correctional officer—he's been deployed overseas on several dozen military operations (he's been to Turkey five times), as part of the Space Shuttle Rescue Team (to Gambia), and to teach ocean rescue (Bangladesh). But those are assignments that generally can be expected. What took Barbara a bit of getting used to are the phone calls from the base—"We've got a mission"—that would have him flying out the door without even stopping to pack a bag or worry about having money in his pocket. She's also become accustomed to the false starts, the close calls: "They run out there, they go crazy, and for one reason or another, they can't go on the mission, or the Coast Guard did it, or another PJ got on it."

On the morning of December 9, three PJs are already in the air on the C-130 that's en route to the site of the shipwreck. Several more are unavailable, in crew rest, having been on the C-130 mission that didn't get back to base until 10:30 the night before. Several others are deployed overseas. Doc gets the first call, primarily because he lives fairly close to the base.

About the same time that Dougherty comes running into the operations building, Sengstacken arrives and heads for the life support supply window, where he meets up with Buschor and their flight engineer, Technical Sergeant John Krulder. Grabbing their gear, they hustle out to Jolly 08, with Buschor filling him in on the details as they go.

Meantime, in the PJ section, Doc is getting the medical supplies together for both helicopters. Mike Moore is going to fly with Buschor, but he's still technically in crew rest, and he's not supposed to get on an aircraft until he's had his allotted twelve hours. The only reason he was at the base at all is that he often sleeps there overnight when he's working several days in a row. He and his family live in central New Jersey, well beyond commuting distance. Moore gets his personal gear, tells Doc he'll meet him on the ramp, and disappears, leaving Dougherty to drag a double load of medical gear and sleeping bags to the Jollys.

Out on the ramp, Buschor and Sengstacken already have the navigational systems on Jolly 08 up and running, while Ed Fleming and Captain Kevin Fennell are doing the same in Jolly 14. The flight engineers, Krulder and Rich Davin, are well into their preflight checklists.

The 106th operations log says, prematurely at 7:50 A.M.: "Helicopters starting to work towards Yarmouth (Nova Scotia). Patrick 130 available and Marine 130 available to tank." The "Patrick 130" is the aircraft that lost an engine and made an emergency landing at Gabreski the previous evening. Maintenance crews repaired it overnight. Reluctantly, its commander agrees to fly the mission after permission was obtained from Patrick. The Marine KC-130 is coming from Stewart Air Base in Newburgh, New York, where a detachment of Marine Aircraft Group 49 is based. They logged a call from 106th ops at 7:30 with an urgent request for tanking support, and in less than two hours Yanky 03, a KC-130T, would be headed for a rendezvous with the helicopters.

Just as Krulder finishes stowing all the PJ paraphernalia that Doc has brought to his aircraft, here comes Mike Moore loaded with enough medical doodads to equip a MASH unit. "Mike, what're you doing with all this?" Krulder asks incredulously.

"Oh, we need this," Moore responds as he hands Krulder a defibrillator.

"Listen, if I start pulling all these people in, this is going out the door," Krulder says, his words accented by an unmistakable New York swagger.

Instead of responding, Moore drops the rest of the gear and runs off, shouting over his shoulder, "I gotta get one more thing."

In a matter of minutes all the gear is stowed, the rotors are turning, and Fleming is set to give the signal for them to depart. Only one small problem. Mike Moore is nowhere to be seen, and they can't leave without at least one PJ aboard each chopper. The delay doesn't sit well with Fleming, who says a few curt words by radio to Jolly 08 as he continually checks his wristwatch, watching with increasing irritation as it ticks off the wasted seconds. As flight engineer, Krulder is the one the pilots abuse when something isn't working right, and a missing PJ with the boss getting antsy is cause enough for them to lay it on. Just as Krulder unplugs his helmet to becomes a search party of one, Moore emerges from the operations building carrying a steaming foil-covered tray which he carefully places aboard Jolly 08. Krulder plugs into the interphone and says, "Moore's on board."

From the front, Buschor asks, "What's that smell?"

By this time Moore is also on headphones, and he

starts to explain that it's one of his special recipes, lasagna with sauteed spinach and mushrooms, only to be cut off with a phrase he's heard before—often: "Shut up, Mike." And with that the Jollys taxi out for takeoff.

SEVEN

In the North Atlantic
About 8:15 A.M. local time

While the shock of being in the water has worn off, Alex Taranov still can't get over the fact that his ship has gone down and he doesn't have a life raft. He believed in the survival training the Black Sea Shipping Company mandated. He took it seriously. But the training never contemplated the ship losing all four of its rafts and, for all practical purposes for most of the crew, both of its lifeboats.

Nevertheless, he's determined to remain positive. That determination is helped a bit when two cans of 7UP come floating by within his reach. He drinks one and stuffs the other inside the thermal suit with some survival rations from one of the rafts that he also found floating among the flotsam. The weather hasn't abated since he was torn from the ship; there's occasional snow, but mostly wind-driven rain pelting his head. Until now he never thought rain could hurt. While the air temperature is only in the high thirties, the water is actually a lot warmer, which is no surprise because he knew the *Salvador Allende* was traveling in the Gulf

Stream to take advantage of the three-knot current that
boosted their speed without any increase in fuel consumption. Part of his job when on watch was to monitor the engine control room gauges, one of which
showed the sea temperature. His last reading had been
18 degrees Celsius—64.4 Fahrenheit—but it actually
feels warmer than that now. Had the ship gone down
outside the Gulf Stream in the Labrador Current, the
water temperature would have ranged from 37 to 43
degrees F. And none of them would have survived the
last three hours in the water.

He tries to share his optimism with the other three
men clinging to the pair of wooden pallets they found
shortly after the ship went down, but one of them
clearly isn't buying it. "I can't handle it anymore. It's
really hard for me."

Alex responds, "Don't worry. Did you see the aircraft? Wait a minute, they'll be back. They will drop
us life rafts. We get a life raft, we go in, take some
water, take some food. When you close the life raft,
it's like a thermos. Four people will make it warm
really quick."

With the awful sea state, it's a tough sell. The waves
are *really* high, especially to men down in the trough
looking up at the crest. Thirty or forty or fifty feet may
not sound like much, but imagine walking down a
street and coming toward you is a solid wall of water
that reaches to the fourth floor of the buildings lining
both sides. And it's going to clobber you because you
have no way to escape it.

The realization strikes Alex that you can hear the
one coming that's going to bury you. You don't need to
see it. Fact is, you're fighting to turn away from it, to
keep your back to both wind and waves. So it rises

over you and then slugs you from behind, forcing your head down. Next, it collapses on top of you, pummeling you with tons of kinetic energy that holds you under and tumbles you over and over and over. Your life jacket is virtually worthless because you're caught *inside* the wave and no amount of kapok or canvas-wrapped air-injected foam is going to win that battle.

Perversely, the life jacket itself is becoming a problem. When the wave smacks Alex in the back of the head, it forces the collar over his head, as though he were removing it. The ropes that he had tied so tightly on the ship have now stretched and the jacket is loose, but the knots are wet and tight, and he can't untie them in order to tighten the ropes around his body. If the jacket had been fastened with up-to-date plastic locking clips, then, wet or dry, all he'd have to do to tighten it is pull on the loose end of the straps. But now his only choice is to wrap both arms around the jacket and hang on, quite literally for dear life. "If this life jacket go out of me," Alex would later say in somewhat fractured English, "I go down for five thousand meters. It was really hard to survive in this."

Aboard Rescue 306
8:15 A.M. local time (6:15 A.M. EST)

As dawn removes night's blindfold and reveals that the worst of the storm has moved on to cause havoc elsewhere, Forrest and Dort bring 306 down to search altitude, expecting at last to be able to fly by sight rather than instrument and instinct alone. Hardly a great expectation, but a reasonable one under the circumstances. Or so they thought until the windscreen clouds over, caked with white salt spray. From sea level to a thousand feet the air is saturated with salt-laden *spray* from the wind-churned waters, leaving only the cockpit's side windows transparent. Once again they're flying blind.

But as the dyslexic preacher proclaimed, the Lord taketh away and the Lord giveth. The gift on this morning comes in the guise of intermittent squalls, normally an annoyance but on this day a phenomenon they actually begin to seek out as they discover nature's own fly-through plane wash.

Seeing through the salt-caked windscreen is only part of the problem. The pilots are also trying to adjust to blinding light when heading east into the rising sun, instantly changing to total darkness when they hit a wall of rain and are enveloped in a squall, back to glaring light when they emerge from the rain with a clean windscreen, and all this while coping with more of the same bone-jarring turbulence they experienced earlier in the morning.

When the crew can see clearly through the windows up front or the Plexi observation doors in the rear, the enormity of their task confronts them. All of them know that Rescue 306 is the only aircraft searching almost a thousand square miles of angry ocean. From experience, SARtechs Ron O'Reilly and Andre Hotton know that a man down there is likely to have only his head above water. And that, intermittently. Even their larger targets will be elusive to eyes scanning from a platform moving at 150 mph, 500 feet up. It's all too easy to catch a glimpse of a raft or lifeboat, only to lose it as it slips down the back side of a wave.

And then there's self-doubt:

Did I really see a raft, or was it my imagination?

Is someone clinging to that board, or was it just more debris?

Should I take us out of the search pattern to go back for another look?

How much longer can I be effective?

What if they're right there and I miss 'em?

What they're doing really *is* brain surgery, or its equivalent. It's being done to save lives, and it requires absolute concentration for long periods of time. A random thought about the child back home with a fever can take your mind away from the task at hand long enough to cost a life. And you wouldn't even know it.

All of which explains the jolt of electricity that shoots through the aircraft when someone spots the lifeboat. Forrest maneuvers the plane so O'Reilly can lock on to it through the left scanning door. From now on the ideal situation would have the plane making only left turns in order to keep him looking at that boat. What does a 25- or thirty-foot boat look like in forty- or fifty-foot waves? A toy in the bathtub? More like a toy in an Olympic-size pool. Based on years of experience, the SARtech is convinced that the worst waves for a small boat are the ten and fifteen footers, because they're breakers. The giant waves he's scanning now have become huge rollers that the lifeboat slowly climbs, then comes racing down, then back up slowly, and down again. It's a roller coaster that never stops. The danger comes if the boat slips sideways and the gunwale is submerged. If they're lucky, it'll straighten out and they can bail like crazy. Otherwise, the force of the wave will roll the boat over, perhaps even driving it under, tossing everybody and everything out, and requiring a huge expenditure of energy to get back into it—if they can.

Dort brings the plane down to 300 feet, more or less. They have to assume that the radar altimeter's reading can be plus or minus fifty feet. They lose another forty or fifty feet when one of the huge rollers passes beneath them. So 300 feet could, in reality, be only 200 feet, and then there's also the gusting wind to consider.

But all that is set aside in the astonishment that they've found the bright orange wooden lifeboat. They make one pass by it. It's empty. They make a second pass. Nothing. They bring it around one more time, and O'Reilly sees a head peek out from beneath the covered bow. And suddenly there's a man waving at them, and another and another. They were concealed by the enclosed bow and stern sections of the boat. Only the center third is open to inspection from above.

The decision is immediately made to drop a SKAD because the people in the boat might need clothing or a desalination kit. It's also a way to get a radio to them, which would give the rescuers an opportunity to get some solid information on how many people got off the ship, how many lifeboats, rafts, etc. In addition, O'Reilly observes that the lifeboat plus two of their life rafts jacks up the odds of survivability.

If mental outlook plays a major role in whether an individual survives a situation like a shipwreck, then just the sight of the huge Herc making repeated passes only 300 feet above them has to bolster the spirits of the people in the boat and jump-start their will to survive. At that altitude, they can see the faces of the pilots in the cockpit, and they can watch the men on the open ramp, waving to them as the plane passes by. Like the earlier contact on the radio, it makes each group of people *real* to the other. The people in the ocean *know* they've not been forgotten, and the people in the plane know precisely who is counting on them. It makes the bruising they've been taking much easier to bear, or even disregard. Looking at that tiny boat being batted around by thirty-foot seas, they instinctively know their discomfort is nothing by comparison. They also know that in a matter of hours they'll be back home. That's a foregone conclusion, a certainty, given their faith in each other and in their aircraft. Unspoken is the knowledge that even if they could rain survival gear on the sailors like manna from heaven, without a boat to pick them up, the inevitable is only being postponed. This sense of frustration, of being so close yet not able to do something definitive to save lives, will only intensify in the hours to come, as the time they have available to help quickly runs out.

Everyone is aware that this drop is not going to be a piece of cake. The only factor working in their favor is the size of the lifeboat. It's a lot easier to line up on than a raft or a man in the water. In the rear of the plane, Ron O'Reilly takes charge. He calls for a four-bundle drop from an altitude of 300 feet, speed 120 to 130 knots—as slow as they can safely go. While the aircraft commander has the final say, the SARtech's years of experience, as well as custom, puts the onus on him to set it up correctly and make it happen.

On the first pass they drop timing smokes—flares that will burn for about eighteen minutes, giving off a white smoke to guide them back around to the target. Forrest directs Dort in flying a crosswind pattern, about fifty feet *downwind* of the lifeboat. They approach it in the opposite direction from which they'll ultimately make the SKAD drop in order to try and keep O'Reilly, who's on the left side of the plane, in constant visual contact with the target. Unfortunately, to fight the effects of the wind they've got the plane crabbed to the left, with the nose on a 45-degree angle into the wind, even though their forward motion is ninety degrees to the wind direction. While this makes it easier for the pilots to see the lifeboat, it's more difficult for O'Reilly, since he's actually angled away from the target.

With a smoke flare ready to drop through a port in his viewing door, as they come abeam of the lifeboat the SARtech begins counting. "One thousand one, one thousand two, one thousand three . . ." and he drops the flare. The plane continues on the same course, and Ron drops two more flares. When they make a U-turn and come back *upwind* of the lifeboat, the pilot will imagine a line connecting the three columns of smoke, and he'll fly parallel to that line. O'Reilly will be able to look out his window on the left side of the aircraft and keep both the lifeboat and the smoke in view. When the plane is abeam of the first smoke they dropped—the "timing smoke"—he'll call the SKAD drop, sending the first bundle off the ramp three seconds before they come even with the lifeboat, and the final bundle of the four will go several seconds after they pass the boat. The end result should have the two end bundles—both life rafts—pushed downwind ahead of bundles two and three, creating a U shape around the target. At least that's how it's taught and how they practice it at SAR school. Given the conditions they're in, a successful drop to that lifeboat is going to require considerable improvisational flying up front and intuitive guesstimating in the back.

As they reverse course, bringing the C-130 around

on final approach to make the SKAD drop, the pilots see a problem. The timing smoke flares produce *white* smoke, and they're losing sight of it in the spray at the surface. Consequently, it's not giving them the visual guide they'd hoped for. Someone mutters that it's time they were given colored smoke, similar to that produced by the smoke grenades commonly used in infantry operations to help aircraft identify ground units. Billows of yellow, red, or green would be hard to miss over the waves. That's something to note in the after-action report. Right now they've got to make it work.

Forrest takes control of the plane and immediately begins to fight the effect of the wind, which is coming from their right, trying to push the aircraft downwind, by crabbing the Herc 45 degrees to the right. It's still moving parallel to the line they flew when they dropped the smokes, still moving perpendicular to the wind, but its nose is pointed 45 degrees into the wind. From his position on the right side of the cockpit, Dort will never see the lifeboat. Forrest expects to see it, but he'll have to be looking out the left-side window and back. He's less concerned with seeing it, however, than with flying a straight line parallel to the track they flew to drop the timing smokes. It's O'Reilly's problem to spot the boat and figure out when to make the drop. It's truly a team effort.

Loadmaster Michaud and SARtech Hotton are now on the ramp, waiting for the order to drop. They've got to rely solely on O'Reilly's call, since looking out the rear of the plane they won't see the lifeboat until after they've flown past it. What they're waiting for is the standard ten second warning, then a measured, "Standby to drop SKAD. . . . Drop SKAD . . . *now*!" But even though crabbing the plane to the right gives the team leader a better view of the target area, he has a hard time keeping the boat in sight. Visibility has gotten worse, and the tiny craft's on top of a wave one second, hidden behind it the next. There's no ten- or five-second warning. What they get is a quick, "Drop SKAD *now*!"

One at a time the four bundles go streaming off the Herc's cargo ramp. All the crew in the back can do now is watch helplessly, and perhaps pray. A moment passes. Then two.

The elation in Ron O'Reilly's voice tells the cockpit crew what they wanted to hear. He's screaming, "Excellent drop. Perfect!" In the cockpit there's complete joy, even bliss, if one can be blissful while having his guts pounded by the turbulence that's still very much a factor. Now the big question: can the people in the lifeboat grab the rope?

They swing the plane into a quick left turn and come back toward the raft, and what they see cranks their euphoria up another couple of notches. This is unbelievable. A Ripley's Believe It or Not drop. Forrest calls it, "The most amazing drop ever," adding modestly, "Bang on target, but I'd say it'd be fifty percent sheer-ass luck." From the cockpit they can see that someone has pulled the rope to the boat and they're already dragging one of the two bundles out of the water.

Now it's a matter of waiting until they can unpack the bundle and find the radio. What Forrest wants to do is take Rescue 306 around in a big circle, trying to stay close to the lifeboat. On a calm day the Herc takes two miles to turn around. This is not a calm day, and they find themselves turning long ovals instead of circles. The wind pushes them three or four miles away, and they're forced to fight their way back upwind of the

boat, only to repeat the procedure, all the while waiting, monitoring UHF frequency 28-28—actually
282.8. Then without warning, there it is: an obnoxious
beep-beep-beep-beep-beep that sounds just like an
EPIRB. Immediate frustration sets in. Were Forrest
given to expletives, this would be the place for one or
more. But the most he'll allow himself in the supersonic transition from elation to irritation is a mini-
mally blasphemous, "Oh, Jesus. They've got it set on
beacon. What do we do now?" The radio transmits in
two modes on the same frequency: beacon and voice.
The beacon allows a receiving aircraft to home in on
the signal and find its source. But when it's emitting a
beacon, it can't send or receive voice.

Frustrated, Forrest continuously keys his micro-
phone on the 28-28 frequency. "*Salvador Allende*
lifeboat, this is Rescue 306. *Salvador Allende* lifeboat,
this is Rescue 306." His hope is that if they're playing
with the switch, flicking it back and forth, they'll hear
his voice and figure out what to do.

As they're turning to make another pass over the
lifeboat, the annoying beeps stop and they hear a voice
speaking in Russian. After a minute or so someone
from the lifeboat says "Hello" to them in English.

Forrest responds, "How many people are in the
boat?"

"Eleven."

"What's your condition?"

"We're cold. We have water and some food."

The language barrier keeps the conversation basic,
but it's apparent that the sailors' spirits have been
lifted by the presence of the plane. They ask if ships
are coming, and are told yes, but it may be a while
before one arrives. As the conversation continues,

O'Reilly, who has been trying to keep the lifeboat in sight, keys the intercom to say that they've got the rafts tied to the side of the boat. Finally, the rafts are working the way they're supposed to. The pockets underneath have filled with water, and the weight seems to be enough to keep them from blowing away in the wind.

The SARtech expresses some concern that the floorboards in the center section of the lifeboat are separating. He can see a black stripe that appears to be water and guesses the boat's been taking a horrible pounding. He has no way of knowing that the lifeboat was damaged when they first dragged it, and then dropped it off the ship. On successive passes over the boat both Forrest and O'Reilly see more black stripes that look like water between the floorboards. They can only hope that the pair of ten-man life rafts lashed to the boat will do them some good.

Having done everything they can for the people in the lifeboat, Rescue 306 moves off to look for other survivors. As they're leaving, Jonathan Forrest has no doubt in his mind that they're going to make it. Logically, he gives them a fifty-fifty chance. Emotionally, he needs to believe they'll survive. "We made the drop of the century, we'd been in radio contact with them." His heart is saying, "They're not allowed to die." But he's flown a lot of rescue missions, and his head knows what the sea can do. "I've always had a personal feeling that on any mission like this, no matter how hopeful you can get [you have to remember] that if they couldn't survive in the 450-foot freighter, they're gonna have a damn hard time surviving in the twenty-foot lifeboat. And that applies to any mission I was ever on. It's just wrong place, wrong time. And Mother

Nature rules, I've always said that. So you give 'em all the credit and hope, but the odds are against them."

In the North Atlantic
8:35 A.M. local time (6:35 A.M. EST)

Time after time the big waves have sent Alex Taranov and his three companions rolling, but fortunately, when they'd fight their way to the surface, they were still very close to each other, and the two wooden pallets were in reach.

They'd been in the water about three hours when the sea state subsides enough for two of the men to climb onto the pallets while the other two float on either side, holding the pair together. Despite the roar of the storm, Alex and the other man in the water manage to carry on a conversation. He was the motorman on duty in the engine room when the *Salvador Allende* was hit by the first rogue wave. The impact knocked him to the deck. Alex asks about the loud sound from the engine room when the ship finally rolled to ninety degrees. Was it a boiler? No. As soon as they realized what was happening, the engine room crew closed all the valves, stopped all the pumps and boilers to avoid a blowout.

While Alex and the motorman are talking, the two men on the pallets take no interest in the conversation. Just hanging on is consuming all their energy. All four of them are exhausted. The ordeal to stay alive these past three hours saps their strength, and except for about an hour while sitting on the stern of the sinking ship, none has had any sleep during the hellish night. Taranov's determination to live has not flagged, but his companions don't have his resolve. He can see that the man who originally said he couldn't take it anymore looks sick. When he tries talking with him, the only response are complaints about the cold, and Alex's continued cheerleading about rescue planes finding them is not helping. He says nothing, but realizes this man is going to be the first among them to die. It only strengthens his resolve to live. Being in the water, even under these circumstances, doesn't threaten him. He's comfortable there. He recalls that he always liked to swim; that's what he takes his family to do every vacation. And he knows it's just going to take time for the planes to find him. Until then he has no choice but to try and make the best of the situation.

Aboard Rescue 306
8:40 A.M. local time (6:40 A.M. EST)

Having done all they could for the people in the lifeboat, they point the Herc southeast, looking for other survivors. Within two miles they find the debris field, stretching north to south: wooden pallets, lumber, and other flotsam from the *Salvador Allende*, all drifting downwind in a slick of oil being whipped by the high seas with the salt spray into a hellish stew that instantly tells an observer something terrible happened nearby.

In what seems only seconds they spot a small wooden work boat. It's a bit of a surprise, since there's never been mention of anything other than four life rafts and two lifeboats leaving the sinking ship. From the back the SARtechs can clearly see there's a man in the boat who appears to be waving. Once again adrenaline surges. They circle around and make a low pass, watching the waves pound the tiny craft. He continues waving, but there's no other movement. Another low pass during which they spot other survivors in the water. As they go over the boat, they see that the man apparently has tied himself in so he won't be tossed overboard, and what they thought was waving is actually his limp arms flopping as the boat gets knocked around. It's apparent that he's either unconscious or dead. Either way, plans to drop a SKAD are quickly canceled. O'Reilly reasons, "This guy's in a boat. We don't know if he's alive or dead. Let's try to save these guys in the water." Now it's a matter of *finding* those guys in the water, again.

Meantime, although visibility has improved, the turbulence is still making their lives miserable. It might actually be worse now than it was at night, because the Herc has burned off at least 40,000 of the 62,500 pounds of fuel they left Greenwood with, and the lighter the aircraft gets, the less stable it is. Aircraft Commander Jonnie Forrest is still using his hands-off system to fly the plane: he's listening to Ron O'Reilly in the back, attempting to watch the target himself, and converting this into specific instructions for copilot Kevin Dort, who actually has control of the aircraft. The commands are terse: "Turn left. Roll out here. Turn right. Roll out." Kevin knows to bank the turn to the max, 45 degrees, to help cope with the effect of the high winds, but he's not flying with a hundred percent efficiency. The vertigo that developed during the night drop when they were having a difficult time reading the instruments is still giving him problems.

O'Reilly spots what he believes to be a life raft in the water and calls for a left turn. Normally, the response is automatic and immediate, but Dort is now in the grip of the worst episode of vertigo he's ever experienced. "I'm thinking to myself, 'I can't turn.' I'm fighting as hard as I can just to stay straight and level. My mind is telling me that we were in a climbing turn, but looking at the A-I, I knew we were straight and level. It was all I could do just to force my mind to say, 'No, we're not turning and climbing; we're straight and level.' You know where you are by the instruments, but your mind is telling you you're somewhere else."

In the rear, O'Reilly can sense that something isn't right. These are good pilots. But they're not responding to his call for a left turn. He tries again. "Turn left!"

In the cockpit, Forrest takes a quick look at his copilot, grabs the yoke and says, "I have control." For the next few minutes he does the hands-on flying, until he's sure that Kevin's okay.

In the North Atlantic
8:50 A.M. local time (6:50 A.M. EST)

Alex sees Rescue 306 coming before he hears it. From the water, a C-130 doing a low-and-slow looks gigantic, invulnerable. He has to believe it's invulnerable, because it's his only link with survival. On the first pass he sees the faces of the pilots, waves to them, and they return the wave. It's a gesture filled with meaning for the merchant seamen. Seconds later he sees something drop from the rear of the plane. It ignites and he sees bright light and smoke, drifting down to settle in the water almost within his reach. His technical mind has already figured its purpose: they need to find the place from which they'll drop a raft.

Taranov watches the plane make a U-turn, and he

knows they're lining up for a drop. The first bundle flies from the rear of the plane, and Alex watches expectantly as it bursts open, inflating on the way down. As soon as the raft hits the water, it starts rolling in the wind. It's stopped short by the rope connected to the second bundle, which seems headed toward him, but gets shoved away by a breaking wave. Bundle three is even farther away, and the fourth package, the second raft, lands about fifty yards from Alex.

His mind goes into overdrive. What did they tell him back in Odessa during survival training? There's safety in numbers. Try and find others and stay together. He looks at the three other men desperately hanging onto the pallets. Sometimes you have to ignore the experts and use your own judgment. This is one of those times. If they stay in the water, sooner or later they'll succumb to the cold. The raft, bouncing crazily about fifty yards away, represents their only visible chance to get out of the sea. He's been watching the horizon for fishing boats or ships that might be responding to the SOS or the EPIRB, and he's seen none. Maybe the big plane will come around one more time and drop another raft closer to them. He looks at the wind-whipped waves and does a reality check. The fact that they were able to get it this close is a minor miracle.

All this goes through his head in microseconds. His decision appears to be instantaneous. He tells his comrades, "We have to swim for it because it's never coming to us." Alex realizes that only two of the three may have a chance of making it. The third has given up. The man's eyes seem light green, sort of foggy, as though they're not really his eyes. And Alex realizes that this must be the moment when you go from life to death. "Let's go to get the life raft," he urges.

The dying man makes what Taranov believes to be a little smile, saying nothing. The other two seem to agree. "Yes, we have to swim," says one.

Alex lets go of the pallets, turns and strikes out for the nearest raft, getting a huge push by the waves that seem to be following him. He expects the other two seamen to duck around the pallets and follow him. But just a second after he commits, a powerful gust of wind picks up the raft and rolls it away from him. When it was just fifty yards away, he was confident. Now it's double or triple that distance from him. No chance. Quickly, he turns around, thinking he can get back to the pallets. But it's too late. They're drifting laterally, away from him. The only way he can get back is to swim uphill, against the waves. His heart sinks. The physical energy he'd need is gone, his strength sapped by the constant fight to keep from being forced under the waves. It's impossible to get back to his friends, and it's impossible to reach the raft. Then, a thought: if he can't swim *uphill* to the others, maybe they can swim *downhill* to him. He stops swimming and starts yelling, waving his hands, screaming, "Swim to me, swim to me," until his voice is almost gone. Two of the men wave to him but make no effort to head in his direction. Another huge wave hits the three men on the pallets, lifting them high above Alex. As the wave rushes toward him, his shipmates slide down the backside and out of sight. Forever.

For the first time since he entered the water, Alex Taranov begins to have doubts. He is now alone in the North Atlantic, convinced for the moment that he's had his last chance at survival. And he cries.

EIGHT

Ron O'Reilly watches with deep disappointment as he sees the first raft roll away and the second land upwind, but to the side of the men in the water. They missed their mark by a scant fifty feet, but it might as well have been a mile. Finding people alive in the water under these conditions is a real high; realizing that your best efforts might not save them is sobering. As he's looking out the scanning window, he's shocked to see someone let go of the pallets and swim for the raft. It's heartbreaking to watch, because he knows there's no way the man is going to catch it. He'd have to swim up a thirty-foot hill, and that's just not going to happen. Ron keys the intercom, "This guy's a goner."

There's no time to dwell on it, however, since the navigator warns that they've only got five minutes to bingo. Bourgoin has been calculating flying time and fuel burn to every airport potentially within reach. And with each new calculation, he'd find them another five minutes on-scene. The closest airports, Saint John's and Gander, Newfoundland, are shut down by snow-storms. The en route weather to any base in Nova Scotia is bad enough that they have to follow Canadian Air Force IFR—Instrument Flight Rules—which has strict requirements for fuel reserves.

It's during this latest recalculation of bingo time that Forrest gets disconcerting news over the radio. The ETA of the aircraft replacing them is well after 306 has hit bingo. "What happened?" he wants to know, sounding distinctly pissed off. The captain running RCC Halifax tells him the Aurora that had been scheduled to replace them on-scene isn't coming.

"Get something out here!" he screams at the duty officer on the other end of the conversation, his voice filled with anger and frustration. "We found these people. I don't wanna lose them." Experience tells him the worst thing you can do is leave something you've found, especially in this kind of weather. In his mind, he's not out of line, he's just making a very direct request. He's saying "This is the situation" and he's doing it point-blank, not mincing words. RCC Halifax tells him the base at Greenwood has scrambled to launch a C-130, but there'll probably be a ninety-minute gap in coverage.

While Forrest has been in conversation with Halifax, he's also been guiding his copilot, who's flying a low-level pattern in an attempt to locate more survivors. Now, with only a couple of minutes left on-scene, they come upon another group of PIWs. Pushing to get another SKAD into the water before the nav calls bingo, O'Reilly guides the pilots into a pass over the people and drops timing smokes. They fight the turbulence and swing around to come in and drop the SKAD, but discover that the people and the smokes seem to have disappeared. The white smoke in white salt spray is just not doing the job, and the bingo clock is ticking louder. So, with the loadmaster and SARtech hanging onto the ramp ready to drop, they're forced to spend several minutes flying around trying to find the survivors again.

O'Reilly knows he doesn't want to go home with rafts in the plane, so he's desperately searching for a target. Suddenly, he sees a couple of guys in the water. "Drop SKAD now. *Drop!*"

From up front Forrest shouts, "No, no."

"Too late," O'Reilly says, "it's already out."

"We're on the downwind side," Forrest says.

The SARtech team leader realizes that in all the circling they'd been doing, trying to reacquire the group in the water, he'd lost track of the wind direction. "Well, I saw 'em, and I didn't think we'd get another chance of dropping it before we have to go."

"No," Jonnie says. "The nav just got us another ten minutes."

There's no time for Ron to dwell on regrets. The last SKAD has just gone off the ramp, they have more time in the area, and they know they're near people in the water. The question voiced on the intercom is terse: "What can we do?"

The entire crew is in on this discussion, when Andre Hotton comes up with a suggestion. "Let's drop the one-man rafts, use a clothing bundle to weight it down, and tie it all together with a pump rope." The one-man rafts are part of the SARtechs' own kits. It's what they use if they have to parachute into the water on a rescue mission.

Quickly, Hotton and Michaud jerry-rig a SKAD. Raft, yellow polypropylene floating rope, clothing bundle, rope, another raft. And then a very quick drop off the ramp into an area near several PIWs.

Up front the nav is logging the latest positions of survivors so he can relay it to the next plane out, while the AC guides the plane through a quick tour of the area. The view of the lifeboat is not encouraging. The floorboards in the open center section now appear to be breaking loose. "Holy smoke," O'Reilly says, "that boat's taking a beating there." Silently, he observes that it's self-destructing before their eyes. The good news is that the two ten-man life rafts are still tied to it, but the eleven people apparently haven't left the covered bow and stern of the lifeboat. Either they don't realize their plight, or are afraid to leave the perceived safety of a hard boat for rubber rafts.

At the moment, a beautiful blue sky and bright, shining sun belie the reality of the situation. Even the rain squalls have moved on. Only the wretched turbulence in the plane and the sight of gigantic, brutal waves below tell the truth as they fly on, making a last pass over the people in the water, wagging their wings, waving to them from the windows and watching them wave back. The crew can only imagine how demoralizing it must be to see them leave and no other airplane come in right away. Bourgoin makes a final call on the frequency of the radio they'd dropped earlier. "We're coming back. Hang on." And as they turn west, the image of the men in the water waving good-bye is indelibly burned into their minds.

They've gone ten minutes beyond bingo. Now there's no time—or fuel—to waste getting home. Forrest asks the nav for a heading, and with his copilot at the controls, it's flaps up and they start climbing. The nav takes note of the weather as they're leaving. Winds are down to 45 knots, compared to the sixty or seventy knots when they were attempting the night drop. The ceiling is 2,000 feet, the clouds are breaking up, and the sun is out. As for the turbulence, Forrest says, "It was bad when we left Greenwood. When we first got there, it was absolutely bloody awful, unbelievable. And when we headed back it was just bad."

Jonathan Forrest can finally let down. "I remember turning to Kevin, and I had the shakes, big-time shakes. I was a basket case, because I went from one emotional extreme to another. Pressure's off. Every single piece of mental energy I have has been used. Physically, I was a basket case, having been beaten around, flown all night. Nothing was left.

"I remember turning to him, and I was going like this. My hands were shaking, and I said to Kevin, I said, 'Did we do everything we could?' He said, 'You did a good job.' That was it. Because I was just—at that point, started coming down. It was, like, we did not want to leave. We had no choice. We'd gone from the high of dropping the perfect drop to the low of— I saw a guy I considered died while I was there, that being the guy in the dory. We missed drops. No drop was successful after the first or the second. The drop at night, that was a shot in the dark. The drop to the lifeboat was successful. The two drops to guys on the pallets were not successful. And then the jerry-rigged drop was a drop and run.

"Everybody in that airplane had been up all night. Everybody in that airplane was completely mentally drained, and then some people had physically been wrecked from the inside out, throwing up. And then there was us, flying, who'd been physically worked. Nobody was recovered from anything."

The flight back to Sydney is very quiet. When the engines are shut down, the flight engineer notes the mission time: 11.2 hours in the air. They'll refuel and fly another hour to their home base at Greenwood.

RCC New York
7:55 A.M. EST

Coast Guard Lieutenant Bill Kelly had gotten a call around one in the morning telling him about the *Salvador Allende* rescue operation, so when he walks into the RCC a few minutes before eight, the scene that greets him is not a surprise. On the huge wall map the location of the *Salvador Allende*'s demise is marked with a ship's icon and the notation "Sunk." The phones are ringing off the hook. Jay Topper, Fred Mletzko, and Gary Parker don't quite look like they'd been keel-hauled, but it's close. And the mood of the place? Intense. Checking one of the computer screens, he sees the lat/long positions of AMVER ships and in his mind can place them relative to the *Salvador Allende*'s last known position. Actually, it looks better than he thought it would. Several vessels looked like they'd be on-scene within hours, rather than days. A glance at the weather reports for the area tells him a different story. It's going to be no joyride for the merchant ships trying to help. And he's acutely aware that unless a ship gets there quickly, the survivors are doomed. What he wasn't aware of till he walked in the door was that the *Salvador Allende* case was now *his* problem: the boss has named him SAR planner for the duration.

Searching the high seas for people in the water, rafts, or life boats requires organization. First, you need to make sure the ships stay out of each other's way, not necessarily a simple task when they're all converging on one small piece of the ocean. Second, you need to make sure you've got continuous air coverage, and that each search plane has a clear understanding of the area it's got to cover and the pattern to fly. Over the next few days Kelly will send each ship specific instructions that tell it by latitude and longitude where to start, how many miles to go, and at what point it should turn and begin the parallel track back. Aircraft will be given similar detailed assignments that take into account the distances they can cover and the relative ease with which they can change course.

Where he commits his assets is based on an evaluation of information from several sources: the Computer Assisted Search Program (CASP), which predicts which way and how fast a specific type of object will drift; the self-locating datum marker buoys (SLDMB), which have been dropped from aircraft; and the reports from aircraft participating in the search, which tell him what's actually happening on-scene. He has to know when to go with what the computer is telling him, and when to ignore the computer's drift projections. The first good look at what the SLDMBs were doing tells him that on this case reality and virtual reality are definitely not one and the same. Before it's over he'll see one buoy drift dozens of miles from the sinking site, while another gets caught in an eddy at the edge of the Gulf Stream and wanders in circles. Both buoys were inserted near something in the water that came from the *Salvador Allende*, and they're now miles apart, in different directions from where the ship went down.

Even mundane scraps of information take on significance. Does anyone know what time sunset is at the wreck site? Searching in daylight is going to be more productive than at night, but it's December 9, less than two weeks from the winter solstice, the shortest day of the year. Topper checks with RCC Halifax. Sunset is 1951 Zulu, around five P.M. in the search area, three P.M. New York time.

Kelly settles in at his desk and begins going over the minutiae not covered in the briefing he received. At 9:07, Halifax Coast Guard Radio calls. M/V *Giovanna* is at position 39-24N, 050-21W, course 130 (almost due southeast), speed sixteen knots, ETA one hour. How could the ship be making sixteen knots in those seas? he wonders. A glance at the high seas weather forecast explains it. The storm center itself is moving southeast at twenty knots, which means *Giovanna* is getting a push from the storm's sixty- to seventy-knot hurricane-force winds. To have a ship on-scene less than five hours after the *Salvador Allende* went to the bottom would be outstanding, but by dint of sad experience, veteran rescue people make it a habit of looking gift horses in the mouth. He asks Radio Halifax to confirm *Giovanna*'s on-scene time, and to tell her to keep an eye out for survivors.

At 9:21, a scant fourteen minutes later, the maxim "If it sounds too good to be true, it probably is," is, unfortunately, proved correct. Radio Halifax again, with a terse message: "*Giovanna* cannot assist due to weather." It's not really a surprise. *Giovanna* is a huge container ship. She's probably got containers stacked four, five, or six high on her decks, which means she's presenting a solid wall the height of a building six or eight stories high to the wind coming from directly behind her. If she tries turning left or right, the wind is going to treat her like a huge weathervane and blow her back onto that southeasterly course. That's if she's lucky. If she isn't, the wind will push her broadside to the waves and she'll broach or come darn close to it. Experience tells the Coast Guardsmen in the RCC that at this moment the *Giovanna* is a 740-foot-long, 100-foot-wide, 32,503-ton surfboard, being pushed along by huge following seas and hurricane-force winds, and there's nothing her captain, crew, and two steam turbine engines putting out 32,450 horsepower can do to change the situation.

Lieutenant Bill Kelly has experienced the phenomenon firsthand, and he can visualize what's happening aboard *Giovanna*. All you can do is hold on. If you're on the bridge, things get very tense. The helmsman has to aggressively hand-steer the ship (no autopilot) on a straight course, although it feels more like the ship is corkscrewing its way through the water, while others are nervously looking at radar and out the window, hoping there's nothing crossing her path. If the situation is really bad, and the *Giovanna*'s apparently is, there's no rudder control whatsoever, and there isn't likely to be unless they can get her engines to drive the ship through the water faster than the speed of the current itself. Quite literally, the only way she can get out of this is to outrun the waves, which clearly isn't going to happen, or wait until the waves abate.

The assumptions the RCC team makes about *Giovanna*'s situation will be confirmed several hours later in a phone call from Halifax Coast Guard radio saying the *Giovanna* had no rudder control and her course was varying by 45 degrees. Ultimately, two telex messages from RCC Halifax pop up on Kelly's screen:

12:53 PM RCC HALIFAX TO RCC NY

IN LAST COMMUNICATIONS WITH THE CONTAINER
VESSEL JIOVANNI THE MASTER ADVISES HE IS
NOW IN PSN 3903N 4921W SPEED 16.5 KTS COURSE
115 NOW 37 MILES PAST LAST KNOWN PSN OF THE
SALVADOR ALLENDE. HE IS ROLLING 40 DEGREES
TO STARBOARD. SEAS ARE 10 TO 12 METERS, VIS 8
MILES NOW REDUCED TO 3 MILES IN RAIN. I AM
UNABLE TO CLEARLY GET THE CAPTAINS INTEN-
TIONS HOWEVER HE IS STILL STEERING AWAY
FROM THE LIFERAFTS. HE ADVISES THAT THERE IS
ANOTHER VESSEL STEERING PARALLEL TO HIM
BUT SPEED 10 KNOTS. THE VESSEL IS THE BENE
QUEEN, CALL SIGN UNKNOWN. HE BELIEVES IT
IS A SMALLER VESSEL PERHAPS A BULKER. HE
BELIEVES VESSEL IS PRESENTLY IN VICINITY OF
THE LIFERAFT(S). HE HAS BEEN UNABLE TO CON-
TACT THE RESCUE AIRCRAFT AND THE BENNE
QUEEN. DESTINATION OF THE MSC JIOVANNI IS
ANTWERP.

1:28 PM RCC HALIFAX TO RCC NY

THE MASTER OF THE CONTAINER VESSEL JIO-
VANNI ADVISES THAT HE IS STILL EXPERIENCING
DIFFICULT STEERING. HE IS UNABLE TO HOLD A
STEADY COURSE AND STATES THAT IT WOULD BE
DIFFICULT AND DANGEROUS TO TURN HIS VESSEL
AROUND, ALSO, IF HE DID MANAGE TO TURN HE
MIGHT STEER INTO A LIFERAFT. NOW HEADING
120 SPEED APPROX. 17 KNOTS. HE IS HEADING TO
ANTWERP WITH AN ETA OF AM 15 DEC WEATHER

PERMITTING. THE CAPTAIN REGRETS HE IS
UNABLE TO ASSIST.
—HALIFAX

In his third year on Governors Island, Bill Kelly has
enough experience to appreciate the camaraderie, dedication, and even heroism of the merchant captains on
the high seas. If a vessel's master says he can't do it,
Kelly accepts it at face value. He's seen too many
times where a merchant ship cruising along in marginal weather with no difficulty on a voyage from
point A to point B has responded immediately to an
SOS and diverted, occasionally even incurring damage as a result. The challenge the master accepts when
he chooses to help is daunting: maneuver a vessel that
can be three football fields long to locate and pick up
people in a life raft, or a single person in the water,
while getting hammered by thirty-foot seas and sixty-
knot winds. Using AMVER, the RCCs try not to task a
supertanker to find a PIW; obviously a ship with an
open deck closer to the water would have an easier
time with it. But with the *Salvador Allende* down and
thirty-one lives at stake, it's no time to be picky.

NINE

Alex Taranov has lost all track of time. Since he was separated from the other crewmen, he's managed to focus on survival, one giant wave at a time. He's aware of his plight, but maintains hope that somehow someone will come pick him up. The two cans of 7UP were a good sign, although he ended up drinking the first one mixed with saltwater and it sent him into paroxysms of retching. The second can is quite literally up his sleeve. Whether it's fear of another bout of vomiting or incredible self-discipline, Alex won't drink this can until he's sure he needs it.

He's drifting amidst the debris from the sunken ship, now strung out over many miles of ocean, and as things turn out, amidst an assortment of rescue paraphernalia apparently dropped from one of the rescue planes. There's something bright orange in the water nearby, and he manages to swim toward it, discovering what he thinks is an uninflated life raft still in its bag. More likely it's one of the supply bundles that make up part of a four-piece SKAD. He can see that one panel on the bundle is partially opened and that a long rope is trailing out behind it. Logic says, "Grab the rope." He does, and pulls the package to him, but as he does so, another breaker hits and tumbles him. Alex refuses to let go of the rope, and when he pops to the surface, he's still got it. But then the realization strikes that the next wave could tumble him with the rope, wrapping him in it. So before he can tear into the bundle, he casts the rope aside.

The rain that had been pelting him earlier in the morning has stopped, and he finds himself drifting from areas of shadow under clouds into bright sunlight. In the distance he sees a plane, and can't understand why it's searching so far away from him. It's frustrating, but he's certain they'll keep looking until he's found. He has to be found. His wife needs him. And his two daughters need him.

He can see their faces as he drifts in the ocean. His wife, Larisa, whom he married in 1979 when he was twenty-one. Their oldest daughter, Lena, born a year after they were married. And the younger daughter, Ludmilla, only three years old. Alex was on vacation with his family when the emergency call came from the Black Sea Shipping Company. They needed him to come back to work immediately. The third engineer on one of their ships in the Estonian port city of Tallinn had been fired for too much drinking on the job. There was no one else available, and they always knew they could count on Alex. So he packed his bags and took the train from Odessa to Tallinn, a two-day trip.

Alex had worked for BLASCO for eighteen years, joining the company right out of the merchant marine academy. He'd spent three years working on Bezitsa-class cargo ships, then moved up to the more modern

Murim-class ships, both of which were built in the sixties. The next step was to Communista-class ships. It was his dream—and apparently everyone else's in the company—to work on the newer, highly automated Zultsa-class vessels, but openings were few and far between. While not in the top class, the *Salvador Allende*, built in 1973, did have automatic controls which allowed the engineers to run her from an air-conditioned control room. He was a bit concerned that he didn't have any time to study and prepare to deal with the new systems, but figured he'd have plenty of off-duty hours where he could hit the books.

The last minute assignment did have one bonus in it for him. The captain of the *Salvador Allende* was Sergey Michailovich Chuluykov, whom Alex had known since he was sixteen years old. Sergey was a year older, but the two of them quickly became friends at marine college. The friendship continued when Alex passed the entrance exam and followed Sergey to the marine academy. In all their years with the company, however, they'd never worked together on the same ship. It was a quirk of fate that brought them together on the *Salvador Allende*, the first ship that Sergey had captained. He had taken over the vessel in July, five months earlier, after having worked as chief engineer and first officer on Greek-owned cargo ships.

It didn't take Alex long to figure out the protocol of shipboard politics. While Sergey was a longtime friend, he was *the boss*, and fraternizing would cause Alex problems with his coworkers and his own supervisor. So whenever he had information about the condition of the ship, he'd pass it along through channels, rather than visiting Sergey and telling him directly. Even if he hadn't had the relationship with the captain, it's doubtful that Alex would have gone directly to him. He'd been reprimanded about a year earlier on a ship carrying cacao from Indonesia to Montreal, and since then he was content to let the chief engineer deal with the master. Ironically, that ship was caught in an early winter storm in the same general area where the *Salvador Allende* went down. Shifting cargo—sixty- or seventy-kilo bags of cacao on pallets—caused the ship to list seven degrees. Alex deduced it was the cargo causing the problem, and he fixed it in twenty minutes by moving fuel oil and ballast water from one side to the other, which couldn't be done on the *Salvador Allende*. She'd been designed so that ballast water or fuel could only be shifted front to back in order to level the vessel after cargo was loaded. Shortly after Alex had corrected the list, the ship's master sent for him and suggested that it was Alex and the other engineers' fault that the problem had occurred in the first place. Perhaps they had screwed up moving fuel from one tank to another. "No," Alex said, "it's shifting cargo."

"Ah, come on, what do you understand about cargo," the captain said angrily, "you're a marine engineer. Go below." When the holds were opened in Montreal, Alex was vindicated. The cargo had shifted completely to one side of the vessel.

RCC New York
8:40 A.M. EST

Lieutenant Commander Jay Topper calls RCC Halifax to ask for times of sunrise and sunset. He's told sunrise is 1033Z, or 5:30 A.M. EST; sunset will be at

1951Z, 2:51 P.M. EST, 4:51 at the wreck site.

Twenty-five minutes later, at 9:05, the 106th calls to report that the two HH-60s, tail numbers 14 and 08, are airborne with an ETA on-scene estimated at 2115Z—6:15 P.M. local time, more than two hours later than had been estimated in the eight A.M. phone call. And well after sunset.

HQ 106th Rescue Wing,
Suffolk County, Long Island
About 9:00 A.M. EST

The 106th Rescue Wing commander, Colonel David Hill, arrives at Gabreski Field expecting a briefing on the status of King 46, the C-130 heading out to the mid-Atlantic to help search for survivors. He's surprised to hear that Jolly 08 and Jolly 14 are also outbound, not on the scheduled gunnery training mission, but to participate in the rescue mission.

Since he and Lieutenant Colonel Landsiedel had done the mission planning for King 46 the night before, he knew the distances involved and the weather that would likely be encountered along the way. A quick check also tells him that at the moment there are only two tankers confirmed, Yanky 03 from the Marines at Newburgh, New York, and King 52, the regular Air Force tanker that had made an emergency landing to repair an engine en route home to Florida from a mission in Iceland. The 106th's own refueler, King 74, was still in maintenance, with crews working as quickly as possible to make it available.

Hill did the math. Once the helicopters get more than 200 miles out to sea, they must have a refueler available or they won't make it back. The *Salvador Allende* went down about 1,200 miles east of New Jersey. Two tankers flying in rotation could theoretically handle the mission if everything worked perfectly. But Hill has spent more than two decades flying aircraft, from jet fighters to Hercs, and he knows machines are not infallible. Hill is adamant. He doesn't want a mission started until all the ducks—or tankers—are in a row. He wants to carefully plan the mission by the numbers, and he wants the flight leader at his side when he does; in his mind, it's not something that's conducive to doing over the radio.

Lieutenant Colonel Ed Fleming also did the math, and he too knows this is a mission that will require three tankers. But given his philosophy of getting the slowest moving aircraft on their way, knowing that the staff will find all the support aircraft that are necessary and they'll be there when they're needed, taking off with only two tankers committed is not a problem in his mind. (The Marine unit at nearby Stewart Airport has, in addition to the one they've already committed, at least a half dozen KC-130 tankers sitting on the tarmac. They also have a gung ho attitude. Fleming knows that one quick phone call is all it would take to get his third refueler.) Besides, his flight plan calls for them to hug the New England shoreline, flying northeast as far as Yarmouth, Nova Scotia, before turning out to sea. If a third tanker isn't available by the time they've reached Yarmouth, it would be easy enough to abort the mission. What's driving Fleming is the notion that there are at least twenty-eight people who have been spotted alive, and under the circumstances, getting helicopters out there today is the only way they're likely to be saved.

About fifteen minutes into the flight Fleming and his copilot, Kevin Fennell, are deep into a discussion about the risks of night hoists—especially over thirty- or forty-foot seas using night vision goggles toward the end of a lengthy mission with the entire crew fatigued—when the radio call comes ordering the two helicopters to return to base. To say that some members of the flight crews are upset is to understate the case. They'd come to work in the morning expecting to be flying a routine training mission. They'd gotten all psyched up about helping to rescue twenty-eight people—after all, rescue is what they train for. And now they're being told to stand down. Someone suggests ignoring the radio call. Feign interference. "Crackle, crackle, crackle. Sorry, can't hear you. Say again." Another crew member describes the situation as a "near mutiny." Buschor believes they can get out there and save lives if they go now. Having been in a similar situation, he can empathize with the crew of the *Salvador Allende*. He knows that with every hour spent in the water, actual physical strength as well as the will to survive diminishes.

Reluctantly, Ed Fleming turns the two HH-60s around and heads back to Westhampton Beach. The 106th ops log says that at 1407Z (9:07 A.M. EST) RCC New York is informed that the helicopters have been recalled because they'd arrive at the scene after dark.

Aboard Yanky 03
9:09 A.M. EST

Heavy with 85,000 pounds of jet fuel in her wing and internal tanks, the KC-130T with call sign Yanky 03

UNIVERSELLE TROCKENGUTCARRIERS VOM »WARNEMÜNDE«-TYP
Die Schiffe vom selben Typ: »Salvador Allende«

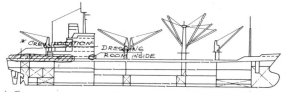

* CREW LOCATION AFTER LIFE RAFTS AND LIFE BOATS
WERE OUT OF THE SHIP

The *Salvador Allende.*

(Handwritten notations made by Alex Taranov)

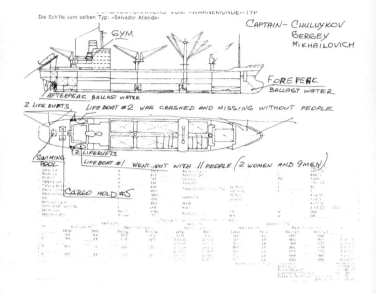

Diagram of the *Salvador Allende.*

(Handwritten notations made by Alex Taranov)

HH-60 PaveHawk helicopter in "pre-contact" position prior to refueling from C-130 Hercules.

(U.S. Air Force photo)

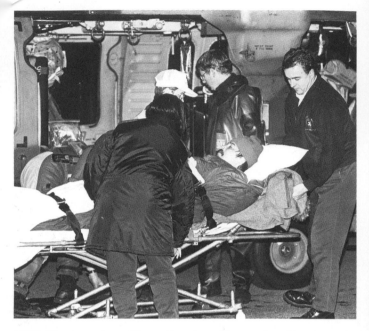

CFB Shearwater, Nova Scotia—Alexander Taranov is transferred from Jolly 14 helicopter to hospital gurney. Man directly above Taranov's head, wearing leather jacket, is Pararescue Jumper Doc Dougherty.

(Reprinted with permission from the Halifax Herald Limited*)*

Lt. Col. Ed Fleming, pilot of Jolly 14 and commander of the helicopter mission.

(Photo by Major Jim Finkle, 106th Rescue Wing)

Crews of Jolly 08 and Jolly 14 (*left to right*): Capt. Chris Baur, co-pilot 14; Lt. Col. Ed Fleming, pilot 14; Major Gene Sengstacken, co-pilot 08; two unidentified civilians; Mike Moore, PJ 08; MSgt. John Krulder, flight engineer 08; Capt. Graham Buschor, pilot 08; Jim "Doc" Dougherty, PJ 14; MSgt. Rich Davin, flight engineer 14.

(Photo by Major Jim Finkle, 106th Rescue Wing)

Returning to Gabreski Airport from *Salvador Allende* rescue mission are (*left to right*): PJ James "Doc" Dougherty, Flight Engineer Rich Davin, and Lt. Col. Ed Fleming, pilot of Jolly 14.

(Photo by Major Jim Finkle, 106th Rescue Wing)

PJ James "Doc" Dougherty, his wife Barbara, and their four children on a family outing that fits right into Doc's physical training regime. *(Left to right)*: Jim ("Doc"), Bobby, Dianna, Barbara, Jimmy and Christie.

(Courtesy of the Dougherty family)

Ann and Graham Buschor and their children Alex and Mary.

(Courtesy of the Buschor family)

Doc and Alex at Newark Airport. Doc has just given Alex the life jacket that kept him alive for thirty-two hours in the ocean.

(Photo by Major Jim Finkle, 106th Rescue Wing)

Inside the helicopter looking at the C-130 trailing the refueling drogue.

(Richard C. Zellner, Sikorsky Aircraft)

Canadian Captain Jonathan Forrest, pilot of Rescue 306.

(Courtesy of Jonathan Forrest)

Exterior of Canadian Herc with observation window in place. Note chute at lower left of door through which flares can be dropped.

(Michael Hirsh)

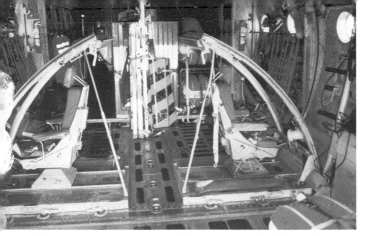

Cargo compartment of Rescue 306 looking toward rear of aircraft. Note two Plexi observation windows in their uninstalled positions. Door with porthole on right will slide up to permit installation of Plexi observation window.

(Michael Hirsh)

Regular door is raised to permit Plexi observation window to be moved into position.

(Michael Hirsh)

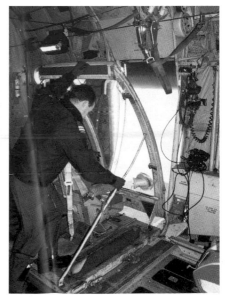

Rescue 306 co-pilot Kevin Dort in cockpit of C-130. Seat at right is flight engineer's position.

(Michael Hirsh)

Dort points out the speed indicator they were unable to read due to extreme turbulence. Instrument to the right is A-I—attitude indicator.

(Michael Hirsh)

rumbles off the ground at Stewart Airport in Newburgh, New York, fifty miles northwest of the 106th's
home base, with Captain Jon Omey at the controls.
Ninety minutes earlier Omey, the Operations officer of
the Marine Air Refueling and Transport Squadron
(VMGR 452) had taken the call from the 106th, asking if the Marines could provide tanker support
because their refueler was down for maintenance.
After a quick check with the CO, Omey said yes, and
while his crew readied the aircraft, he was briefed on
the mission over the phone. The thirty-three-year-old
pilot had been flying KC-130 tankers for nine of his
eleven years in the Corps, had worked with the helicopter pilots of the 106th before, and always enjoyed
the experience. He's quick to say that the pilots trained
by Ed Fleming are the best he's ever seen in action,
and a mutual respect had been built between the two
units.

Yanky 03's assignment is to rendezvous with the
two HH-60 helicopters over the ocean east of Mon-
tauk, Long Island, and to escort them out to the scene
of the search, refueling them on an as-needed basis.
Just as they were going "feet wet," they receive a radio
message from Stewart: "Return to base, mission
aborted."

Since they were already all dressed up and now
had no place to go, Yanky 03's crew decides to land
at Gabreski Field, home of the 106th, to try and find
out what's going on. Their landing coincides almost
precisely with the return of Jolly 08 and 14, and as
crews from the three aircraft walk into the unit's
operations building, it's quite obvious that most of
the helicopter people are not happy to have been
called back.

RCC New York
9:35 A.M. EST

> FM ARS: HELOS CAN'T GO TONIGHT BECAUSE
> PILOTS NO NIGHT QUALIFIED. DO YOU WANT US
> TOMORROW.//RGR. PREPOSITION TO LAUNCH AT
> FIRST LIGHT.//RGR.

While the Air National Guard helicopters can't launch immediately, and the weather is making it difficult for the RCC team to get surface vessels to the scene quickly, SAR planner Kelly appears to have the air coverage situation well in hand. He's got an interlaced schedule of C-130s and CP-140 Auroras from the Canadians at 14 Wing Greenwood, C-130s from Coast Guard Air Station (CGAS) Elizabeth City, North Carolina, from CGAS Borinquen, Puerto Rico, from CGAS Clearwater, Florida, from the 106th Air National Guard at Westhampton Beach, and P-3 Orions from the U.S. Naval Air Station at Brunswick, Maine. If the schedule holds, he'll always have one aircraft as OSC—on-scene commander—to communicate with other search aircraft and with merchant ships participating in the search, and it's beginning to look as though there'll be at least one other aircraft flying search patterns at all times.

Now it becomes a matter of coordinating the search, dividing thousands of square miles of ocean into sectors, choosing into which sectors to send the ships and planes, and telling them what type of pattern to use for their search. In addition to the computer-aided search program (CASP), he's got real-time reports from the aircraft telling him which way the debris line and oil slick are moving, and at 9:32 A.M.

one more tool is added to the mix. The International Ice Patrol in Groton, Connecticut, faxes over the first position reports from the self-locating datum marker buoy that CG 1503 dropped earlier that morning. It shows the buoy moving to the east-southeast at 1.6 knots, just under two miles an hour, and water temperature at almost 68 degrees F. No surprise; just confirmation of what they'd already figured out based on reports from aircraft.

106th Rescue Wing HQ
9:35 A.M. EST

Colonel David Bennett Hill, Jr., began his Air Force career as a fighter jockey flying F-4 Phantoms. When he joined the 106th in 1970, the unit was flying KC-97 tankers. In '72 they began flying the F-102, and he was back in his element. He vividly remembers sitting on alert in Jacksonville, Florida, in the early seventies watching TV, boots off, waiting. And suddenly the call would come: an unidentified aircraft entering U.S. airspace. Three minutes later his boots were on, his flight suit's zipped, and he's run out to the tarmac, jumped in his F-102, cranked it up while getting into the rest of his gear, pushed it out, and received immediate scramble clearance. "You just hit the runway, hit the afterburner, and you're in the air. In three minutes. That's no time at all."

But in December 1994, with nineteen years of rescue experience behind him, he is decidedly not running a unit that's expected to be airborne within minutes of receiving a rescue call. First, it's an Air National Guard unit. People aren't on call twenty-four hours a day; if they were, he knows that a twenty- or thirty-minute response time would be appropriate. Second, he knows what it's like to lose an aircraft, to spend hours agonizing over the fate of the crew. So he's cautious, and unapologetic for being so. "We want to respond appropriately rather than immediately," he says, adding that "[in] a rescue, one or two minutes is probably not going to make the difference. Three or four hours certainly can."

In the case of the *Salvador Allende*, calling back the helicopters meant not just a three- or four-hour delay, but at minimum, a twenty-four-hour delay in getting to the scene. Nevertheless, after assessing the situation, Hill is convinced he's made the right decision. It would be risking the lives of the crews to send them 1,200 miles out to sea after dark in horrific weather, to attempt to locate survivors, hover over them with no visible horizon, no moonlight or starlight, and try and have a PJ ride the hoist down into thirty- or forty-foot seas to pluck them to safety. And do it not just once, but perhaps twenty-eight times. Even with night vision goggles, Hill says those are not odds he wants to play, and since the buck in the 106th stops at his desk, it's his call to make.

Truth is, he's not even thrilled with the concept of sending his men and his aircraft 800 miles out to sea (from Halifax) in daylight, especially when there's weather out there that's responsible for knocking over a 450-foot ship. The *Salvador Allende* rescue is, in Hill's mind, on the ragged edge of impossibility. Definitely in the "high risk" category. Just the thought of approving an operation that requires his men to spend the amount of time it's going to take to get there and back in the cockpit of an HH-60 is enough to make him waver. Before he'll let his men go, he's going to make sure they plan the hell out of this mission to minimize the jeopardy to both man and machine.

Hill's biggest concern is the weather. "Nobody can tell you what the weather is. They tell you they can tell you, but the fact is, 800 miles at sea, nobody has a clue. There's no weather reporting stations out there. They can give you a satellite photograph of what it looks like, but you can't tell how thick it is from the photograph, you can't tell how low it goes, you can't see the height of the waves . . . that is always the question when you go on one [of these rescue missions]. Yes, the equipment can make it. Yes, I believe the men and the crews can do it from a training standpoint and from an endurance standpoint, but always, the question is, 'Can you do it with the weather? Is it predictable enough? Is there enough latitude for it to be successful?' "

People who have gotten to know Ed Fleming over the seventeen years he's been at the 106th say there's no one better at evaluating a mission to determine if it can be safely carried out, and then leading his air crews on that mission. And there's virtually no one worse at playing unit politics. That's why it was anyone's guess as to how things were going to play out when Fleming met with Hill behind closed doors to discuss the helicopters' participation in the *Salvador Allende* rescue.

It's no secret Fleming believes the helicopters should have been tasked from the beginning. But that's water over the dam. He also believes they should have been allowed to proceed, not called back for "planning." "Planning" was not an issue. They'd done it. They'd lined up two tankers within minutes, knew that a third would be coming out of 106th maintenance shortly, and that the Marines at Stewart could put another KC-130 in the air on short notice. The veteran pilot's plan was to top off the HH-60s' tanks whenever they'd burned 1,000 pounds. Before taking off, he'd received weather information from four separate sources: the Meteorological Office at McGuire AFB, from the Coast Guard, from NOAA, and from the Internet. He knew that in an emergency they could put down on the offshore oil platform known as Gorilla Rig, or on Sable Island. What he hadn't stopped to do was prepare the briefing charts, timelines, and map overlays the brass loves, but which he'd never have time to use. With the lives of up to thirty-one people at stake, graphic design just wasn't his priority.

Hill's position hadn't changed from the previous night. This was not a mission for helicopters. When Fleming walks into the meeting with the colonel, he knows they'd lost any chance of getting out to the scene in daylight. All they can do now is relocate to Halifax and prosecute the mission from there the next morning.

For nearly two hours, Hill has Fleming go over his plan step-by-step to the point where the veteran rescue pilot feels he's being badgered by his commanding officer. Hill won't be happy until he's sure the mission is planned to the nth degree. Fleming's position is that a mission like this *can't* be planned to that extent. Some decisions have to be made in real time as the operation unfolds, and he's quite comfortable doing it that way.

The differences in style are irreconcilable. Finally, they reach a compromise of sorts. The helicopters can relocate immediately to Canadian Forces Base Shear-

water, near Halifax, since the flight from there to the
search area is at least three hundred miles shorter than
from their home base to where the *Salvador Allende*
went down. Once at Shearwater, the helo crews will
go into a mandatory twelve-hour crew rest period, during which time a separate group, flown up there on a
C-130, would create the charts, maps, graphs, refueling plans, and alternate refueling plans that Hill feels
are necessary. The mission out to sea will launch at
five A.M. Saturday, December 11, almost twenty-four
hours after the *Salvador Allende* went to the bottom.

In the back of Fleming's mind is the notion that
while Hill realizes there's an expectation by now at
higher headquarters that this mission will proceed, the
commander is hoping that by the time they're due to
launch one or more ships will have picked up the survivors and the helicopter operation can be scrubbed.
Colonel Hill readily acknowledges that the loss of a
helicopter and a PJ three years earlier, in the so-called
"perfect storm" of October 1991, weighs heavily on
his decision-making process.

Having reached their accord, the two head for the
ready room to address the assembled flight crews and
support personnel. Hill explains the plan and assigns
Lieutenant Colonel Robert Landsiedel, the commanding officer of the 102nd Air Rescue Squadron,
to take charge of the overall operation, thus putting
Fleming directly under the thumb of the man who
replaced him as squadron commander just three weeks
earlier.

Landsiedel's pronouncement that he'll take a planning cell to Halifax to get everything in place so the
helicopters can head out before dawn the next morning doesn't sit well with a number of people in the

room, which has subtly divided itself into factions.
The tension is heavy, and the Marine C-130 tanker
commander isn't about to help ease it.

"You guys are kidding, right?" asks Captain Jon
Omey, more than a bit incredulous. "We could have
been halfway out there by now. We could at least have
made an attempt to get out there and find someone.
Now these guys are stuck out in the water for at least
an additional twenty-four hours."

The counter that they couldn't have made it out to
the scene before dark isn't washing with the Marine
contingent. Omey's navigator, CWO4 Jack Guthrie,
did the research while their plane was being prepped
at Stewart. His chart shows sunset in the longitude of
the search area—almost due south of Saint John's,
Newfoundland—is at 4:40 P.M., but nautical twilight—which means you can still see the horizon well
enough to use a sextant—continues until 5:54 P.M. Had
they not turned back, with favorable winds the HH-
60s escorted by Yanky 03 could be out there by six
P.M., perhaps a few minutes earlier. They may have
still had some twilight, and when that was gone, orbiting C-130s could drop enough parachute flares to provide usable light. Since aircraft had been over many of
the survivors all afternoon and would presumably
remain there till the Jollys arrived, they could vector
the helicopters directly to them. The Jollys would have
immediately been in "rescue" mode, no searching necessary. Certainly there would have been a good shot at
picking up the eleven people they knew were in the
lifeboat. It wouldn't have been easy, but the stakes are
high.

As the briefing continues it becomes clear that not

only is there friction between the 106th's C-130 officers and the helicopter crews, but that the regular Air Force tanker crew that has been dragooned into service isn't sending any "having great time, wish you were here" cards to the folks back home at Patrick AFB in Florida. They're resistant to the notion that they could possibly get up to Shearwater and be ready for a predawn launch, escorting the helicopters out to sea. The Air Force aircraft commander, a young captain, raises his hand and says, "I don't see how we can get up to Halifax, Nova Scotia, and get into crew rest, and have adequate crew rest so we can launch out at three o'clock in the morning."

The tension that had merely been an undercurrent till then pops like an overripe boil. Omey, abandoning all pretense of interservice diplomacy, turns around in his seat and says, "You guys are kiddin' me. Those guys are bobbing around in a little boat in sixty-foot seas right now."

Which prompts Colonel Hill to ask Omey, "When can you guys leave?"

"Right now," Omey responds. "We're ready to go right now." His tone makes it clear that he means, "Out to sea, up to Halifax, wherever the hell you want us to go. It doesn't matter what the regs say about 'crew rest,' let's just get this show on the road and try and save lives."

Hill answers him with a simple, "Okay. You guys have got first launch." As the briefing breaks up, Ed Fleming makes his way over to Omey and pointedly expresses his thanks that the Marines are there. It won't be the last time on this mission those sentiments are expressed by one of the helicopter crew.

Aboard Rescue 222
12:20 P.M. local time (10:20 A.M. EST)

Colonel Bill Stratemeier has his hands full flying the
C-130 in search mode. And the scanners in back aren't
exactly having a picnic either. The winds 500 feet
above the ocean are sixty knots; the seas below are
running forty to fifty feet. They're alternately flying
through fog and rain, and salt spray is constant. Before
they left the Air National Guard base at 7:30 in the
morning they'd been briefed on the weather, but
Colonel Hill was right: it's one thing to hear or read
about it, it's another to fly through it.

Rescue 222 is being guided by the Canadian Aurora
now assigned by RCC New York as on-scene commander. The Aurora is using its infrared radar to find
hot spots in the water, and then tries to vector the
American Herc to check them out. At the same time,
222 is also trying to fly sector searches and expanding
square searches in an attempt to spot survivors.

The constant switching from searching to investi-
gating the Aurora readings is problematic. Even
though the navigator can bring the aircraft back to
precisely the same spot where they broke off a sector
search to chase down a lead, there's no telling if a
survivor drifted through the area while they were
gone. It's a nasty, constantly shifting seascape below
them, and more than once the phrase "needle in a
haystack" passes through the minds of the crew
members.

After several hours of futile searching, one of the
scanners in back spots a good target: two survivors
clinging to what looks like plywood. He quickly
deploys a smoke and informs the pilots, who put the

plane into an immediate turn. Now that they've found people, Stratemeier doesn't want to lose them. "Everybody keep an eye on him, don't lose sight of him. Don't break eye contact with him. Just keep staring at him, because you may never find him again."

While the Herc is coming back around, the loadmaster and PJs are getting the ramp opened and the five-bundle kit ready to go. A quick discussion, and the decision is made to drop the rafts so they *won't* inflate on the way down. It's a risky choice. The reason for having the rafts at either end of the kit inflate on the way down is so they'll catch the wind and drift faster than the three bundles in the center, forming a U around the target. Dropping them uninflated, they have to be dead on target, or the people in the water will never get near it. The alternative is to make a normal drop, with the risk that the inflated rafts will be blown away by the sixty-knot winds.

Rigging the two rafts with long lanyards that can be easily located and pulled by the people in the water to inflate them is apparently taking longer than expected, because Stratemeier and his copilot, Captain Gregg Lagrand, have got the Herc on course for the drop, and they can already see the two men in the water waving frantically at the plane. But they haven't been told that the back end is ready to deploy the rafts. Consequently they do a fly-by and have to come around again. Frustrated by hours of wrestling with the controls and accomplishing relatively little, Stratemeier explodes at this blown opportunity. Letting loose a string of deletable expletives, he brings the plane around again, saying, "C'mon guys, we can't afford to miss it this time. These guys' lives are dependent on us. Let's make it good this time." His big concern is that even though the two men in the water seem to be okay, he's afraid of losing sight of them. It wouldn't take much for them to get tumbled by a breaking wave and disappear in the spray.

Fortunately, it doesn't happen. They bring the Herc in low and slow over the pair and the pilot calls for the drop. With the loadmaster kneeling on the ramp and anxiously watching them fall, the five bundles sail out of the plane. A few seconds go by and then they hear him shout, "He's got it!" He can actually see one of the two men hauling in the rope, which landed no more than five feet away.

For Colonel Stratemeier, it's like kicking a winning field goal with one second on the clock in a nationally televised game. He's ecstatic. Everybody goes nuts. Back at the base they practice drops with winds up to fifteen knots. To have sixty knots of wind with moderate turbulence and drop it in their laps is remarkable. But the exuberance is short-lived because moments later the Aurora is calling them to check out an additional sighting. "Okay, we can come back to these guys. They have it in their hands." And with that they turn the plane to chase down the new target.

An hour and a half later they go back to check on the first two men they'd located. They're gone. Fuel concerns force them to give up the search, and as they head for Shearwater to join the others relocating there from Suffolk, one ominous truth weighs heavily on Stratemeier and his crew: in all the time they were searching, covering hundreds, perhaps thousands, of square miles of ocean, they didn't see a single surface vessel heading into the area. Everyone aboard Rescue 222 knows that even if the survivors found every raft and supply package they'd dropped, unless a ship can reach them relatively soon and get them out of the water, they have almost no chance of surviving the beating the angry sea is visiting upon them.

TEN

Minutes after leaving the ready room, Fleming meets with the pilots of Jolly 08, Buschor and Sengstacken, and with the AC of Yanky 03, Captain Jon Omey. At the moment he's still short one pilot. Kevin Fennell had a family emergency and has called Chris Baur at his U.S. Customs job, to see if he can come in to replace him. Baur agrees, puts in paperwork for a short leave, runs home to grab a bag with a couple of flight suits and a toilet kit, and heads to the base.

Baur's relatively new to the unit, having joined it two years earlier following a six-year stint in the Army and four years in the Coast Guard. When he enlisted in the Army after flunking out of college because he was working three jobs, they made him an MP and sent him to the proving grounds at Yuma, Arizona. Wanting to continue the flying he'd begun to do in college, he applied for and was accepted into warrant officer school, where, he says, "They shout at you all day long." Ultimately he flew Scout helicopters near the

172

DMZ in Korea, and Hueys in Hawaii and Thailand. He left the Army and joined the Coast Guard—he'll tell you he "came for the food and left with a commission"—where he spent 1987 to 1991 flying out of the Coast Guard Air Station in Brooklyn. That's where he got his first taste of search and rescue, flying missions in their up-to-date Dolphine HH-85 helicopter. His day job now is flying helicopters and fixed wing planes for U.S. Customs, as well as occasionally working as an undercover agent.

All his helicopter experience got him into the 102nd Air Rescue Squadron, but he still has to complete the qualification course in the HH-60 PaveHawk. Rather than sending him away to flight school, they've allowed him to take his training while flying with the unit. While Baur has performed midair refuelings, it's always officially been as a "student," with the AC logging time as instructor.

Ed Fleming has flown with Baur and likes him, but he knows he'd be better off with a fully qualified pilot in the left seat. It's one of the quirks of trying to fly emergency missions out of an Air National Guard unit. Less than half the people assigned to the base are fulltimers, which means it's not unusual for the best qualified individual for a given mission to be working his civilian job and unavailable to take the call.

Fleming's concern about Baur is a personal one. Since it's his policy to assign the most experienced pilot to fly with the least experienced, Baur's going to be his copilot. The lieutenant colonel is forty-seven years old and has had bouts of sciatica over the years. He knows how long they're going to be in the seats, how physical this mission is likely to be, and would have preferred someone in the left seat who could handle half the load.

With Baur, he knows that as a matter of course he's going to do most if not all of the refuelings. *C'est la guerre*. Sorry 'bout that. He knows he'll just have to deal with it. It isn't the first bit of adversity he's run into on this mission, and it certainly won't be the last.

Fleming's briefing for the first leg of their mission is short. The flight northeast to the Canadian Air Force Base at Shearwater, Nova Scotia, just a few miles southeast of Halifax, and almost right on the beach, should take about four hours, and the plan is to refuel at least twice along the way. Once everyone is squared away on route and radio frequencies, they head for the aircraft.

By the time Baur arrives on base, picks up his gear, and gets out to Jolly 14, the rotors are already turning, and as soon as he's aboard, they lift off, this time without any culinary delays. It's not until they're airborne that he has an opportunity to ask Fleming where they're going. "To Halifax. To crew rest." The brevity and tone of the answer speak volumes.

RCC New York
2:45 P.M. EST

The phones are keeping three people busy as the first afternoon of the search wears on. Aircraft already on the scene are calling directly with reports of individual sightings. Unit headquarters are checking in with reports of planes ready to launch or returning to base. Representatives of companies associated with the *Salvador Allende* keep coming out of the woodwork. There are calls from the commercial managers of the vessel in Hamburg, Germany; from the spokesman for the ship's

agent; from the American Bureau of Shipping; from a
shipping company in Miami; from the vessel's insurer;
from someone claiming to represent the charter company, followed an hour later by someone else claiming
that *he* is the ship owner's charter representative in
Freeport, Texas. If the duty officer has time, he briefs the
caller; if not, they're told to call Public Affairs, which is
also handling media calls. In frustration they begin
telling the callers claiming to be associated in one way
or another with the Black Sea Shipping Company to get
together and choose just one person to call the RCC.

In the North Atlantic
4:45 P.M. local time (2:45 P.M. EST)

Darkness comes quickly in mid-ocean. One minute
Alex can see the waves coming at him, the next it's as
though someone turned off the lights. He's got the
food package he found in the water stuffed inside his
orange exposure suit, but even though he hasn't eaten
anything in more than twelve hours, he's not hungry.
The waves are still forcing him to swallow huge
amounts of saltwater, and he's constantly vomiting.
He has no way of knowing that he's drifted more than
fifty miles from where his ship went down. What he
does know is that none of the search airplanes that he
can occasionally see in the distance come anywhere
near him. At last light he is all alone.

Snippets of memories come to him between struggles with the huge breakers. He remembers that what
first attracted him to the sea was not a love of ships,
but the uniform that the high school boys in the after-

school sailing classes wore. He looked good in that uniform. And later, when he had to choose a shipboard specialty, he remembers the warning from friends: "Don't be a navigator. If you go to navigator school, you can only be a navigator. Navigators are nothing on shore. You go to be a mechanic. Because mechanic is mechanic on the ship and also mechanic on the shore."

He thinks about his father, Julian Avner, which is strange because he hasn't seen him since the late seventies, doesn't even know if he's alive, isn't even sure if he really did go to Argentina. For years after his parents divorced, Alex kept his father's name, a distinctly Jewish name in a decidedly anti-Semitic country. When he married, he took his wife's name, Taranov, accent on the *rá*, very Russian-sounding. Suddenly, promotions at work came much more easily. Thinking about his wife, then his daughters, brings tears to his already swollen eyes. He shakes his head as if to clear the memory bank and come back to the present. He looks around and listens. Nothing. He's still very much alone.

RCC New York
4:05 P.M. EST

A telex message arrives from the German tanker *Torungen*:

```
WE ARE PROCEEDING TO DISTRESS POSITION
3939.5N 05006.1W ETA 092235UTC MASTER
```

Other than having the search planes pinpoint the survivors' locations, that's the best news so far.

With the M/V *Benny Queen* also getting close, it
means that two merchant ships will be in the search
area between 5:30 and 6:00 P.M., New York time,
unfortunately after sundown in the mid-Atlantic.

A call comes in from the operations center at Suffolk:

WILL THERE BE ANY RESCUE VESSELS BETWEEN
SHEARWATER AND THE SEARCH AREA IN CASE A
HELO HAS TO DITCH?

PJS WANT TO KNOW IF ANY PLACES TO LAND IN
CASE THEY DITCH. CAN YOU CALL THEM? //
RGR. THE ONLY PLACE IS ONE [OIL] RIG.

Ten minutes later, at 6:05 P.M., Rescue 306 is on the
phone with another good news/bad news call. Finally,
they've got a surface vessel on scene, but no survivors
to be found.

SIGHTED SEVERAL L/R'S W/ NO POB IN POSN 39-
19N 049-45W. M/V TORUNGEN IS O/S

A half hour later they learn that the second merchant vessel has actually made it to the search area.
The M/V *Benny Queen* has been vectored to a position
by one of the Coast Guard planes.

NEGATIVE SIGHTINGS. VSL REPTS O/S WX AS WIND
NNW FORCE 6, VIS 15 + NM, SEAS 20FT

More good news/bad news. *Benny Queen* didn't
find anyone, but the weather appears to have moder-
ated after dark. Force 6 winds are about thirty mph,
and while seas of twenty feet aren't to be taken

lightly, they're a lot better than the thirty- to sixty-foot seas that had been reported at various times earlier.

At 9:18, CG 1501 calls:

```
RESCUE 760 D/S (DEPART SCENE) IN 15 MIN. CAN-
FOR 306 O/S. TORUNGEN ATTEMPTING TO LOCATE
2 POB IN RAFT POSN 39-18N 49-49W.
```

At 10:28 P.M., Rescue 103 reports its position. The plane is dropping illumination flares and has spotted "multiple survivors."

At fourteen minutes past midnight on Saturday, December 10, about twenty-five hours after the *Salvador Allende* got knocked over, they get the call they'd been hoping for. It's Rescue 103:

```
M/V TORUNGEN RECOVERED ONE POB IN POSIT 39-
13N 049042W AT 0356Z (10:56 PM EST) BELIEVE
ITS THE SECOND MATE. HAVE SIGHTED TWO
STROBE LIGHTS IN POSIT 39-07N 049-39W. VEC-
TORING M/V TORUNGEN INTO POSITION. HAVE
STROBE IN POSIT 39-10N 049-41W M/V BENNY
QUEEN GOING TO INVESTIGATE. HAVE THIRD
STROBE IN POSITION 39-02N 049-39W. DO NOT
HAVE ANYBODY TO DIVERT TO IT//RGR. WE WILL
TRY TO ID SOMEBODY TO GO LOOK//RGR.
```

How did the Merchant Vessel *Torungen*, an 850-foot-long oil tanker, manage to maneuver in heavy seas to pluck the *Salvador Allende*'s second mate from the water? And can the survivor tell them anything about the sinking of his ship that might be of use in the continuing search for his mates?

Canadian Air Force Base, Shearwater, Nova Scotia
11:00 P.M. (10:00 P.M. EST)

For Lieutenant Colonel Robert Landsiedel, planning
the logistics for this mission is the closest he's come to
going to war. It means moving fixed and rotary wing
assets to a foreign country, putting together primary
and backup crews for each aircraft, making certain
that "crew rest" regulations are considered as the
crews are scheduled, getting authorization from higher
headquarters for potential extensions of the allowable
duty day for the helicopter crews, requesting a waiver
to permit the Jollys to exceed the recovery range
between air-refueling control points, and obtaining a
waiver to permit the HC-130P tankers to operate
20,000 pounds heavier than normal, so they can carry
"the maximum amount of fuel to be onboard so HH-
60s can remain on station the maximum amount of
time to recover all survivors."

Arrangements also have to be made with the Canadians at Shearwater to provide fuel, food, and transportation, and to locate hotel rooms convenient to the base.

Earlier in the day, as the helicopters were taking off
for Shearwater, he had base operations contact the
officer-in-charge of the weather station at McGuire
AFB in New Jersey and request a "weather close
watch" for a mission departing Shearwater at 0900Z
on the tenth, out to N39-30N, 51-16W, at or below
2,000 feet. Approximate arrival time on-scene would
be 1400Z (eleven A.M. local time). McGuire AFB is
asked to provide all pertinent information, including
ceilings, visibility, winds, sea state, and water temperature. And most important, to monitor the flight corridor and report any changes in forecast or conditions

as the mission proceeds. This was a lesson learned from the 1991 experience, when McGuire didn't know that the 106th had aircraft searching for a boat 200 miles out to sea. Their weather office knew of the storm that would ultimately cut Jolly 110 off from returning to base on a direct course, but the 106th didn't call to ask, and McGuire had no reason to offer the information. The end result was that the helicopter flew into the storm, was unable to refuel, and ditched in the Atlantic no more than sixty miles from Gabreski Airport.

The helicopters and Marine tanker escort arrive at Shearwater in mid-afternoon, following an uneventful flight, unless you count Gene Sengstacken's door flying open at altitude with an explosive bang so loud that it scared the hell out of everyone. They immediately slowed to seventy knots and somehow muscled it shut, managing not to lose the gear he had stashed nearby. But as soon as they came back up to 130 knots, it exploded open again. Enough was enough. Jolly 08 put down in an open field outside of Yarmouth to give Krulder and Moore a chance to secure the door with a cargo strap. They'll get it repaired at Shearwater.

Following a quick visit to base operations, the crews went by taxi to the Holiday Inn. More precisely, they went in two taxis, to two *different* Holiday Inns. Who knew there was more than one when they hopped into the cabs and said "Holiday Inn"? It took a couple of hours before they finally connected with each other. During dinner, Fleming, Buschor, and Sengstacken had some time to discuss the mission. Then, they were supposed to go into the uninterrupted twelve-hour "crew rest" period. That's what the official paperwork says they did. It's right there in the 106th's operations log.

1930Z (3:30 P.M. Halifax time) Jolly flight and Marine Bird Yanky 03 land at Shearwater. Will be in crew rest.

Crew rest regulations notwithstanding, Ed Fleming needs to meet again with the pilots before the morning briefing to get procedural details out of the way. The session takes place in his hotel room with HH-60 pilots Buschor, Baur, and Sengstacken; Yanky 03's drivers, Jon Omey and Jim Hall; and the regular Air Force pilot who had expressed great concern about adequate crew rest earlier that day. Fleming's message to the helicopter pilots is that the two ships are to stay together as much as possible during the entire mission. No one needs to say it out loud, but they all know that if something happens to one of the HH-60s, they'll be depending on the other one for rescue. He makes it clear that they'll top off their tanks whenever the opportunity presents itself. Each of the helicopters can carry 4,500 pounds of fuel; Fleming wouldn't be unhappy if they refueled as soon as they've burned 1,000 pounds. While it sounds supercautious, all the pilots know that the only fuel they can absolutely count on is what's in the main tanks, which hold 2,200 pounds. The engines can't take fuel directly from the internal auxiliary tanks. That gas has to be pumped into the main tanks first in order to be usable. If a tiny fuel pump fails, whatever's in the auxiliary tanks becomes nothing more than ballast.

The rest of the briefing is devoted to coordination of communication frequencies, assigning squawk frequencies that will allow the C-130s to easily identify the helicopters on radar and TACAN channels that the helicopters use to determine how far apart they are. Those details taken care of, it's back to crew rest.

The notion of "crew rest" on the night before a high risk mission, while officially taken quite seriously, is somewhat of a joke amongst the crews. "Hello, men. Tomorrow morning you're going to fly into what amounts to a hurricane, end up so far out to sea that if the coupling breaks off the refueling probe you're dead meat, then try and pull thirty or so people from the water, who will die if you don't succeed. The crew van will pick you up at 0400. You launch at 0500. Oh, by the way: have a good night's sleep." It's like telling your kids to go to bed early so they'll be rested up for a big day at Disneyland tomorrow. It's not going to happen.

No matter how keyed-up the men are about the morning's mission, in their calls home they downplay everything. Some wives, like Ann Buschor, don't want any details, and Graham doesn't volunteer any. Others, like Barbara Dougherty, get the picture in broad strokes. "A ship is going down. We're in Halifax and flying out in the morning." Nothing's mentioned about nine or ten midair refuelings, 900 miles out to sea, and weather they wouldn't fly in unless it were a matter of saving lives.

Barbara Dougherty is content knowing that when it's over, she'll hear the whole story. When Doc leaves on a mission, or when he calls, all she'll ask is if he's mountain climbing, or scuba diving, or jumping into the water. "It would drive me crazy if I let it get to me, if I really thought about all the details," she says.

From a practical point of view, it really doesn't

matter to her what kind of mission Doc is on or where he's gone. She has to carry on with the house and four kids. The situation is not quite the same as that of Army or Marine wives whose husbands are deployed overseas, perhaps into combat, with an entire unit for an extended period of time, or for a Navy wife whose husband is scheduled to be at sea for six months. Everyone assigned to the 106th lives off the base in civilian housing; with their families, if they're married. And half the unit's personnel are actually civilians who usually take a military leave from their job in order to fly a mission.

That said, many of the PJ's wives whose husbands have been part of the 106th for, in some cases, more than twenty years have developed their own mutual support group. According to Doc's wife, the running joke between herself, PJ John Brehm's wife Peggy, and John Spillane's wife Laura is that "if anything ever happens to the men, we'll just live in a big house all together, the three of us, two of us will go out to work, and Peggy'll stay home with the kids. We have this all planned out." Then she adds, "The other was, we would never want all three of them to be on a mission at the same time, 'cause God forbid anything happened, y'know, we'd still want at least one man if we could." Doc's response? "We're always saying, 'I hope I'm the guy.' "

The reality is, when a mission goes out, the wives are in constant phone contact. "Do you need anything? Do you need help with the kids?" This preplanning came into play in October 1991 when word came that one of the unit's helicopters was in trouble in a horrific storm sixty miles out to sea. Unable to refuel, they were preparing to ditch. PJs Rick Smith and Spillane were aboard. Doc Dougherty had gone through PJ school with both of them.

The wives got word of the trouble five minutes before Jolly 110 went in. As soon as the call came, the support group snapped together instantly. John and Peggy Brehm brought their daughter to the Dougherty's house to baby-sit the kids. Then Peggy and Barbara went to Laura Spillane's house while the two PJs went directly to the base to get involved in the search. Just before they left, Peggy kissed her husband goodbye, then threatened him with death if he didn't call to report every scrap of information that came in.

Laura was five or six months pregnant with their first child at the time, and the women didn't want her getting too stressed-out. They kept urging her to lay down for a while, saying, "Everything'll be okay; John's well-prepared. Don't think the worst."

On the outside, Barbara Dougherty is very controlled. Inside, however, there's dread. "You want to believe, but there's the other thing saying, 'Oh my God, what if something does happen? How am I going to console my best friend? What can I do for her? I mean, I can't bring him back myself. I can only be here to pick up the pieces.' "

Barbara knows how easily she could be the one whose husband is missing at sea, the one who's hearing beguiling words of comfort from her closest friends. Her coping mechanism is to stay busy. When Doc's on a mission, furniture gets rearranged, walls get painted, carpets get replaced. That night at Laura Spillane's house, Barbara worked off her nervous energy by wallpapering a room.

Every time the phone rang, Peggy Brehm would leap for it. She's the designated recipient of any news;

if it's bad, she's the one who'll have to handle it. The first call told them that four of the five men had been picked up. But no names had been relayed to the 106th command center. The next call came an hour or so later. Laura's husband John had been picked up, but he was badly hurt. Period. Still no word on which of the crew was missing.

It was after sunrise when they finally got the news that although he had multiple internal injuries and broken bones, John Spillane was going to make it. That's also when they learned that the missing man was PJ Rick Smith, whose wife, Marianne, had just had a baby three weeks earlier.

It was a devastating blow to the unit's PJs, and to their wives. They all know the dangerous nature of the job. The women married them knowing that being a PJ was really more than a job, it was a calling. They know "That Others May Live" is more than a noble motto, more than a nifty military creed. In order that others may live, one of their husbands may die. It's an existential situation that requires more than an ordinary dose of courage—from both husbands *and* wives.

Halifax Holiday Inn
1:40 A.M. (11:40 A.M. EST)

After twenty-two years as a PJ, the last fifteen with the 106th, Mike Moore's approach to crew rest is realistic. You're given twelve hours during which to get eight hours of uninterrupted sleep, which means that you consider yourself lucky if you get four. Rather than holing up in his room, the veteran PJ takes a little tour of the Holiday Inn, befriending anyone with keys to the pantry. By the time they finish exchanging recipes, Moore's larder is stocked for the trip.

Back in his room, he calls his wife, Betsy, at home in New Jersey. She's already been notified by the base that he's gone on a water rescue mission off Nova Scotia, so her only question is, "Are you going to be home for Christmas?" She's also been through this enough to know not to ask for specifics. Sometimes he can't tell her because it's classified; other times he won't tell her because he doesn't want her or their four children needlessly worrying. Of all the wives of the part-timers, Betsy Moore is probably one of the most understanding of her husband's affection for his PJ work. Mike's day job is director of emergency medical services programs at Fort Monmouth, New Jersey. It's okay, but being a PJ is better.

Coursing through Doc Dougherty's mind as he tries to fall asleep is his reaction to what he saw in the Canadian Air Force operations planning area shortly after they landed at Shearwater. "This is big. If we do this, it's gonna be something." Of all the people on the mission, getting a good night's sleep is probably least critical for Doc. He has no problem sleeping in the back of the helicopter, and he knows it's going to be a six-hour flight out to sea. He still isn't convinced the mission is really going to happen. He can imagine a scenario where the mission planners work all night, wake them up and hand them a package of operational plans, and then Lieutenant Colonel Fleming will decide if they're going to go, that is *if* they even have permission to go. Bad weather is predicted for Shearwater in the morning, and it's still bad in the search area.

Doc is beginning to get the feeling that they're getting all dressed up only to be told not to go. It wouldn't surprise him. In his years with the 106th, he's gotten used to the gun getting cocked without anyone ever pulling the trigger. It happened to him just a week before this mission. He was at home, the phone rang and he was out the door, racing to the base. There was a boat on fire, people in the water. He and Mike Moore grabbed their gear and piled into an HH-60 whose rotors were already turning. A quick taxi away from the buildings, and they were airborne. Just as they were about to clear the fence, there was a radio call: "C'mon back. The Coast Guard's got it."

Now, Doc flips on the TV and plops onto his bed. The late CBC news carries a quick story about the rescue mission, and he begins rethinking his doubts. "Yeah, there's something out there, something going on. Maybe we are going to do this. We're here. We're in crew rest." But as he tries to fall asleep, his dominant thought is that they'll show up for the morning briefing and be told to go home.

Senior Master Sergeant Rich Davin has been a flight engineer since 1977, the last seven years with 102nd. For him, the notion of getting a good night's sleep before a mission like this is a fairy tale. Try as he might, at midnight he's still tossing and turning. Three hours later he hasn't gotten a lot of rest. In fact, he'd call it the worst night of sleep he's ever had.

Marine Captain Jon Omey is still not onboard with the concept of "crew rest." Sure, he knows the Marine Corps has regulations that cover it, but they're not nearly as anal about it as the Air Force seems to be. Omey describes the difference between the two services this way: "The Marine Corps tells you what you *can't* do; the Air Force tells you what you *can* do, and precisely how you're allowed to do it." It's a difference that will be seen again and again on this mission, in situations a whole lot more critical than crew rest.

CFB Shearwater Operations Center
11:00 P.M. (10:00 P.M. EST)

The mission planning cell flew up from Long Island on a C-130 several hours after the helicopters, set up shop in the operations building at Shearwater, and by late evening are well into the task of figuring out the logistics for sending two helicopters farther out to sea for a longer period of time than had ever been contemplated when Sikorsky designed the HH-60. The first job was to sort out their personnel so they could cover the facility around-the-clock without having anyone run afoul of workday or crew rest restrictions. Mission commanders are Lieutenant Colonels John Flanagan and Robert Landsiedel, with the latter taking the overnight shift while Flanagan, who is a night-water, hoist-qualified HH-60 pilot, worked until around eleven P.M., then went into crew rest in case he was needed to fly the following day. Mission planners are Major Mike Weiss, a C-130 pilot, and Major Mike Canders, an HH-60 pilot, along with Senior Master Sergeant Jack Brehm, a veteran PJ.

Their main task during the night is to try and figure out how much fuel the HH-60s would be burning and how much the C-130s would be using to get out and back. They have to take into account weather, altitude, weight, and speed, then "what if" it to death. A C-130 flying home at 25,000 feet with fumes in most of the tanks might burn less than 5,000 pounds of fuel an hour (6.5 pounds = one gallon). The same plane with a full load of fuel, playing mother hen to the helicopters below 1,000 feet, could eat up 9,000 pounds in an hour of flaps-down orbiting. Subtracting the Herc's needs from what a fully tanked plane could carry tells them how much gas they can give to the helicopters. Knowing the burn rate of the helicopters tells them how long the transferred fuel will last, which is what determines when the next tanker in the rotation needs to be out there.

Landsiedel doesn't want the helicopters out there without two tankers available to them on relatively short notice. The plan would be to have one Herc with the HH-60s, another one en route to them, perhaps no more than half an hour away, while the third one returns to base, refuels, and prepares to launch on a predetermined schedule. Shortly after midnight the what-iffing leads them to call the Marine unit at Stewart and ask if they have another KC-130 available. Once again the Marines come through, and prepare to dispatch Yanky 01 on a flight plan that would have it landing at Shearwater by six A.M., ready to fly as a backup in case something happened to one of the other three tankers.

The mission planners pencil the contingency on the bottom of the tanker schedule.

If Yanky 03 aborts, AFR 852 takes off at 0600Local
If AFR 852 Aborts, Yanky 01 takes off at 0745Local
If AFR 974 aborts, Yanky 02 takes off at 1030Local

Now it's a matter of waiting to see if the weather will be good enough to launch the helicopters.

RCC New York
Saturday, December 10 1:25 A.M. EST

An hour after the M/V *Torungen* pulled a live survivor out of the water, RCC New York gets the first bits of information about him. Canadian Rescue 103 relays that the man's name is Igor Skiba, he's thirty-six years old, and was the second mate on the ship.

Five minutes later a call comes in directly from *Torungen*. They've checked four other life rafts and found no one. The second mate is asleep. Anxious to learn more about the sinking and possible survivors, *Torungen* is told that RCC will call back in four hours to debrief him.

CFB Shearwater
2:15 A.M. (1:15 A.M. EST)

At 2:15 the Canadians give the planning cell the latest weather. It's relatively good news. Favorable conditions on the way out. High seas and high winds on scene. And nothing in the forecast to give them concern about the trip back in. Weather is Landsiedel's biggest concern. Even though this is an operational as opposed to a training mission, he doesn't want to send them out there without a minimum 1,500 foot ceiling. "I was a helicopter pilot before I went to fixed-wing, and I was out there on missions at 100 feet with ceilings at 150 feet. And we've been out on missions where we had to air refuel at 400 feet. But we weren't out 700 miles having to do that, we were out maybe 100, 150 miles. You don't try to get yourself in a situation like that." But convinced that the weather is good enough to support a decision to launch, Landsiedel confirms that the Canadians will pick up the crews at the hotels, then grabs a short nap on a nearby couch.

In the North Atlantic
4:30 A.M. (2:30 A.M. EST)

Alex Taranov has been in the ocean nearly twenty-four hours. Now he's floating in total darkness, in a driving rainstorm, still being battered by giant waves. Occasionally, a shaft of moonlight cuts through a break in the clouds, and on a couple of occasions he can see the orange light of flares being dropped by search aircraft, but none comes anywhere near him. Even if they did, he knows there's no chance of being spotted by one of the airplanes because during the day the waves ripped the flashlight from his life jacket.

His biggest concern is that his life jacket will be stripped from him by one of the large breakers. He can't see them coming, but he can feel and hear them. He knows the ones with the more powerful sound are the ones that will tumble him and force him under, and each time he hears one coming, he grabs the canvas between the sections of the jacket and holds on, quite literally for dear life.

Alex is fighting to stay awake, because what he's hoping for is that a ship will come nearby. He knows that if there are planes searching overhead, there have to be ships coming to pick up survivors. At one point he's convinced that one of the lights in the distance must be a ship, but listening intently, all he can hear is the far off sound of a search plane. No ship materializes.

CFB Shearwater Ready Room
3:45 A.M. (2:45 A.M. EST)

Both helicopter crews, as well as the Marines from
Yanky 03, are treated to a Canadian Air Force breakfast of scrambled eggs, bacon, hash browns, and coffee during the early morning briefing. The Marines,
who have a lavatory on the C-130 and the opportunity
to get out of their seats to use it, chow down, as do the
mission planners. The helicopter crews are a bit pick-
ier. Ed Fleming and Graham Buschor have coffee.
Gene Sengstacken munches on some dry toast. Chris
Baur eats some of the eggs, but seems to be distracted
and uncharacteristically quiet. He hasn't mentioned it
to anyone, but he's had premonitions about this mission. Because Baur's been doing sneaky Pete work for
U.S. Customs, he's told no one where he's living on
Long Island. Before he left home for the base, however, he'd taken the unusual step of calling his mother
to give her his address. And just a few minutes earlier
he debated whether to actually check out of the hotel,
finally deciding to leave his bag in the room.

The briefing lasts half an hour. As the crews come
in they're given an inch-thick briefing book that has
been put together in the last few hours. The Canadians
tell them what kind of weather to expect. The mission
planners go over the refueling plan, unaware that
Fleming has already issued his own, and Landsiedel
makes it clear that they want the helos turned around
and heading back no later than 12:30. Sunset that far
out in the ocean would be at 3:30 Halifax time, and
they don't want a tired crew having to air refuel in the
dark using night vision goggles. He also emphasizes
that the HH-60s are not going out there to search.

They're going out to pick up survivors that have been pinpointed by the C-130s. Unless they're told that survivors have been located, he wants the helicopters to go no farther than 150 miles past Sable Island, a small spit of land 150 miles out to sea.

"We don't want the helicopters out there as a search platform. That's the C-130s' job," the mission commander emphasizes. The statement flies in the face of SAR reality, but neither Fleming nor any of the other helicopter pilots see fit to raise an objection. They know that while a C-130 flying at 120 knots, just above stall speed, can cover a lot of territory, it can't effectively work lower than 300 feet. If the Herc spots something, it'll need at least a mile to make a U-turn and come back to positively identify it. The helicopters, on the other hand, are the perfect platform for low-and-slow searching once the drift line of debris has been located. It's how RCC New York will instruct their on-scene commander to use them.

As the briefing ends and the crew is attending to last minute details, Baur walks up to the Marine C-130 pilot Jon Omey and his navigator, CWO4 Jack Guthrie.

"Hey, I have a couple of questions for you," the helicopter pilot says. "Our guys are a little worried about going out on this mission. You know the background. We lost a helicopter a couple years ago doing pretty much the same thing."

Omey acknowledges that he'd heard the story.

Baur continues, "What are you going to do if we get out to the site and we're bingo, we don't have enough gas to get back home, and you guys lose an engine?"

"I'll tank you on three engines," the Marine pilot answers. "I'll tank you on two engines. I'll tank you until we start going down ourselves."

The Marines aren't at all put off by the pointed questions. Omey understands where Baur is coming from and what he's getting at. The animosity between the 102nd's C-130 people and the helicopter crews, while not flagrant, has been obvious in the little digs they've been taking at each other. There's no question in Omey's mind that the HH-60 crews hold the tanker pilots responsible for the loss of Jolly 110 three years back.

Baur tries another scenario. "Well, what happens if we get out there and the weather's bad?"

Omey knows that Air Force regulations say you're not allowed to tank below a 1,000-foot ceiling. "If we go out there and the ceiling's bad and you guys need gas, we'll tank you as low as it takes. If we have to tank you at 200 feet, we'll tank you at 200 feet. Whatever it takes. We're not going to leave you out there."

Those were the words Baur wants to hear. He smiles. "I'm glad we have some naval aviators here. I knew that would be your answer, but I just needed to hear it so I could go tell my crew."

Then Baur makes two unusual requests. If one of the helicopters should ditch, he wants the Marines to check and see if anyone managed to get out. They agree. Then he gives them a high frequency channel he used when he was flying rescue for the Coast Guard, and asks them to monitor it throughout the mission, "Just in case we need you." Once again the pilot and navigator agree, and Baur leaves, feeling relieved. A couple of minutes later Ed Fleming comes over to thank them, and emphasizes once again how glad he is that the Marines are flying with them.

A few final details are straightened out, and the helo crew members who hadn't put on their mustang suits at the hotel change into them now. For the PJs, the insulated canvas survival suits are just temporary. Once onboard they'll change into their cold water working gear. Doc's planning on wearing long johns under his dry suit. Mike Moore's dry suit is in for repairs, so he'll be using a heavy wet suit.

Walking from Operations to the crew van in the snow, everyone seems lost in their own thoughts. That changes quickly once the van is rolling. From the rear, where Baur is sitting, comes an extremely loud farting noise, followed by Chris moaning, "God, I feel sick." All the way out to the helicopters the farting sounds continue, and the Americans are falling apart with laughter. When the van rolls to a stop and everyone piles out, the Canadian driver walks around the vehicle, opening all the doors, mumbling about having to "air it out." This sets off another paroxysm of laughter. Once again Baur's managed to lighten things up, but the laughter is short-lived. It's 5:15 A.M. At that moment RCC Halifax is on the phone to RCC New York. "Both HH-60s will be airborne in fifteen minutes. ETA on-scene is 1500 Zulu."

ELEVEN

Ten minutes from launch the laughter that filled the van on the way out to the helicopters is only a distant echo in the night. It's snowing heavier now, and looking into the distance, they get a good idea that perhaps the weather briefers were a bit optimistic about the conditions they'd be flying through early in the mission.

To watch them prepare, one gets the impression that they know precisely what they're doing, precisely what they've signed up for. They have faith in themselves, in each other, and in the team that keeps the HH-60s in the air. The maintenance crews that flew up with them have been working through the night to make certain the aircraft are prepped. They, more than anyone else, know that Sikorsky recommends minor maintenance after every four hours of flight, and a major, day-long overhaul after ten hours in the air. Now they're about to send them out on what will be a fifteen-hour mission.

As Rich Davin talks with the ground crew, it doesn't even cross his mind to question the wisdom of undertaking this mission. Not now. He's in a zone, locked into what he's doing. Making sure the ship is ready, and that he's ready for whatever might happen, including the worst. He checks and rechecks his survival gear; he wants to be comfortable knowing he can survive on his own, if it comes to that.

After years in this business Davin is convinced that the people who sit in operation centers and make decisions about whether a mission should press on or turn around don't always have the best understanding of the situation. "Sometimes when they want us to come back, the old radio doesn't work. The 'We can't hear you' type of thing. We're more prone to say, 'Let's press on and do it. We can do this.' "

Dougherty says, "We're not suicidal. We're going to plan a mission and make that conscious decision: 'Can we do this and survive?' Yes, we can. Do we know it's dangerous? Yes, we do."

Even veteran helicopter pilots can get queasy about a mission when they suddenly find themselves on the hot seat in operations, monitoring the radios while the troops are out in the weather doing their thing. It happened to Ed Fleming one winter afternoon when one of the helicopters responded to a call for help from the Coast Guard station in Hampton Bays. An eighty-foot fishing boat was anchored about a mile offshore with a torpedo hung up in its net. The boat's captain had ordered the net hauled in when he felt an unusually heavy drag on the vessel. Before he could stop it, the net was hanging from a high boom with a live WWII twenty-foot torpedo pointed business end down, right over the deck.

By the time the Coast Guard got involved, the vessel had heavy cable hanging off its stern and an anchor line off the bow. Together they were keeping the boat broadside to the huge swells. As a result, she was rolling heavily, with the torpedo acting like a doomsday pendulum. A Navy explosive ordinance disposal (EOD) team was flown into the base at Suffolk and driven to Hampton Bays. After determining that the torpedo was live, that it was a type carried by Navy destroyers in WWII, and that it had a blast (concussion) radius of 2.5 miles if it detonated above the water, they planned to take a small boat out to the trawler, board it, and, much to the chagrin of the skipper, plant explosive charges in the holds, which were filled with fish, and sink it, taking the boat and torpedo to the bottom.

The fishermen were taken off their boat by the Coast Guard, but by the time the EOD team arrived, the swells were too big to permit them to board the trawler from a boat, and they asked the 106th for help. It was going to be a tricky mission. In heavy seas they had to lower five EOD men to the bow of the boat—the only deck space that was clear of antennas, booms, winches, and outriggers—wait for them to plant the charges, then pluck them off the boat before the charges fired. When Fleming back in operations learned precisely what was being asked of the helicopter crew, he ordered them to scrub the mission. Putting men on the deck of a fishing boat bristling with obstacles and rolling in heavy seas while a live torpedo swings from a boom didn't seem worth the risk.

Davin got on the radio and reminded Fleming of the mission they'd flown together to pick the woman with the bee sting off a similar boat, in a sea state very much like the one they were now dealing with. "Colonel Ed, we can do this. It's doable." Reluctantly, Fleming consented.

They loaded the EOD crew on the helicopter, along with a pair of PJs, Paul Bellissimo and Chris Baker, and in a matter of minutes were over the fishing boat. The EOD team leader leaned out the door, saw how badly the boat was rolling, and said there's no way to get us down there on a hoist. Davin assured them that if he didn't believe he could safely get them on the deck without banging them up, he'd stop the hoist and haul them back in. The Navy team agreed to go for it.

With Lieutenant Colonel Dave Ruvola piloting the HH-60, they went in low and slow and dropped the PJs in the water as close as possible to the boat, then backed off to watch as the two men struggled to get aboard. Fortunately, there was a net draped over the side of the vessel amidships, and when the boat rolled toward them, they grabbed the net and hung on. Suddenly, they were dangling ten feet over the water as it began rolling back the other way. When it cycled again, they were able to climb a few feet up the net. They did the same thing through two more cycles, and finally managed to scramble over the railing.

The next step was for them to get to the bow and signal the helicopter to move in with a tag line—a weighted line that can be used to guide the hoist directly to the boat's deck. One by one the five EOD men were lowered to the boat. Next, they went below to plant the charges in the unrefrigerated holds filled with a two-day-old catch of fish. After lighting the twenty-five-minute fuses, they came back on deck and immediately puked their guts out. The live torpedo dangling over their heads bothered them considerably less than the odors of decomposing fish mixed with diesel fumes in a rocking boat.

The helicopter moved back into position over the

bow and, one by one, plucked the boat's captain, the EOD team, and then the PJs off the deck. Minutes later they were back on shore at the Coast Guard station, waiting there until the charges went off, taking the boat and torpedo to the bottom. Though the boat's owner was less than thrilled with the solution to his problem, he was assuaged with the promise of being given another fishing boat, one that had been seized in a drug raid. It took two years, but he got the replacement boat.

With the *Salvador Allende* mission, the shoe is more or less on the other foot for Ed Fleming. It's the unit brass that have had misgivings about this operation from the get-go. And he's the one who has looked at his team, looked at their plan, and assured Colonel Hill, "We can definitely do this."

The PJs' original plan was to bring an abundance of medical equipment. But as they look at the size of the HH-60's cabin and contemplate picking up fourteen or fifteen people in each helicopter, it becomes clear that they have to strip down to the bare essentials. For Dougherty that means a single forty-two-pound rucksack filled with IV fluids, chemical heating pads, cold packs, traction splints, a minor surgery kit, blood pressure cuffs, and stethoscopes. What he knows they're going to need most is stuff to keep the survivors warm.

When they landed at Shearwater yesterday, the Canadian Air Force support people asked what they'd be needing. This morning they delivered. A bobtail truck filled with wool hats, gloves, blankets, and sleeping bags backs up to the helicopters. Mike Moore stopped counting at sixty blankets stuffed into every available nook and cranny on Jolly 08. The cold steel floors in both aircraft were covered with blankets and sleeping bags. The thinking is that if it gets in the way, they can always toss it out, but anyone they pluck from the ocean is likely to be hypothermic, and the back of the HH-60 is notoriously cold, especially when they're flying with the door open. All that wool will be put to good use.

While the PJs are getting everything squared away in back, the pilots have started the engines and are going through preflight checklists. Outside each ship the crew chiefs are on a headset, talking to the cockpit. As the rotor head gets up to speed, they check to make sure the drop stops have popped out, allowing the four fifteen-foot blades to flap as much as necessary for flying. Next they check the lights, then watch as the pilots manipulate the flight controls, making certain the stabilator is moving up and down properly. At the AC's command they pull the chocks that have been blocking the wheels. Normally they'd put them inside the cabin, but the flight engineers wave them off. They have no plans to be landing anywhere but right back here.

Each crew chief is in charge of maintenance for one specific helicopter, and as they disconnect the interphone cable and move away from the aircraft in preparation for giving the signal to taxi, it's not difficult to read the concern on their faces. They've spent the night going over every inch of these helicopters, but they're acutely aware that all it takes is one part to go bad and the HH-60 could plummet into the ocean. When the pilots have finished their checklists, they blink a light at their crew chief, and in return get a thumbs-up. The helicopters begin to taxi away from the ramp, and once clear, they accelerate, get a running start, and lift off the ice-covered runway into light snow.

It's 5:30 A.M. They're right on schedule.

Inside Jolly 14
5:35 A.M. (4:35 A.M. EST)

And they can toss most of the preplanning out the window.

It seems no one told the weather gods about Fleming's hard and fast rule for this mission—the Jollys are to keep each other in sight at all times. Before they leave dry land they are in pitch-black, no visibility whatsoever, instrument flight conditions. The problem now is the flip side of the coin—they can't get too close to each other. Flying the second ship in the formation, Graham Buschor doesn't have a visual on Jolly 14, yet he's got to maintain separation somehow. They've already got their TACAN dialed in, so they know the distance between them is half a mile. What the TACAN on the helicopters can't answer is, "Half a mile in which direction?" Baur calls on the radio to give them the lead ship's heading, altitude, and airspeed. That's a start, but it would be nice to know where the other helicopter is with some degree of certainty.

The radar on the HH-60 is designed to show them weather formations such as heavy clouds and thunderstorms, coastlines or ground terrain, and vessels on the surface. It's not designed to track other aircraft. Nevertheless, they manage to tweak the antenna until it paints the other airframe. Then, by maintaining the same altitude, heading, and airspeed as 14, they're able to keep him in the twelve o'clock position on the radar screen, which lets them know that he's dead ahead. As a check, they bring up the forward-looking-infrared-radar—FLIR—and paint 14 at the twelve o'clock. Now that they're certain of his location, they can concentrate on flying through the increasingly heavy weather.

A few minutes later, 14 calls, reminding them to run their refueling probe out to its full twelve-foot length and leave it there. If there are any problems with the probes on either helicopter, now is the time to discover it, not when they've already passed the point of no return, are bingo on fuel, and have no attractive alternatives. Leaving the probe out is a trade-off. They deal with a little bit more constant vibration in exchange for the comfort of knowing that it can reach the drogue on a C-130 whenever they need it to. The probe is driven by the same tiny fuel pump used to transfer gas from the interior auxiliary tanks to the mains. Problem is, the flight engineers don't completely trust the pump.

At his position behind the pilot, Rich Davin is seated sideways, looking out a window, and he doesn't particularly like what he's seeing. "It was snow, it was sleet, it was rain. But each time the position light would flash on my side—it's a green light—it would illuminate all this moisture going by. And it looked a lot like flying through a meteor shower. You'd see it. Then you wouldn't. You'd see it. Then you wouldn't." Davin has to force himself to stop looking at the phenomenon, because it has a mesmerizing effect. For all practical purposes, except for the reflected flashing lights, they're in a black hole whose depth is infinite.

While Buschor and Sengstacken are concentrating on flying, and Davin is monitoring his instruments, Doc is fashioning his own version of Motel 6 by pushing the blankets and sleeping bags around until he has a nice, comfortable bed. He doesn't even need a quarter to make it vibrate. Although outwardly tranquil, his mind is pumping out unanswerable questions: are we going to come back with fourteen people in this helicopter? Can we do it? How long is it going to take? How long am I going to be in the water if I've got to get in? And how am I going to treat fourteen patients in a helicopter when I won't have any room to move? There is one thing about which he has no doubt. He needs to be well-rested in order to perform at the highest levels, both physically and mentally. So with a wisecrack aimed at Davin about his mission being to keep the bed warm for prospective patients, and without taking off his flight helmet, Doc quickly falls asleep.

Dougherty's comfort is too much for Davin to bear. He's been prepping a supply of ammo—wadded balls of tape are the best—and when he senses he can get away with it, whips one at the sleeping PJ, then quickly turns back to his console as Doc sits bolt upright, wondering what's going on.

Inside Jolly 08
5:55 A.M. (4:55 A.M. EST)

Unlike his counterpart in the other helicopter, PJ Mike Moore is keeping himself busy prepping equipment and filling the role of observer on the left side of the aircraft. Though he's been doing this for a long time, he's uncomfortable knowing there's another HH-60 nearby that he can't see. There's something else bothering him as well. Most of the PJs hate aerial refuel-

ing, but Mike Moore says the procedure scares him
more than anything else he does. The problem is lack
of control. While the PJ's job entails doing a lot of
dangerous things, they're in control. They know that
aerial refueling, especially in marginal weather, is a
dicey proposition, and it's totally out of their hands.
That's why on training missions, if at all possible,
they'll ask to be dropped off at the base before the
flight crews begin practicing refueling techniques.

Moore has never seen a refueling mishap occur, but
he's acutely aware of the potential for one. When the
time comes for refueling, he becomes hyperalert, figuring his attentiveness might be a little more fine-tuned
than the others. So even though he hates it, he prefers to
be involved during the entire midair refueling process.

Part of that involvement will be saying prayers
prior to each one of the refuelings they'll do on this
mission. Before jumping into the ocean, he doesn't
pray; before refueling, he does. Mike was raised in the
Roman Catholic Church, but the more time he spent in
the military, the more he got involved in nondenomi-
national churches, and then, as he puts it, "I started
getting into the natural stuff. So I would spend time on
the Jersey shore on the jetties, I guess talking to the
Main Man while the ocean waves would come crashing in. So I've let my church be well beyond the doors
of a regular church."

Aboard Yanky 03
7:25 A.M. Halifax time (6:25 A.M. EST)

The Marine KC-130 tanker left Shearwater right on
schedule, at six A.M., half an hour behind the helicop-

ters. The refueling plan calls for them to meet the HH-60s precisely at seven A.M., but once again the plan is foiled by the weather. At seven A.M. it's still dark and the helicopters are still caught in weather that's not conducive to aerial refueling. The good news is that they've only burned about a third of their gas.

When they do break clear of the severe weather, it's nautical twilight, just barely enough light to see a horizon. The helicopters are now able to regroup and fly in formation, the way the mission was planned. Ed Fleming is anxious to get the first refueling out of the way as soon as possible. His concern? "What if the drogues won't extend from Yanky 03? What if the hoses fail? Both have happened before." If it were to happen now, they'd have two choices: have Shearwater get the next tanker in the rotation of three out there immediately, or return to base.

The Jollys call for a rendezvous with the Marines at 1,000 feet, just below the cloud layer. The refueling procedure is a ritual as standard as the swearing in of a President. It's always done the same way, using the same words, no matter if the refueler is from the Jollys' own unit, from the regular Air Force, or from the Marines.

Standard practice is for the helicopters to arrive at the agreed upon location two minutes early, and the tanker to show up two minutes late. The flight engineers on both aircraft will have called off the refueling checklist during the approach to the rendezvous site, so when they arrive, they're ready. While it's possible to refuel both helicopters at the same time—one off each wing—it's rarely done, primarily because it's physically easier to refuel off the left wing of the C-130.

The refueling probe is on the right side of the HH-60, directly in front of the pilot. To hit the left drogue, he doesn't have to tuck the ship in as close to the C-130 as he would have to do going for the right drogue. In addition, rotation of the C-130's propellers result in more turbulence for a helicopter coming up behind the right wing than the left.

As the flight leader, Jolly 14 will gas up first, while the other helo hangs back and observes. The plan calls for a running rendezvous, with the tanker approaching from behind and to the right.

"This is Yanky 03 coming up abeam of you at three o'clock."

"Roger, we've got you in sight."

"Yanky 03 has the lead." At this point the C-130 has got flaps extended, the refueling drogues fully extended from pods on each wing, and is slowing down to 110 knots, which is only ten knots above its power-off stall speed. It's not comfortable flying for the pilots, because the Herc is sluggish and not very responsive to the controls, even more so when it's heavy with an almost full load of fuel. While the helicopter crews are equipped with night vision goggles, the Marines haven't adopted them as standard equipment, and the interior and exterior lighting on their KC-130s hasn't been modified for their use, but to provide a reference and learn what they can do, copilot Jim Hall and the loadmaster, Staff Sergeant Robert Brought, have put them on.

"Jolly 14, you're cleared to observation position."

Fleming responds, and moves the helicopter to a spot about 100 feet off the Herc's left wing.

"Jolly 14 is cleared for wet contact to the precontact position."

"Roger, Jolly 14 is cleared to the precontact position." Fleming slowly brings the helicopter to a stabilized position about fifteen or twenty feet behind the drogue. "Jolly 14 is in the precontact position."

As soon as the loadmaster watching from a side window tells him everything is in order, Omey lets the helicopter link up.

"Jolly 14, you're cleared for wet contact. Two thousand pounds."

"Roger. Jolly 14, I'm cleared for contact."

This is where things get dicey. In order to get fuel, Fleming has got to plant the probe squarely in the center of the fifty-three-pound coupling. Picture an archer standing on a trampoline and attempting to shoot an arrow into a bull's-eye that is continuously and unpredictably moving around. Difficult, but not impossible. Now tell the archer that instead of shooting the arrow, he's to run forward on the trampoline toward the target and jab the arrow squarely into the bull's-eye—and if he jabs too hard and misses, he dies.

That's essentially what an HH-60 pilot is trying to do with the fuel probe. It's moving in three dimensions, and the drogue is moving in three dimensions, but they're not synchronized.

To help the helicopter pilot find the four-inch coupling at the center of the drogue, it's surrounded by a cloth-covered basket about the size of an automobile tire. The objective is to get the probe into the basket, then slowly move it to dead center and forward, locking into the fuel coupling. What makes it sporting is that both the drogue and the helicopter are reacting not only to the propeller wake coming off the airplane's wing, but to the gusty winds they're flying through. They also have to keep in mind that the probe only

extends four feet beyond the rotor blades, and that
while the C-130's horizontal stabilizer is still well forward and to the right of the HH-60, an overaggressive
move that sends the probe punching through the cloth-
covered spokes on the drogue could put the rotor blade
dangerously close. The tips are going around at 493
miles an hour. Contact would certainly shatter the
blade tip, knocking the entire rotor assembly out of
balance, causing it to vibrate itself to pieces, resulting
in the helicopter dropping like a rock. Conversely,
according to the pilots who fly it, the C-130 is a tough,
powerful airplane and it could survive the collision
without catastrophic damage.

But Jon Omey isn't expecting any problems like
that, even with the gusty winds. In his seven years of
flying the KC-130, he's tanked a lot of helicopters, and
says there's no question Ed Fleming and the pilots he's
taught are the best in the business at aerial refueling.

While hitting the basket on the first try is the idea,
when Fleming trained the unit's pilots, he made sure
they understand that's not the most important thing to
worry about. If they miss the first try, they can always
do it again. What matters is that their moves are
always smooth and even; he doesn't want them rushing at the basket and risk punching through, having
their momentum carry them into the wing.

When they first set up the rendezvous, Fleming told
Omey that he wanted 2,000 pounds of fuel, and the
flight engineer, Staff Sergeant Chris Jablonski, has set
up his gauges to deliver it. On the flight engineer's
panel is an indicator light telling him when a good
contact has been established. Only when he sees that
light will he start the fuel flowing at the rate of 1,000
pounds a minute.

Following the standard refueling protocol he's taught countless pilots, Fleming waits for the okay from the tanker, then uses a light touch on the controls to bring Jolly 14 closer and closer to the drogue, until he's sure the probe is centered in the basket. Then he applies a bit more forward speed, and locks the probe into the socket on the first try.

The instant he's sure the probe is locked into position, Fleming moves the helicopter up and to the left. If something were to happen and they had to break away, the drogue would drop, making it virtually impossible for the rotors to hit it as they pulled away.

"Jolly 14, fuel is flowing."

When the gauge hits 2,000 pounds, Jablonski shuts off the flow and tells Omey.

"Jolly 14, you have 2,000 pounds of fuel. Do you need more?"

In the helicopter, Rich Davin has been controlling which of the four tanks the fuel flows into. He can quickly determine if they're able to take any more, and he passes this information to the pilots.

"Yanky 03, this is Jolly 14. You can give us another 500 pounds."

"Roger. Another 500 pounds." Jablonski releases the fuel, carefully monitoring the flow.

"Jolly 14, we show you topped off. Are you satisfied?"

"Yanky 03, roger, we're satisfied. Request disconnect."

"Okay, Jolly 14, caution your playmate, you're clear to disconnect off to the left."

Disengaging from the coupling requires as much precision as connecting to it. The helicopter is now 2,500 pounds heavier than it was when it connected.

But the additional weight hasn't required the pilots to add any power, because they're in the vorticity of the C-130. In other words, the air coming off the wings is supplementing their power, giving them additional lift. It's almost like one race car drafting off another. The helicopter is actually flying more efficiently right behind the Herc than it does when it's plopping along on its own. What this means in practical terms is that the pilots don't feel the effect of the additional ton of fuel until they disconnect from the hose, then all of a sudden they drop. It requires an almost instantaneous adjustment in power, but Fleming says it becomes instinctive, you don't even think about it. When the maneuver is performed correctly, there should be no drop at all, which is the safest way to do it, because if the helicopter drops on disconnect and the drogue rises to the position it naturally flies in, the potential exists for it to come up through the rotors. That's why he teaches his pilots never to descend during disconnect.

Completing his refueling without incident, Fleming backs straight out as Doc Dougherty watches from the left window to make sure they stay clear of the other HH-60. Once the pilot can clearly see Jolly 08, he gains a little altitude, hops over him, and slides left, making room for Graham Buschor to bring 08 in for gas.

The simple statement that the helicopters refueled in midair sounds so routine, so mundane, it belies the skill and concentration required to do it quickly and safely. It's an incredibly complicated piece of precision flying, where the threat of disaster looms just a few feet away. When Leonardo da Vinci dreamed up the helicopter around the beginning of the sixteenth century, he could never have imagined how complicated a beast he had conceived and the level of skill it would take to keep one in the air.

Just by manipulating the main rotor and a small tail rotor, an HH-60 pilot must be able to make the aircraft move forward or backward, left or right, and up or down. He also has to control the attitude of the helo as it moves through those three dimensions; that is, he has to be able to keep the craft from yawing so it flies with the nose headed in the intended direction, he has to keep it from rolling to the left or right, and he has to be able to control the pitch—the up/down angle of the craft.

In a single main rotor helo like the HH-60, all of this is done by controlling the speed of the rotor, the pitch of the individual blades, and the tilt of the disk created by revolution of the four blades in a more or less flat plane. (It's "more or less" because the blades are designed to flap.)

All the forces a pilot can manipulate are interrelated. A change in pitch requires a change in throttle setting. An increase in forward speed requires an adjustment in the speed of the tail rotor. Some of it happens because the controls are linked, but much of it requires the complete and undivided attention of a human mind; there is no autopilot on this generation of helicopters.

Graham Buschor says the Pentagon's attitude is that as long as they're paying pilots to do the work, an autopilot is an unnecessary frill, leaving him to conclude, tongue firmly planted in cheek, that "we're nothing more than sophisticated heavy equipment drivers." The grin belies his true feelings about flying helicopters, which he sums up by saying, "It's probably the most fun you can have with your pants on."

Here's Buschor's notion of fun: to move a helicopter where they want it to go, each pilot has two hand controls and two rudder pedals. And whichever pilot has control better be on them at all times, or the laws of physics, of aerodynamics, of rotating bodies, and of gravity will be strictly enforced. The pilot uses his right hand on the control known as the "cyclic," which gives him directional control by tilting the main rotor. Tilt the main rotor to the right and the helicopter should move right. The cyclic stick also has a trim release button that must be periodically applied to equalize pressures in the control system. Also on the stick is a trigger switch: activate it one way and you're talking directly to the flight engineer over the intercom; trigger it the other way and it keys a transmission over a previously selected radio frequency outside the aircraft. Whichever pilot is not actually flying the ship hands-on at a given moment is responsible for keeping the radios tuned to the frequencies that keep them in touch with Jolly 14, and with their refuelers in the C-130s.

In normal flight the pilot's left hand is on the "collective," a lever that adds or reduces power to the rotor system. Pull up and you add power to climb. But then you have to concurrently compensate by retrimming of the cyclic. Lower the collective, reduce power, and the helicopter descends smoothly, assuming that your right hand has compensated on the cyclic. Want to hover? The Flying Wallendas' high-wire balancing act was a stroll in the park compared to the dexterous digital dance even an ordinary helicopter pilot continuously performs.

Then there's the tail rotor. Without it, the main rotor would spin in one direction and the aircraft body in the other, doing a mechanically terminal imitation of whirling dervishes. The tail rotor is controlled by the foot pedals, which also provide additional control for the direction of flight. If you want to fly straight and you add power, you have to add left pedal and some cyclic all at once. If you subtract power to slow down or descend, you have to add right pedal and adjust the cyclic with your right hand. The HH-60 PaveHawk is an advanced helicopter and its controls are more sophisticated than your basic traffic copter. Sikorsky designed it so the tail rotor input is automatically applied. That works just fine in good weather. In a gale over the Atlantic, the pilot must continuously and relentlessly apply the adjustments. Sit down on a bar stool with your feet off the floor and try patting your head, rubbing your stomach, circling your left foot clockwise and your right foot counterclockwise at the same time, and you'll have a sense of the concentration required to keep the ship in the air. Lapses of attention, however brief, are not recommended.

But no matter how difficult it sounds, maneuvering the HH-60 to refuel is relatively simple compared to trying to hover the helicopter a precise height above the water's surface to do a hoist, especially while that surface is varying by plus or minus thirty feet. When you're snuggling up to a C-130, there's a very large visual reference just a few feet in front of your nose. There's no such visual point of reference to guide you over the ocean 700 or 800 miles from the nearest rock. It's as though the horizon is pitching up and down a distance equivalent to the height of a three-story building. Disorientation and motion sickness are a constant threat when your entire visual field is rising and falling. What you do, says Ed Fleming, is "cage your eyeballs and keep struggling against nature."

The only situation that could be more arduous for a rescue helicopter pilot is to do a maneuver like that at night. Learning how to perform a night water hoist is the most difficult skill Fleming has to teach new pilots. It's a death-defying act that takes a long time to learn. In Fleming's estimation, aerial refueling is the second most difficult skill he's had to teach, and he says there are some very good pilots who never become very good at refueling. Next in degree of difficulty is teaching low-level operations while wearing night vision goggles. This is basic to combat rescue missions, which is the actual raison d'être for keeping aerial search and rescue units in the active duty Air Force and Air Force Reserves.

As formation lead on the *Salvador Allende* rescue mission, Ed Fleming is responsible not only for pulling off the rescue, but for the safety of the crews. It's a continuous real-time study in operational flexibility. Unlike combat missions, the only option he does *not* have is to disengage from the enemy. He, along with his aircraft and crewmen, is locked in battle, and there's no getting away from it. No matter how vivid his imagination, there's no way da Vinci could have foreseen what Ed Fleming would be doing on this miserable December day, heading to a point 600 or so nautical miles out in the North Atlantic.

In the North Atlantic
9:10 A.M. (7:10 A.M. EST)

Alex Taranov has now been in the water for about twenty-eight hours, and for most of that time he's been alone. When dawn broke, it was apparent that the seas were nowhere near what they'd been yesterday. Instead of thirty to forty feet, they're now running twenty to thirty feet. The wind has diminished significantly and he no longer feels like he's caught in a hurricane. Even the heavy rain has dwindled to an occasional shower, and every so often the overcast breaks and he can actually see beautiful blue sky overhead.

Since the waves ceased treating him like a rag doll in a Maytag, he hasn't been swallowing as much seawater, and the constant vomiting has diminished. His big concern now is his life jacket. Aside from being loose, he senses that it's waterlogged and has lost buoyancy because it's not keeping his head as far out of the water as it did yesterday. Constantly alert to his surroundings, he spots a life jacket floating nearby and decides to try and get it to put under his legs. He realizes that to an aircraft flying overhead, he's nothing more than a pumpkin-sized ball. With the second life jacket, he thinks he'll be able to float with almost his entire body above the surface, making him easier to be seen from the air.

Swimming to the life jacket, he's upset to discover a body. Taking hold of the man's hair, he lifts the head from the water, sees who it is, and releases it. He realizes it's the seaman who had said, "This is the end for us." Alex's guess is that the man, Igor Korbidat, didn't put the life jacket on correctly before leaving the ship. It was able to ride up, wrapping the ropes around his neck, choking him to death during one of those moments when he was being tumbled by the breakers. He opts not to try and strip the jacket from the body, and pushes it away.

Just as he's turning away from the body something
that feels like sandpaper slides against his leg. His first
thought is "shark." But then he asks himself how
sharks could be in stormy winter weather. Sharks like
warm water, in the south seas, not the North Atlantic.
His mind is starting to play tricks on him. Quickly, he
swims away, trying to put as much distance as possible
between himself and the dead man. Even though the
seas have calmed considerably, the effort is exhausting
and he's unable to get very far.

During the regular safety and survival classes held
by the shipping company, the importance of maintaining a positive mental attitude was emphasized. Thinking about sharks, therefore, is counterproductive. So
Alex decides that it couldn't have been a shark. It was
a dolphin. It's not so unusual for dolphins to nudge
people in the water. That's what it was. A dolphin.

But now exhaustion is setting in. Though he's
stopped vomiting and would like to eat something, he
hasn't been able to reach the food package he'd found
floating near one of the survival bundles. Somehow,
when he tucked it into his survival suit it slipped down
below his waist, and he can't get to it, and as his
energy fades, it becomes more difficult to stay awake,
and he finds himself drifting in and out of consciousness. He begins to dream.

Alex is back on the ship because he needs something to drink. He knows that in his cabin are two
twelve-can packs of Coca-Cola. Then he sees a
lifeboat and he brings it to the ship. He goes up to the
bridge, where he sits at a table with three people—the
chief engineer, the second engineer, and the chief
mate. They tell him that they've sent many people
away to a place where they won't be in any more dan-

ger. Alex asks, "Why didn't you guys send me? Send me there." But they say, "No."

"But I need to go to that place too. Send me," Alex pleads.

"No," one of the men says. "You have to fly and search for dead body." Alex leaves to go to his cabin, and on the way he sees the first lifeboat they had tried to launch, with number 2 painted on it. Beside the lifeboat a dead body is floating. He thinks, Oh, that's good. These people [on the ship] will take him out of the ocean. He gets to his cabin, finds the Coke, and brings it to lifeboat number one, the one that launched with eleven people aboard. Then he goes up to the bridge and begins seeing some white aircraft flying around the ship. He looks around, trying to get oriented, then uses the ship's radio to call the company, asking them to come get him. But when they do, they put him back on the ship.

A breaking wave hits and unceremoniously brings him back to reality. Looking around, it dawns on him that he'd been dreaming. He fights to stay awake, but it's a losing battle, and once more he drifts off to continue the same dream. In part two, he goes back to the ship and begins exploring. Turning a corner, he sees a man who looks like God. Not Jesus Christ. But God. He never does see the man's face, but knows it's an old man with long white hair, a white beard, and white clothes. Probably a robe; definitely not a shirt and pants. He tries to get a good look at the man, but another crewman tells him, "Nobody can see God." So Alex leaves the ship and dreams that he's beginning to cross a desert. At which point he's awakened by another wave.

Without understanding why, he has a sudden impulse to know what time it is, but his watch is pushed back from his wrist, well under the cuff of the survival suit. He manages to cut or tear the cuff, trying to make an opening big enough to not only see his wristwatch, but to remove the second can of 7UP that he'd stored in his sleeve. Looking closely at his watch, he's shocked to realize that all he sees is a white circle, nothing else, and thinks, I guess this means I'll never see again, because I saw God.

The contemplation of God isn't what would be expected of an avowed atheist who grew up in a communist country. Alex realizes it's strange, but attributes it to missionaries who brought Russian language Bibles to the ship. He took time to read it, the first time in his life he'd ever done that, and found it interesting. During his time in the water, thoughts that he'd read in that Bible keep coming up, and he realizes they're totally beyond his control.

Aboard Yanky 03
8:15 A.M. Halifax time (7:15 A.M. EST)

As Yanky 03 continues escorting the helicopters out to sea, it appears more and more likely the Marines are going to have to make good on Omey's promise to tank the HH-60s well below the approved minimums. Since their first refueling, the ceiling has been dropping down, forcing the three aircraft to fly lower and lower through the wind and spray trapped between the bottom of the clouds above them and the huge waves below. It's not a problem for the huge KC-130, but the helicopters need to avoid going through the clouds, where they'll begin to pick up a coating of ice.

While Ed Fleming wanted to refuel at every "soft

spot" they fly through—and what they're in right now would not necessarily be considered soft—everyone recognizes that things could get much worse before they get better, so he opts to tank up. As the tanker is flying by Jolly 14 to get in position, the cloud layer drops another couple of notches lower. Now they're below 400 feet and everyone is getting a real good look at the ocean below. A few minutes earlier the Marines had flown over a couple of merchant ships fighting their way through the seas. It made a lasting impression on Omey. "There was nobody on deck. The ships looked like when we were kids and played with toy boats in the bathtub. It was pretty impressive, these big giant ships getting tossed around everywhere by huge seas. And I guess they weren't nearly as big as they were the day before [when the *Salvador Allende* went down]."

Neither Omey nor Fleming mention it on the radio, but both know that the lower they go, the smaller the margin of error gets. The Herc pilot has to concentrate on staying below the cloud deck to keep the HH-60s out of icing conditions, but not so low that there's a risk of the helicopters getting hit by the top of a rogue wave that might happen by. At 110 knots of speed and less than 500 feet of altitude, Omey is flying right on the ragged edge of their envelope, where one screw-up could lead to a bad stall situation.

Ed Fleming has another way of putting it. "Altitude is time." The lower you are, the less time you have to react to an emergency; and the lower the cloud deck, the greater the effect the winds have on the helicopter. What they're getting are winds coming down from above and the ocean pushing air up, causing a rough, rugged ride because it's compressing the winds in between. Add in the Bernoulli effect and you're fighting very intense turbulence at the same time you're trying to score a bull's-eye with the fuel probe.

While the refueling goes without incident—and Fleming's pilots continue to amaze the Marines with their ability to hit the basket the first time, no matter how much turbulence there is—Yanky 03 is burning fuel at a rate that's beginning to cause concern. The flight engineer and navigator put the numbers together and calculate that their burn rate flying low is more than 9,000 pounds an hour, nearly double the 5,000 pounds they burn at altitude. It's not that they're concerned about running out of fuel, just that the more they burn, the less they can give to the helicopters.

The only way to significantly reduce consumption is to take the Herc up high, where its turbojet engines operate much more efficiently. This presents a problem. Omey's style of flying a mission like this is to be a mother hen, keeping her chicks in sight at all times. He's not going to go above the clouds and keep in touch by long distance. But the helicopters can't climb up through the clouds without the risk of picking up a lot of ice, and even if they should get up there safely, they need a way to come back down to do what they came out to do. The problem isn't ice forming on the windshield. They've got deicers and defoggers to deal with that. It's ice forming on the blades, an especially critical problem for Jolly 08, which took off from Shearwater with its rotor deicers not functioning. The danger is that when the blades pick up ice, they begin to lose aerodynamic effectiveness. In addition to that, the airframe will begin icing up, making it increasingly heavy, possibly to the point where there isn't enough power to keep it airborne.

Even when the blade deicers are working properly, as they are on Jolly 14, there can still be ice problems. The front of each of the four blades has a heated mat that sheds the ice off continuously, but not necessarily uniformly. It'll shed a chunk over here, another over there. Result: the blades aren't balanced and the aircraft starts to shake, sometimes violently. If it gets bad enough, it can lead to structural failure. The optimum solution is to avoid icing conditions entirely.

Knowing this, the Marines pop up through the clouds to take a look at the weather. Up top they see solid overcast, but every forty or fifty miles there's a hole big enough for the Jollys to use to come up or go back down. He radios his findings back to Fleming, and moments later both Jollys climb through one of the holes to 5,000 feet, where they're safely out of the clouds. Meantime, Yanky 03 climbs to 10,000 feet, which cuts their burn rate back to 5,000 pounds an hour yet still allows them to keep the helicopters in sight. The next tanking is, relatively speaking, a piece of cake.

RCC New York
8:06 A.M. EST (9:06 A.M. Halifax time)

Lieutenant Commander Jay Topper takes a call from the 102nd's mission commander at Shearwater. "Our aircraft are entering a critical point where they either need to go rescue somebody or return home," says Landsiedel, making an educated guess that the HH-60s are coming up on 150 miles past Sable Island. And he's not far off. Topper promises to contact CG 1503, which had returned to the area three hours earlier to assume duty as on-scene commander, and get back to him.

When the RCC staff first discussed the helicopters participating in the mission, Lieutenant Bill Kelly, the search coordinator, observed that if they went, they wouldn't be able to stay on-scene too long, which meant, theoretically, they should be used as a response asset rather than a search asset.

Now that the helicopters are apparently out there with no sightings to respond to, the only thing for them to do is search, and there's nothing the Coast Guardsmen running the RCC can do about the situation. So much for theory. Kelly says, "It's a timing thing. If you wait until you spot something to launch the helos, they won't get there for hours. If you try and time it so they arrive shortly after the fixed-wing aircraft, and in daylight, they can't stay long." A classic Catch-22.

Meantime, the helicopters and their Marine escort have crossed the Landsiedel Line. They know their instructions were to go no farther than 150 miles past Sable Island, about 325 miles out to sea, unless they knew survivors had been located. Landsiedel had made it clear: they're a recovery asset, not a search platform. But as they approach that line, it's evident from radio traffic that there are no identified survivors for them to just swoop in and collect.

An hour earlier Trident 760, a P-3 Orion flying out of Patrol Wing Five at the Naval Air Station in New Brunswick, Maine, reported sighting six life rafts and two bodies. No survivors. CG 1503, the on-scene commander, also tells New York they've been unable to relocate any of the survivors that were identified last night, including the eleven people in the lifeboat.

What they had no way of knowing was that the survivor picked up by the M/V *Torungen* was one of
those eleven. Since being pulled out of the water, he's
been sleeping and they've been unable to debrief him.
Two other factors complicate this problem: no one on
the German vessel *Torungen* speaks Russian. And his
leg was injured, possibly broken, as they hauled him
aboard using a heaving line attached to a life ring that
he was able to swim into. When they finally are able to
debrief him, with an officer aboard the merchant ship
Tromso Trust translating via radio, they'll learn that
the lifeboat was continually swamped during the
night, and with each successive dumping, fewer survivors managed to climb back in. Finally, he was the
only one left, and when the lifeboat finally disinte-
grated, he survived by climbing into one of the life
rafts that had been dropped to them by Rescue 306.

CFB Shearwater
9:45 A.M. Halifax time (8:45 A.M. EST)

Lieutenant Colonel Robert Landsiedel is beat. Since
learning yesterday morning that he's going to be sent
to Halifax as mission commander, he's had, at best, a
half-hour nap on a lumpy couch just before the four
A.M. briefing of the helicopter crews. So it doesn't
improve his demeanor when he learns that the Jollys
have gone beyond his line-in-the-water without knowing if survivors had been located for them to pick up.
He and Hill had decided that even with three tankers
available, they didn't want to risk using the HH-60s as
a search platform more than 700 miles out to sea. His
first reaction upon hearing that his orders have appar-

ently been ignored is to get ticked off. "Damn, I briefed these guys not to go out beyond that 150-mile point, and all of a sudden they're going."

Back on Long Island, when Colonel David Hill learns that the helicopters are proceeding out to the scene without having survivors located, he's also considerably less than delighted. "They know my position on searching at deep sea with a helicopter. That's not what we do. We rescue with a helicopter; we search with a 130. And we don't bring that helicopter and expose it to risk until we know that we have a survivor."

But putting himself in Fleming's situation, he can rationalize the decision. "What if you're there and you decide, 'Hey, nobody's told us they're out there alive,' and you start heading back, and you fly a couple hours back [and they find a survivor]? You just jeopardized the whole mission. So I can understand the reasoning of the helicopter pilots. As far as they're concerned, they were launched for survivors in the water and in lifeboats, and they should go."

Landsiedel, too, rationalizes Fleming's decision to search with the HH-60s. "They probably got some information, they talked about it on the aircraft and said, looking at the time, how long we're gonna be here, 'Hey, the weather's good. Let's go for it.' And they might've gotten information from the C-130s on-scene. I don't know. I wasn't there when they made that call."

Declaring that a helicopter assigned to the 106th Air Rescue Wing is not designed to be used as a search platform on an overwater mission is an absurdity that flies in the face of the 106th's history. Yet that's the position the Wing Commander declared to be his policy; that's the position his appointed Mission Commander briefed earlier that morning. At the time, none of the helicopter pilots chose to debate it.

Now, Lieutenant Colonel Ed Fleming is more than three hundred miles out to sea and has chosen to continue beyond the line-in-the-water in order to get involved in the search effort. "I'm already out there. Whether I circle and hold or search, I'm in the same amount of danger. If I lose a gearbox, it doesn't matter whether I'm holding or I'm searching." The message the veteran helicopter rescue pilot sends back to Shearwater and out to the on-scene commander is, "We would like to search."

TWELVE

"Gene, you have control," Graham Buschor says, handing over control of Jolly 08 to his copilot, Gene Sengstacken. Even though he stands only five-six and has more wiggle room in the confining seat than any of the other chopper pilots in the group, Buschor needs a chance to take his feet off the pedals, his hands off the controls. Flying the HH-60 is physically and mentally draining; trading off provides a little relief. While he's now responsible for monitoring the radios and instruments, being able to relax gives his mind an opportunity to step back from the aeronautical task at hand, the micromission, to the macromission: save the lives of thirty-one people who are already in boats, rafts, or worse—in the water.

Graham Buschor is the only person involved in this rescue mission who knows precisely what Alex Taranov is going through at that very moment. Graham Buschor is the only one flying this mission who can say, "Been there, done that, and I didn't believe I'd live to talk about it." It's also why Buschor believes

227

they're going to find people in the water, alive. He figures he survived it; others can. But there's no knowing
for certain. They have to go out there and look. "If
there's somebody out there, we'll get them."

At the same time, Buschor has no difficulty admit-
ting that this mission scares him. "Whenever you do
stuff like this, everybody gets scared to a certain
degree. Everybody does. If you're not scared, you're
somewhat stupid. Either incredibly brave or incredibly
stupid. I don't think there's much difference between
the two sometimes. That's what we do for a living,
that's our job."

Three years earlier Buschor was copiloting Jolly
110 when it ran out of fuel and had to ditch at night in
an Atlantic storm only sixty miles from home base.
Four of the five men aboard that helicopter lived to tell
the story. The body of the fifth, PJ Rick Smith, was
never found.

Even before that experience, Graham Buschor had
developed a healthy respect for the sea and what it can
do. He spent six months of each of his second and
third years at the Merchant Marine Academy at sea,
working as an apprentice engineer. Most of the ships
were general cargo carriers—"break bulk" in the parlance of the business—and were about 600 feet long
(compared to the 450-foot *Salvador Allende*). At the
age of twenty being at sea, even in the merchant fleet,
wasn't just a job, it truly was an adventure. He still
remembers going up on deck to watch the ship work
its way through fifty-foot waves—what the South
Africans called "Cape rollers"—taking them on the
quarter stern or quarter bow, bracing himself as the
ship rolled from side to side, being hit by waves that
were bigger than houses. His biggest problem was not

seasickness, but trying to get some sleep. Standard procedure was to stuff life jackets underneath your mattress so it would squeeze you against the bulkhead and keep you from being tossed out of bed.

Buschor came out of the Merchant Marine Academy with a college degree and a commission as an ensign in the Naval Reserve. He also had a third assistant marine engineer's license; coincidentally, the same position that Alex Taranov held on his ship. Unlike Taranov's situation, jobs in the U.S. Merchant Marine fleet were scarce, so after a short stint in the Naval Reserve, he abandoned that career in favor of flying.

By late on the afternoon of October 30, 1991, Buschor had already flown several Coast Guard searches in the HH-60. A pleasure boat in trouble off the Hamptons. A fisherman washed off the rocks in Rhode Island. It wasn't a great day for flying, but it wasn't terrible. Winds were twenty knots, gusting to thirty. Visibility was ten to fifteen miles, clear skies with an overcast above 10,000 feet. The ocean was gray and nasty, churned up by a hurricane that had fizzled, the remnants of which were miles out to sea.

Back at the headquarters of the 106th, just west of the fashionable Long Island Hamptons, the men were relaxing when they were tasked yet again. In the flight planning room, the briefer filled them in on the mission. A forty-foot sailboat in trouble in heavy seas. In 1991 the most sophisticated weather data they had consisted of charts faxed from McGuire Air Force Base in New Jersey. There was no World Wide Web to tap for satellite imagery over the ocean; there was no easy access to the data from the deep water weather buoys that NOAA had permanently moored in as much as 16,000 feet of water. They had no way of knowing what the sea heights were, what the winds were like.

What they had going for them was the powerful Sikorsky HH-60 PaveHawk helicopter, in the Air Force inventory for barely three years. The HH-60 had not yet been optimized for SAR work with the installation of range-extending internal fuel tanks, so a flight 200 miles off the coast would require at least four, perhaps five, air refuelings. Nevertheless, the twin-engine HH-60—call sign "Jolly" because it replaced the HH-3, which had been known in the Vietnam War as the Jolly Green Giant—had proved to be a reliable ship known for being long on power, albeit short on comfort.

Jolly 110 took off in late afternoon, heading southeast over the ocean, escorted by one of the unit's C-130 aircraft. They did two refuelings without incident. No problem at all. First contact, banged it, took on the gas and pressed on. The planners figured they'd arrive on-scene around sunset, but had neglected to take into account that as you fly east in each time zone, the sun sets a bit earlier. Calculating sunset just by time zones alone, rather than by applying a fairly complicated formula, is usually good enough; in this case it wasn't. Making contact with the Coast Guard C-130 that had been on-station over the sailboat, the crew of Jolly 110 put on their night vision goggles and went down for a look.

Even though the weather was horrific, the boat was in fairly decent shape. Head-up into the waves, with a sea anchor holding the position. No question, however, that the lone Japanese yachtsman taking forty-foot swells in a forty-foot boat was getting the ride of his life.

The sailor was in radio contact with the orbiting C-130, which was relaying his ever more desperate requests to be taken off the boat. Despite the fact that the two PJs were ready to jump, no one argued with the decision when the aircraft commander, Lieutenant Colonel David Ruvola, said that with the sea state so bad, there was no way to be certain he could recover his own men, much less the hapless yachtsman. Even the notion of lowering a basket on the penetrator cable was ruled out; wind conditions made controlling the basket at the end of a long cable impossible. There was no way they could pluck the man off the deck, and even though he had volunteered to jump into the water to make a pickup easier, they demurred. This mission was beyond their capability. All agreed that he was better off riding it out in his boat until he could be picked up safely in daylight. The 106th's C-130 made a final pass over the sailboat to drop a large life raft and bundle of rescue gear to the man, then turned and joined Jolly 110, already headed for home.

Their first refueling on the way back was without incident. The crews were contemplating a fast trip back to Westhampton Beach, and a long overdue hot meal. It wasn't meant to be. Suddenly, without any warning, all hell broke loose and they were bouncing around the sky in stomach-churning winds that had gone from twenty knots gusting to thirty, to winds in excess of eighty knots—more than ninety miles an hour. In all his years flying, Buschor had never experienced turbulence like this. Anything that wasn't tied down was flying around the cockpit, and just keeping the ship on course was nearly impossible. Refueling in these conditions was not going to be easy, but they had no choice.

Ruvola made stab after stab at the basket trailing off the C-130's left wing, but it would have taken a miracle to hit it in that weather. It was like trying to fire a rifle at an unpredictable, moving target while being repeatedly punched in the shoulder by a drill sergeant with heartburn. It wasn't going to happen.

By this time Buschor says they were had by what he calls the sucker factor. "We're checking weather back home, and it's the same as it was when we left. So we're thinking we're gonna break outta this stuff into clear weather, be able to air refuel, and get home." He was sure that everyone in the helicopter and their escort C-130 was under the impression that this was an isolated storm which they'd break out of momentarily. So they kept flying northwest, toward home. Unbeknownst to them, they had flown into a storm that was moving toward the southern portion of Long Island. They were in the storm, and moving with it. The storm extended miles to their left and right. They couldn't fly around it. They couldn't fly fast enough to get ahead of it, and the sucker factor kept them from opting to reverse direction. (The "sucker factor" describes the phenomenon of getting sucked deeper and deeper into a problem because you think it's going to get better. It applies to flying into storms as well as continuing to put coins in the slot machine. It should not be confused with the "pucker factor," which was also in play on the flight home.)

The weather radar on the C-130 was a late 1960s system, and it didn't show any clear weather to fly into. And while the ops office back at the base knew of their plight, they had no weather information to provide that would have helped. So Jolly 110 tried refueling at 500 feet; no luck. They tried 5,000 feet. Still no luck. No clear air, no way to get gas and go home.

Complicating matters was the fact that the drogue off the left wing of the C-130 was falling apart from being whacked at so many times by the refueling probe on the helicopter.

Unfortunately, Murphy's Law (if it can go wrong, it will) and its corollary (at the worst possible time) came into play. Their C-130 refueler lost its left outboard engine. When it shut down, the mechanism that monitors the fuel hose coming out of the underwing pylon sensed a change in the airflow and drew an incorrect conclusion. It assumed that too much hose was out, and retracted it. They were left no choice but to move around to the right side of the plane and try a last desperate stab for gas. But both aircraft were bouncing all over the sky, and even with NVGs they were unable to maintain visual contact with the plane, which, on three engines, was flying dangerously close to its stall speed in severe turbulence.

That's when Ruvola reluctantly made the only rational choice. They were going to ditch a perfectly good $10 million helicopter that happened to be running out of gas into the ocean. He'd use the twenty minutes of remaining fuel to fly the ship to just above the wave tops, and hover so the crew could jump. As radical a decision as it may sound to nonaviators, they all recognized it as better than continuing the futile attempt to get fuel, run out of gas at 1,000 feet, and plummet into the ocean.

With Ruvola flying, Buschor was working the radios. The Coast Guard cutter *Tamaroa,* already en route to the area to assist in the boat rescue, was twelve miles to their nose. With enough gas, they could have flown to the cutter and ditched next to it.

But they were down to their last 150 pounds of fuel and it wouldn't take them the distance.

While Buschor was on the radio talking with *Tamaroa*, their number one engine failed. With less than 100 pounds of fuel left, they all knew that number two was basically running on fumes. It was 9:20 at night, the average seas were running at about forty feet with max tops up to sixty feet. Winds were in excess of eighty knots, and with the salt spray, visibility using the landing lights was barely a few feet.

Ruvola managed to bring the helicopter to a hover and ordered the four crew members to jump. Buschor was wearing his Mack 10 exposure suit—the mustang suit—that would function almost like a wet suit if they had to ditch. His survival vest carried a radio, flares, first aid kit, whistle, and compass. It also held the HEED bottle—the Helicopter Emergency Egress Device, a two-minute scuba tank they carried just for situations like this one. And he had his LPUs—the life preserver units that fit under his arms and would inflate from CO_2 cartridges that fire when the lanyards are pulled.

He popped open his door, stood, flipped the NVG goggles down so he could see the waves, and just a second after the two PJs exited through the rear door, he jumped, trying to time the leap so he could catch the top of a passing wave. Even using NVGs, it was like leaping into a black hole.

Meantime, flight engineer Jim Mioli had prepared the nine-man life raft and shoved it out the door behind the PJs. But as it inflated, it turned into a giant kite and went sailing away. Seeing the raft go, unbeknownst to Colonel Ruvola, Mioli opted to stay in the aircraft till it hit the water.

Ruvola's job at that moment was to make sure that his helicopter didn't drop on top of the crew. Using the last of the gas, he hovered it a short distance away, waited until the number two engine failed and the four rotor blades were no longer turning, and rode it into the water. (Hitting the water with rotor blades under power would result in a violent crash from which escape would be all but impossible.) The HH-60 immediately filled with water, but the two men were able to swim out of it and get to the surface without any problem, pull their LPUs, and link up with each other almost immediately.

Buschor found himself uninjured, but alone in the turbulent water. His first thought after realizing he'd survived the jump was to find the others. In the distance through the spray, he saw a strange moving light, apparently on the life raft. He tried to swim for it, but the wind-driven water thwarted him. It was almost like Disney animation. The waves were Neptune and Poseidon, personified and angry, and they were taking it out personally on Graham Buschor. They were not going to permit him to gain the apparent safety of that life raft. Much later he learned that the flashing light had been PJ John "Mickey" Spillane in the raft, trying to attract the attention of the crew. But the gods had other plans for him as well, and they repeatedly dumped him from the raft. Finally, he watched it sail away for good.

The feisty pilot thought back to survival training, which included practicing egress from a submerged helicopter. "There's safety in numbers. Stay together in the water," the instructors had said. Right, he thought, looking around. Maybe next time.

What else had he been taught? Curl into a ball to

conserve body heat. Another winner. Imagine being in a washing machine permanently stuck in the spin cycle. Buschor quickly learned in seas like that you don't just ride up one wave and down the next one. You get close to the crest, and it breaks on top of you. "Remember when you're a kid and you're playing in the surf and you get nailed by a wave?" he asks. You get tumbled, you can't breathe, it's up your nose and ears and everywhere. Now multiply that force by ten, or a hundred, or a thousand. You swallow volumes of saltwater. You manage to break the surface and immediately vomit. Think *Exorcist* vomiting. It comes out like a fire hose. And once your stomach has rid itself of the saltwater, you get the dry heaves. All you can do is wait for the next big wave to come and hammer you, and do it all over again.

Waves travel in sets, and not all of them break. But Buschor knew when the big breakers were coming. The real big ones, fifty- and sixty-foot monsters. Waves as tall as a five-story building. He could *hear* them coming, *hear* them breaking, and seconds later he'd get hammered. It took all the strength he could muster to fight his way back to the surface and catch a breath. It took so much strength that he questioned whether he'd survive the night. Not that he wasn't going to keep fighting. But the reality of the situation was grim: he was 65 miles southeast of Westhampton Beach, Long Island, alone, at night, puking his guts out in the middle of a vicious storm, and his survival radio was filled with water, inoperable. He'd been working since seven in the morning and was tired. He didn't know what time it was—the Velcro band on his watch had been torn open when he jumped from the chopper—and had no sense of how long he'd been in the water.

Then hypothermia started setting in. With his core body temperature dropping, he got the shakes. Buschor's last meal had been lunch, about ten hours earlier. There were no energy bars in his survival vest—they were in the raft kits—but even if there had been, he'd never be able to keep them down. While he didn't give up, with exhaustion setting in, Graham Buschor acknowledged that he wasn't going to make it.

Strange thoughts came to mind: Do I have enough life insurance? Who's gonna take the kids trick-or-treating tomorrow night? The Halloween parade at school is a very big deal, and I'm going to miss it. Will somebody ever find my body?

Still, he forced himself to remain hopeful, and he kept waving the handheld strobe light above his head. And kept getting it batted out of his hand with each breaking wave. The light was tied by a three-foot lanyard to the survival vest, but having to hold it in his hand was a definite conceptual flaw, obviously devised by someone whose idea of rough water was the end of the log flume ride at Disneyland. (He wrote it up in the after-action report. Now, in addition to the lanyard, the lights have a Velcro strip that sticks to patches on both the survival hood and flight helmet.) Having flown SAR, he knew the strobe light was his best bet, easily visible on a clear night ten to twelve miles over the black ocean. He still had several small emergency flares in the vest, but they flamed out in a snap and weren't worth using.

What he was waiting for, hoping for, were the rescue aircraft that he *knew* were looking for them. They had given home base an accurate reading of their position before they ditched. They *knew* that a rescue effort was being ginned up even before Jolly 110 hit the water. And suddenly there it was. In the distance he could see the landing lights of a low-flying Coast Guard Falcon jet flashing on and off. The plane had come out of its base at Cape Cod and begun flying an expanding square search pattern. Beneath the plane he could see what he now knows were strobe lights, winking through the haze. What he also learned after the fact is that Dave Ruvola, John Spillane, and Jim Mioli had somehow linked up and tied themselves together, which must have slowed their drift rate. That explains why Buschor was more than a mile ahead of them.

Buschor remembers watching the Falcon almost skimming the tops of the big breakers, and thinking, "That guy has some set of balls." Seconds later that guy was over him, flashing the landing lights on and off, on and off. He'd been spotted. So much for "search." It was time for "rescue." But he remained a realist. Weather conditions were awful. Any attempt to pluck them from the ocean at night was doomed to failure. Or disaster. In his words, "We're still screwed." But better to be screwed together than apart, so he started to swim against the current, toward the trio of fellow crewmen. With the big inflated balloons of his LPU under each arm, he wasn't doing any stroke officially sanctioned by the International Olympic Committee. He describes it as feeling like he'd become a motor spastic. His object was to head in a straight line for the guys, but just keeping them in sight was nearly impossible. He'd get hit by a wave, drop the strobe light, come up gasping and puking, then try to visually reacquire them. After several minutes of this—he has no recollection how long he tried swimming uphill—Graham realized he had no idea how far away the light actually was; he wasn't *really* certain that a fellow crew member was attached to that flashing light—it could have been a strobe on a partially submerged raft. Concluding that if he kept trying to swim he would unnecessarily tire himself, he opted to conserve energy, to literally go with the flow and hope for the best.

That's when he saw the Coast Guard Dolphine, a small helicopter flying out of Brooklyn. Buschor knew almost immediately that this was not going to be his salvation. The Dolphine has limited range, and this mission was taxing it to the max. It's also got limited power, and was not winning the battle with the elements. Graham watched as the pilot turned downwind pulling maximum power to keep from dropping into the sea, and retreated to its base.

But the Dolphine pilot must have seen the strobe lights, because shortly afterward Buschor spotted a Coast Guard Pelican, an HH-3 helicopter with enough range and power to do the job. What he didn't know was that the HH-3 crew had already attempted to drop a cable to the three men in the water, but the winds were so fierce they blew the heavy cable down the side of the aircraft, dangerously close to the tail rotor. Time after time the pilot tried to pick them up, but hadn't been successful. Abandoning that effort, the Pelican flew directly over Buschor, tossing flares into the water.

Yes, he thought. He's coming to pick me up. But instead the Pelican disappeared in the weather. It didn't make any sense. It didn't compute. What were the flares for? Moments later the question was answered. At first he couldn't make out what it was. Saltwater had taken its toll on his eyes to the point where they hurt constantly. Everything was foggy. There was something out there, with lights on. As it approached, he realized it was a Coast Guard cutter. It was the *Tamaroa*, fighting her way through horrendous seas, heading toward the flares. Soon he could see the trademark white boat with the big red stripe near the bow, lit up like a Christmas tree. Suddenly, he'd become the principal player in another one of those good news/bad news rescue scenarios. They *sort of* knew where he was—that was the good news. The bad news was that *sort of* was just close enough to beat his brains in. As the *Tamaroa* got closer he could see almost the entire crew on deck, each one of them tied to a safety cable that ran down both sides of the ship, hanging on for dear life as they tried to spot him.

"These guys are screaming their brains out, so I figured they're gonna tell me some magical way to get on this vessel. And I couldn't hear what was going on, so I had to take the exposure hood off, and all I kept hearing was 'Swim, motherfucker, swim!' And I thought, 'What do you think I'm doing?' "

The winds at this point were still in excess of eighty mph, and the seas hadn't abated at all. One minute he was in a trough below the ship, the next on a crest above it. The 205-foot *Tamaroa* was broadside to the waves, rolling 55 degrees to either side, as she tried to provide some protection for Buschor while drifting down on him. That's standard rescue procedure. Put the rescue vessel upwind of the swimmer, provide a lee, and drift toward him. Standard procedure, however, didn't contemplate the maneuver in seas like that. Truth be told, it didn't contemplate *any* rescue maneuver in seas like that. The ship's skipper, Commander Lawrence Brudnicki, had obviously made a decision to put his vessel and crew at risk to save Graham Buschor.

With continued verbal encouragement from the *Tamaroa* crew, the now completely exhausted pilot continued his struggle toward the ship, swimming into the oncoming waves, fighting to catch one of the lines ending in a cork buoy and chem light that were being thrown at him. Finally, he grabbed one and hung on as the Coastie at the other end hauled him in, hand over hand. At the same instant they both realized that Buschor was going to be swept under the bow, or more likely, the bow was being lifted by a wave and would sweep over him. So as the *Tamaroa* lifted up, her bow completely clear of the water, Buschor dropped the line and slipped underneath the keel plates, about ten feet back from the bow of the vessel.

Popping up on the starboard side of the ship, he could hear the crew screaming, "He's over here now!" Once on the windward side, Buschor was fighting a different problem: no longer was he trying to swim into the waves to reach the ship, he was now upwind of *Tamaroa* and trying to keep from being bashed into the constantly rolling steel hull by wind and waves. Although the ship's engines were at a dead stop, she still had forward motion, and as she brushed past him, he was able to grab one of the cargo nets draped over the side. Immediately, the net was hauled in with Buschor hanging on for dear life. Months later he would meet the guy who got to him first and started shaking him, asking if he was all right. "I remember exactly what you said to me," the Coastie told him. "You said, 'I'm fuckin' tired.'" It was as though someone had let the air out of a balloon. He'd been in the water, fighting to live, for almost five hours.

A few minutes later the three other survivors were hauled aboard, and Graham Buschor went to sleep, amazingly unscathed. Pilot Dave Ruvola was also relatively unhurt. Flight engineer Jim Mioli, who hadn't worn his mustang suit aboard the helicopter, and at the last minute had to choose between putting it on or launching the life raft, was in bad shape. For hours Ruvola had hugged Mioli to him, trying to give him a little warmth, some protection from the waves, and a lot of encouragement. No question that Ruvola saved his life. When they got Mioli aboard *Tamaroa*, his body temperature was down to 87 degrees and cardiac arrest was a real concern. PJ Spillane, who had jumped with his fellow PJ Rick Smith, had severe internal injuries, as well as a broken arm and leg.

The assumption is that Smith was similarly hurt when he jumped into the water, became unconscious and drowned. He left a wife and three daughters, the youngest only three weeks old. The search for Smith's body went on for nearly two weeks. Finally and reluctantly, but with the blessings of Smith's wife, it was called off. With a need to bring closure to the tragic episode for the PJ's family, friends, and coworkers, a memorial service was held at a nearby cemetery. Incredibly, as he was leaving the cemetery on his motorcycle, Pararescueman Al Baldwin, who'd been a Navy SEAL for twenty years before joining the PJs, was fatally injured when he struck a car that made an unexpected left turn in front of him. He was airlifted to Stony Brook Hospital, where he died of spinal cord injuries. At his family's request, his organs were donated, so that others might live.

That evening, to the chagrin of many members of the unit, Colonel Hill inexplicably reopened the search, accepting the offer of a Long Island psychic who claimed to have helped police locate missing persons, and who had been pressuring Smith's wife for money as payment for using his powers to find her husband. Hill sent a C-130 out over the ocean, then permitted the psychic to sit in the Operations room, gaze intently at the map of the North Atlantic, and issue instructions that were relayed to the aircraft. After several fruitless hours of vectoring the plane hither and yon according to the psychic's directions, the plane was ordered back to base and the search for Rick Smith's body was finally ended.

THIRTEEN

Alex can't understand why he couldn't taste the fresh water. He's holding the garden hose. He can see the cool, clear, clean water rushing from it. But he can't drink from it. Can't get it to fill his mouth, rush down his throat and take away the vile, salty taste of the seawater.

He also can't tell whether he's asleep and dreaming, or awake and hallucinating. Doesn't matter, really. Either way he's just as thirsty. And just as alone.

And then he sees the plane. It was in the clouds, then out, then back in. A big plane. It had to be looking for him. He grabs the whistle attached to the life jacket and starts blasting it. He thinks for a second, and starts whistling the Morse code SOS. Dot dot dot. Dash dash dash. Dot dot dot. And again. Dot dot dot. Dash dash dash. Dot dot dot. After a minute he realizes they can't hear him. There's no point to continuing. So he stops, and all he can hear is the sound of the ocean.

Seeing the plane disappear is a turning point for Alex Taranov. This is the low point. The moment

244

when he's ready to give up hope and face the reality of his situation. All the strength and energy drains from his body. But there's still that glimmer of life within him. It begins to grow; he feels the power within him. Suddenly, he punches the onrushing wave with a fist. "Fuck you!" he shouts in Russian. He's determined that the sea will never kill him.

Whether his mind was finally succumbing to the ordeal he's going through or whether it really happened, he can't be certain. But he says that just after the plane left, he heard a voice. He knew it was his voice, but different. It was coming from deep inside him. Russian words. *Gospodi, pomilui!* (God, have mercy upon us.) A wave turns him around, and in the distance he sees a rainbow. He knows it's real, not another dream, not a hallucination. Yes, it's cloudy, but far in the distance he sees shafts of sunlight streaming down through a break in the clouds. And the rainbow. His rainbow.

With Jolly 14, 08, and Yanky 03
11:20 A.M. Halifax time (10:20 A.M. EST)

Having topped off for the fourth time, Lieutenant Colonel Ed Fleming is anxious to get below the clouds and see what's going on. He's got the HH-60 flying in favorable winds just above the cloud deck, at about 6,000 feet, but can't see any clear spots that would make dropping down easy.

Telling Jolly 08 to stay up there until he calls, Fleming takes control and begins dropping down through the clouds. In less than a minute he sees the aircraft is picking up ice. Heavy ice. This is not something he wants to mess with, so as fast as he dropped below the cloud deck, he climbs back out of it, telling Buschor and the Marines that they'll have to find another way down.

After tanking the Jollys, Omey takes Yanky 03 up to 10,000 feet. Now he's getting concerned because although they're not yet anywhere near the search area, he sees that the holes in the clouds up ahead have closed up, and he's just heard what happened when Fleming tried taking his ship down through the clouds. There's just one more opening that he can see, about twenty miles in front of them. While he'd rather not go down and increase his fuel burn rate, there isn't much choice.

When they took off from Shearwater, the KC-130 was carrying 85,000 pounds of fuel. In the first two refuelings, he gave each Jolly 1,500 pounds. In the next two tankings, each helicopter got 2,000 pounds. His fuel plan had estimated that he'd burn almost 23,000 pounds, himself, by this time, but they hadn't anticipated an 8,000 or 9,000 pound per hour burn rate early in the mission. Right now the flight engineer is telling Omey that they've got just about 30,000 pounds of fuel remaining. The nav does some quick calculations and determines that the flight back to Shearwater at 25,000 feet will eat up 20,000 pounds, leaving them a reasonable reserve.

The Marine captain is comfortable with that. He knows that Air Force Rescue 852, the C-130 from the 71st Rescue Squadron at Patrick AFB, Florida, is not far behind them, coming out at high altitude to replace them. His concern is staying with the Jollys until 852 arrives and they know their hoses are work-ing. If something happened with 852, Omey can tap into his reserves and keep the Jollys flying until another tanker gets out there. Right now he needs to make sure the helicopters can get down below the cloud deck. On the radio he tells Fleming that the hole coming up is the last chance he sees to get them down in the clear.

The hole in the clouds is small, less than a quarter mile in diameter. Fleming scopes it, and then tells Buschor the plan. They're going to spiral down through it, maintaining a thousand-foot separation. "Okay, I'm going to start down. I'm going to call you at five thousand feet. I want you to roger it and then start down. Our rate of descent will be a thousand feet a minute." The trick is going to be keeping the spiral tight enough to stay in the hole and out of the clouds. Hitting the fringes won't be too bad, just so long as the hole doesn't begin closing up while they're in it.

Knowing that the faster he's going, the wider the turn radius will be, Fleming and Baur slow Jolly 14 down from a cruising speed of 150 knots to 90 or 100. And then they drop into the hole at a forty-degree angle of bank and begin the corkscrew descent. Fingers of clouds reach out to grab them, swirling in the rotor wash as the HH-60 comes flying down, now at almost a 45-degree bank angle.

"Jolly 14 at five."

Sengstacken comes back. "Roger. At five. Jolly 08 starting down." And the second HH-60 seems to leap into the hole, lays over in a heavy bank, and races around the circumference of the open space.

"Jolly 14 at 4,000."

They've got the rate of descent locked in. "Roger. Jolly 08 at 5,000."

It's a protocol Ed Fleming learned in the early seventies during the Vietnam War. He continues down, getting thrust toward the cloud wall by the turbulence. The rate of descent is better than sixteen feet a second, fast enough to take an elevator from the top to the bottom of Chicago's Sears Tower in seventy-seven seconds. But the sensation is even faster, heightened by the centrifugal force pushing them out from the center of the hole, by the bank angle, and the fact that they're covering almost four-fifths of a mile around the circumference even as they're dropping.

"Jolly 14 at three."

"Roger. Jolly 08 going through 4,000 feet." With the helicopter banked to keep the circle tight, Mike Moore looks out his window and sees 14 continuing its spiral beneath them.

They're executing the maneuver perfectly. Buschor and Sengstacken have locked onto the 1,000-foot-per-minute rate of descent. If there were no weather-related turbulence, they might get bounced around a bit by the vortex rising from 14's rotors, but considering what Mother Nature is already providing, it has no perceptible effect.

At a thousand feet Jolly 14 pops out of the hole into clear air and quickly resumes an easterly heading that will carry them to the search area. "Jolly 14 is clear at 1,000 feet, heading 095." A minute later Jolly 08 pops out like it's the end of a carnival ride, and immediately turns, sees the other helicopter, and speeds up to get back in formation. "Roger, 14, Jolly 08 has you in sight."

Now the two helicopters are flying below the cloud deck at an altitude of 1,000 feet, and their mother hen in the guise of Yanky 03 is at 7,000 feet above the clouds. If the Yanky C-130 were regular Air Force or

Air National Guard, he'd stay up there, observing the protocol that says stay out of the weather, stay out of the ice, have better fuel consumption.

But pilots Jon Omey and Jim Hall, navigator Jack Guthrie, flight engineer Chris Jablonski, loadmaster Bob Brought, and first mech Scott Blackman are Marines, and even if it sounds like recruiting propaganda, they truly are a different breed. They see themselves as part of this three ship team.

Just because the hole is only a quarter mile wide is, in Jon Omey's mind, no reason to separate from the helos. Yanky 03 calls 14 on the radio, gets their heading, and in effect says, "Be right there."

With the deicing equipment on the KC-130, Omey could have gone IFR and brought the plane down through the overcast. But that would have meant the Jollys were out of his sight for longer than he's comfortable with. So to the amazement of the helicopter crews, Omey lets them know they're coming down through the hole, and with that Yanky 03 does a wing over and dives in. The AC says the maneuver is nothing special. Just a routine "ridge line crossing" procedure that they'd normally do in mountainous terrain. Sixty degrees angle of bank and bottom rudder; the rudder is in the same direction as the turn, which makes the nose fall, putting the plane into a steep dive. Minutes later the Marines come roaring out of the hole, check their TACAN and distance measuring equipment radar—which shows the two helicopters on a small color radar screen in front of the pilot—turn, and once again the mother hen is orbiting over her chicks.

Now that Buschor and Sengstacken have had their fun flying the HH-60 like the world's most expensive amusement park thrill ride, and another refueling is a ways off, Mike Moore's thoughts turn to things gastronomic. In addition to prepping his medical gear, Moore sets up shop to prepare his food. His scrounging mission the previous night turned up grapes, cheese, and trail mix. In the morning, the Canadians gave everyone box lunches with peanut butter sandwiches. But Moore disdains premade peanut butter sandwiches "because they get squishy." So there he is, on the floor of Jolly 08, calmly smearing peanut butter and jelly onto slices of whole grain bread.

Sensing that Moore is at it again, Buschor asks what's going on. In his distinctive Long Island accent with more than a trace of attitude, Krulder says, "He's making peanut butter and jelly sandwiches." Here they are, bouncing through the remnants of a storm, 750 or so nautical miles out to sea in a machine that was built for two-hour sorties, and the guy who's going to have to jump in and fish the survivors out of a wretched ocean is impassively making sandwiches. No one will own up to it, but Moore distinctly hears someone on the interphone scream at him. It sounds like, "Take a spoon and eat the fuckin' jelly out of the jar." He handles such comments with purposeful equanimity, which just seems to have the effect of goading his crewmates on. It doesn't seem to bother him, perhaps because he knows he's the one who could be dropping into the ocean shortly, and, as a forty-year-old with eighteen years of doing this and plans to stay in good enough shape to do it for another fourteen, he knows what kind and how much food it takes to stoke his body's fires in order to get him through the physical and mental stress of a rescue.

While Moore works out of both helicopters and C-130s with equal skill, he does acknowledge that the opportunities to cook are much greater on the huge Herc. With a microwave and a convection oven on the plane, he's been known to whip up some gourmet meals, often starting with food he's prepped at home before the mission. And with a straight face he also claims to be working on a recipe book for long missions, which would certainly be the first of its genre. Truthfully, while Moore's obsession with food can get under the skin of his colleagues, when elements of the unit are being deployed to Turkey or Iceland for an extended period of time, there's a concerted effort to get assigned to the group Moore is in, since it's common knowledge he'll volunteer to cook and they'll eat like kings.

Finishing with the food, Mike Moore changes from the mustang suit into his wet suit. A dry suit is more preferable for winter waters, but his is being repaired. He completes his preparation by getting his fins, mask, and snorkel ready, along with the kit he'll take with him if he has to jump. That done, he takes up the observer position on the left side of the aircraft.

In Jolly 14, Doc Dougherty is going through similar preparations, but he's getting into a dry suit, with long johns underneath. In front, Ed Fleming checks in with CG 1503, the on-scene commander who's shocked that a pair of helicopters are this far out to sea. Fleming asks that all airspace below 500 feet in the search area be assigned to the Jollys. He gets a yes from the Coast Guard pilot, and asks for assignment to search the debris line of oil and flotsam that has been moving southeast from where the *Salvador Allende* went down.

Aboard Yanky 03
11:50 A.M. Halifax time (10:50 A.M. EST)

With the ceiling varying from 400 to 800 feet, the Marine tanker is once again burning fuel at a rate that's a lot faster than their plan had anticipated. Visibility is good, and they're watching forty-to-fifty-foot seas rolling underneath them. Much as they want to stay with the Jollys, Omey knows it's time to head back to Shearwater. Since he's got control at the moment, he asks copilot Jim Hall to call Rescue 852, which has been conserving fuel by orbiting at 18,000 feet, and tell them it's time to come down.

Hall contacts the regular Air Force Herc, talks for a moment, then clicks the interphone and tells Omey, "They won't come down. They say they can't cancel their IFR flight plan." The Marine pilot wasn't thrilled with the attitude of the 852 pilots from their first meeting yesterday at the 106th operation ready room when they expressed more concern about crew rest than about the people in the water. "I'd kinda had enough of them already." Now he's gone from "had enough" to "totally pissed off." This is not some theoretical training exercise they're flying on a simulator. They've got two HH-60 helicopters carrying a bunch of ballsy guys the Marines really like, they're 800 miles out to sea, the helicopters have begun searching for survivors, and even if they wanted to, they couldn't climb up through the clouds to meet the Patrick crew at altitude because they'd ice up and risk crashing. Besides, no matter what the Air Force regulations say, he knows they can cancel their instrument flight plan and claim "due regard," especially on a SAR mission, and go down to deal with an emergency situation.

"Jim, tell them they need to come down now 'cause we're out of gas and we can't leave these guys alone down here. We don't have time to screw around."

The copilot relays the message—and the tone. Listens for a few seconds, then hits the interphone again. Omey is not going to like this.

"They asked me what the ceiling is. I told them 800 to 900 feet and vis is great, and they just need to let down."

Omey already senses that "pissed off" is not going to be an adequate response for what he's about to hear. "What'd they say?"

"They said, 'No, we can't come down below a thousand feet; it's our legal limit."

Omey's response is not something he learned in flight school. It was something he picked up from gunny sergeants during his two years as a Marine infantry officer. In short, he kind of loses it.

"Tell them to get their . . . asses down here."

"Air Force Rescue 852, this is Yanky 03. Get your asses down here, *now*. We need you down here right now. We can't leave these guys alone!"

Apparently, the intensity of the Marines' feelings, perhaps coupled with the knowledge that they're all likely to meet in person back at Shearwater, persuaded them. And a few minutes later they emerged from the clouds.

Omey wants to see the Air Force plane with his own two eyes before they depart. His concern is that they leave the Jollys and then the other tanker comes down and isn't able to find them, or has a bad hose, leaving the HH-60s not so high and very, very dry.

"We could have probably tweaked out another couple of thousand pounds to them if we had to, and got back with no reserve at all. I didn't want to put ourselves in that situation if we didn't have to, but I wanted to make sure that they actually had their eyeballs on the helicopters before we left."

FOURTEEN

Lieutenant Colonel Ed Fleming's head is pounding, his back is killing him, and his legs are cramping up. The constant vibration of the chopper makes him feel like he's been strapped into an earthquake simulator that's been abandoned by the attendant. All in all, this is not the condition the commander of a high risk rescue mission wants to be in.

For helicopter pilots, even experienced instructors like Fleming, this mission calls for the most difficult kind of flying possible. It requires that both he and copilot Chris Baur pay constant attention to driving that aircraft. On the fringes of a storm far out to sea, with a violent ocean below that offers no discernible features, no landmarks, nothing to give them a point of reference left and right, up and down, the task is mind-numbing. Visibility is hampered by salt spray that goes up to 1,000 feet, and to top it off, they realize that a search for the proverbial needle in a haystack would be a snap compared to the task they've undertaken. When the mission began what seems like

255

a hundred years ago, the 106th volunteered to do the job based on the reports that there were at least twenty-eight survivors of the *Salvador Allende* desperately hoping for a miracle. When they began the mandatory crew rest period at Shearwater, they had word that a Canadian C-130 had spotted a lifeboat with eleven survivors, successfully dropped a SKAD to them, and established radio contact. But overnight, contact with that lifeboat was lost and the other seventeen souls had similarly disappeared. Now they've reached the area where the ship went down, about 900 miles from the nearest landfall, and find themselves bouncing around a dirty sky and accomplishing precisely nothing.

In the back of the ship flight engineer Rich Davin is feeling the frustration of spotting target after target in the water, only to discover that it's just another piece of flotsam from the sinking, with no sign of life nearby. Davin and Dougherty in 14, and Krulder and Moore in 08, are scanning the ocean, operating in the belief that any survivors would have to be on top of wreckage or in a raft, not actually in the water. The *Salvador Allende* had gone down almost thirty-two hours earlier; succumbing to hypothermia is virtually assured if they couldn't get out of the water.

After a couple of hours searching, Davin figures he's vectored the helicopter to nearly eighty different targets in the water. Nothing. They've seen pallets, dunnage, crates, even a refrigerator, but no survivors. What's also frustrating is that he knows, with each passing hour, the size of the search area expands. Between the wind, waves, and current, the survivors could be anywhere in several thousand square miles of the Atlantic.

Aboard Jolly 08
1:40 P.M. Halifax time (12:40 P.M. EST)

Going into search mode is not PJ Mike Moore's idea
of a good time. Searching takes a lot out of him, personally. It takes a lot out of the whole crew, even out of
the aircraft. They were hoping, perhaps naively, they'd
be on scene for a half hour to an hour before heading
back in with a full load of survivors. Previous experience tells him this could take three or four hours,
maybe longer, with lord knows how many more aerial
refuelings. And despite the fact that all six ARs to this
point have gone like clockwork, Moore is still not
ready to put the procedure on his "Things I Want to Do
on My Next Vacation" list. The tanker is flying at 500
feet, which means the helicopters are lower, so there's
not much room for mistakes. He feels particularly vulnerable when the tanker approaches and appears to fly
directly over them to get into position. "If they start
losing power, they start sinking down. . . ." But what
worries him most with the low ceiling is that there are
other search planes in the area, flying just above them,
occasionally in the low clouds. Human nature being
what it is, he figures that even though the Jollys are
supposed to own the airspace below 500 feet, one of
those planes might just drop below that 500 foot mark
in order to stay out of the cloud cover and keep their
eyes on the water. If that happens while the helicopter
is connected to the tanker, they can't maneuver very
quickly. So Moore's eyes are focused above them,
watching for a four-engined surprise. The only reason
he's not a white-knuckle flier during refuelings is
because there's nothing to hold on to. "I think the
pucker factor is way up there, it really is, during that

part of the procedures." And he prays silently.

Each time someone calls a target, the PJ's adrenaline starts rushing. The mindset is "We're going in now," and both he and Doc in 14 have to be instantly ready. They're flying search patterns centered on the debris line, usually a creeping line or ladder pattern that has them flying back and forth across the debris field, moving farther out to sea with each sweep. But it seems every time they get a rhythm going, one of the C-130s will call. "If you can come two miles to your three o'clock and check this out . . ." Usually the Herc will drop a flare to mark it, and they can locate the target quickly. But then they have to try and pick up the ladder search right where they left off, hoping that a survivor didn't drift through while they were gone. So far, each HH-60 has played that game half a dozen times to no avail. The microtasking is also beginning to annoy the pilots, because it's pulled the two helicopters in different directions, one time resulting in a three mile separation. Since each helicopter is the primary rescue platform for the other, that adds to their anxiety.

What's beginning to get Moore down is the disappointment of knowing that there were all these people out here that had been seen; eight hours ago they were briefed that they were still alive, and now they can't find them. It's disappointing and anxiety producing. The realization is beginning to sink in that sooner or later they're going to have to give it up and leave those people to their fate.

The frustration gets expressed by crew members in a variety of ways over the interphone, some of them tasteful, some not. "We might just be out here for nothing, doing the world's longest search," someone says, adding, "Maybe these guys are all shark bait."

While they're talking about what they've seen, the notion that something might go wrong with their helicopter that would put them in the water remains ever-present. But it's just that—a notion—until Buschor tries to lift the ship out of a hover after going down to check out yet another empty raft. He pulls on the collective, but it doesn't budge. He pulls harder. Still nothing. With concern growing, he says, "Gino, it's not coming up." Not comprehending the nature of the problem, Sengstacken says, "Well, what're you telling me for?"

Rather than argue, Buschor yanks on the collective with all his strength. Suddenly it gives, there's a *pfhhht!* and water sprays all over him and his side of the cockpit. The source is one of the little water boxes the Canadians had given them. Somehow, it had gotten jammed in the collective, and there was no way to gain altitude until it got unjammed. For a moment all Buschor can imagine is what the accident report would cite as the cause of the loss of a $10 million dollar aircraft. Wiping himself off, he's able to join the others in a much needed laugh.

Aboard Jolly 14
2:45 P.M. local time (12:45 P.M. EST)

Each time a new search plane rotates into the area, it begins calling targets that the Jollys have already checked out. All the rafts that have been dropped tend to look alike, and with the wind picking them up and blowing them across the wave tops, there's no way to identify them for the next Herc as having already been checked out. It's also not a matter of just flying over a raft and seeing that there's no one in it. Most of the rafts have covers, and they need to make certain that an exhausted survivor isn't hidden beneath it. On some searches, including the one for PJ Rick Smith, the HH-60s actually dropped a PJ in the water to climb aboard the rafts in order to make certain they were empty. Given the sea conditions here, that's not going to happen.

"They need to start putting numbers on these things so we don't play this game the next time," Davin demands. Up front, Baur responds, "Or we have to bring an M-60 [machine gun] along so we can sink the damn things."

Too tired to join the discussion, Fleming looks at the fuel gauges, then tells Baur to set up another rendezvous with the Air Force tanker while the weather holds. Baur calls Jolly 08 to give them the word, then radios AF Rescue 852. This will be their seventh refueling of the mission, the third off this tanker. As 08 forms up with them, Davin is looking at the water 100 feet below, at an area with considerable floating debris, while at the same time he's reading the AR checklist. That's when he sees Alex Taranov waving at him. "There was a pause, probably about ten or fifteen seconds. I'm looking at him and I'm thinking, 'I was never looking for anybody swimming in the water.' I was always looking for somebody in a raft, 'cause I was under the impression the water was the same temperature in that area that it was back in Halifax, like 37 degrees.' " The flight engineer's brain is doing cartwheels. He's actually shocked. He's experiencing textbook cognitive dissonance. "This is some thirty-odd

hours [after the ship went down]. There's no way anybody's swimming in the water, I don't care what kind
of suit they have on, it wouldn't matter. It makes no
sense to me at all. The only thing I could think of, after
my brain finally accepted the fact that there's a guy
swimmin' in the water, was that he had recently fallen
out of a raft or lost whatever he was hanging onto."

Davin says, "Hang on, there's something in the
water over here."

Ed Fleming hears someone yelling, "Break right,
break right."

Davin's concerned that his eyes are playing tricks
on him. "I mean, we're how many hours into this day,
already? Y'know, and I'm lookin', I'm lookin', I'm
lookin', and that's what I said. 'There's a guy waving
in the water over here at two o'clock.' " They'd finally
spotted their first survivor, seventy miles southeast of
where the *Salvador Allende* had gone down thirty-two
hours earlier.

No matter if it was "Break right!" or "There's a guy
in the water," Fleming's gut churns, his hands squeeze
the controls tighter. The tremor in Davin's voice tells
him this one is not a false alarm. After eight hours in
the seat, and seeing nothing but debris, he just senses
this is real. Not flotsam, not another reflection off the
breaking waves that looked like a man. There really is
something—someone—down there. He immediately
slams the HH-60 into a hard turn, heeling the ship over
as it responds to his hands, adjusting power and
changing direction. He has to resist looking for the
survivor right away, because it's a sure way to drive
the ship right into the water. So he keeps his eyes on
the power parameters, on the things he's supposed to

be monitoring inside the aircraft. But human nature says, "Where is that *ta madan*?" Stress tends to bring out the Gaelic in Fleming. So he concentrates on following Davin's instructions around the turn, constantly adjusting power, and remembering that what he's turning *over* is changing altitude beneath him. As he comes down from 100 feet, the radar altimeter is constantly going up thirty, down thirty, up thirty, down thirty. Without Davin's eyes, there's no way this maneuver happens with a happy ending. Meantime he's got Baur paying maximum attention to the engines and power. Down that low they're sucking salt into the jet turbines. The water deposits salt on the blades, it dries and crystallizes, putting drag on the blades, which causes the engines to work harder to cool themselves, which raises their temperature. And that affects the power that Fleming needs to keep the ship hovering where it's supposed to hover. If the engines start sucking up a lot of salt and the situation turns critical, he won't be able to make the rapid power adjustments he needs to clear the waves rising in front of him. If it gets *really* bad, the engines are going to stall. His copilot can tell him what the instruments say, but his hands have to transmit the constantly changing acceleration characteristics of the engines to his brain, which needs to function faster than a Cray supercomputer in order to tell his hands and feet how to respond. It has to happen in microseconds.

In the back, Davin has slid the right-side door wide open. Doc strips off his helmet and immediately moves next to Davin, in front of the open door. On a normal pickup they'd drop a smoke to mark the target and then come around into a hover. But now there's no time to do it by the book. All they can think of is getting this guy out of the water, and they'll improvise if they have to.

PJs have a variety of techniques for exiting a helicopter. The choice of method depends on location, mission, and circumstances.

The fast rope is just what it sounds like. A three-inch-diameter rope that PJs slide down. Think of it as a portable fire pole. It's used when speed is of the essence: combat, hostage rescue, runway takedowns, rooftop assaults. Generally, fast rope is used for heights of twenty to thirty feet. There've been instances of 100-foot fast rope infiltration, but since it's only the PJ's physical strength holding him to the rope, it can become a real challenge with a sixty- or seventy-pound rucksack on his back.

Rappeling is used when the helicopter can't come in low enough to deploy PJs via fast rope: on a steep mountainside, in areas of tall trees, or in the desert where the rotor wash would cause a brownout from the dust. Rappeling is also used with heavy equipment because there's a mechanical breaking device—a figure 8 in the rope—with which the PJ can stop himself. Also, if things go wrong in a combat situation, the PJ can tie himself off to the figure 8 and the helicopter can fly away with him still on the rope. Rappeling from 250 feet—about twenty-five stories—is more or less a routine operation.

The hoist can be used in any situation where the aircraft can't land. This was the primary method used over the Vietnam jungles, where the "penetrator" at the end of the hoist cable was invented to get PJs down through heavy jungle canopies. The biggest drawback is that it's slow. For peacetime rescue operations, especially from boats and from the water, it's ideal.

It's very safe, doesn't require a lot of strength to use it, and can be used from ten to 250 feet. They can also put a victim in a stokes litter—a wire basket—and haul him up with the hoist. The danger of using the hoist over water is that loose cable beneath the surface can wrap around the PJ or the victim. If that happens and the helicopter goes up or a wave goes down, in the words of Doc Dougherty, "Kiss your ass good-bye!"

The primary method for deploying into water is the low-and-slow approach. Desired height and speed for them to jump from the helicopter is ten feet and ten knots off the top of the wave. If PJs are deploying to a ship with tall masts or wires, they'll low-and-slow into the water, swim to the vessel, and climb or be hauled aboard. Hoisting off ships like this is a challenge, but Dougherty says, "That's the pilot's problem."

The method used to get back into the helicopter also depends on circumstances. The hoist works well, but it's slow. The other option is the rope ladder, used most often when there are numerous PJs coming out of the water or off land. Maximum height is twenty to thirty feet, and smart PJs wear a heavy canvas "first line belt" which can be used like a rappel harness, with a carabiner to clip into the ladder in the event hostile fire forces the helicopter to leave before they've made it into the cabin.

Before they left Shearwater, Ed Fleming had briefed that the PJs were to ride the hoist down, grab a survivor, and ride it back up. The decision to do it that way was predicated on each helicopter having to do as many as fourteen pickups. It's much more efficient if the PJ doesn't become a free swimmer and, in essence, another survivor who needs to be pulled out of the sea. In the hours they'd been out there, Fleming had never changed his orders, even though it was apparent they weren't going to be doing mass rescues.

Davin says, "I think when we actually saw what we had to deal with, and the size of the waves . . . I'm thinking, 'If I'm going to put Doc down on a hoist, at one point he's going to be getting slapped by a wave. And at the next point he's going to be hanging twenty-five, thirty feet above the trough of a wave.' It just didn't seem like the right thing to do."

Doc also knows the danger of riding the cable down. The penetrator at the end of the cable has flotation. Any slack cable sinks out of sight. That's a problem. "Once there's twenty feet of cable in that water, it gets a loop, and it gets around your leg, your neck, your arm. And then the wave drops out, and now you're hanging by whatever was wrapped in that cable. When we're in the water, our biggest concern putting somebody on that hoist is that cable. There's always one hand on that cable so you know where the lead end is. And then you've got the other hand on the patient, trying to get him out. You don't want to let go of that cable."

In the cabin, Davin is acutely aware of the problems that can develop with the cable. He's wearing heavy gloves, and will always keep a large loop of the cable in his hand so he's got an extra measure of control until the PJ and survivor are on their way up.

There's no time to discuss changing the plan. At this point Fleming is flying the aircraft, and he can only go by what Davin tells him. Fleming can't see anything. Not the man in the water. Not whether they're centered over him. Not even how high they are above him. Fleming flips the switch on his interphone so all he can hear is Davin. Every other source of audio is cut off.

The flight engineer is virtually driving the HH-60 by remote control. Davin has a wide angle view of the situation. He can see the waves, he can see the survivor in the water. He's calling off approximate footage, but his tone and the rapidity of the count also convey information to Fleming. "Right fifty, forty-five, forty, thirty, stop right. Forward ten, nine, eight, seven, continue forward, hold."

As the helicopter gets closer to the survivor, Davin's field of view narrows. Now he's no longer looking *out*, he's looking *down*.

Davin wants to go lower. "Down five, down five, four, three, two, one." Davin's directing Fleming to bring the ship as low to the waves as he possibly can. He and Doc are watching the waves go by, trying to keep Alex in sight, and they're also checking each other. Nothing's said, but they both know Doc's going to jump. He's ignoring the hoist that's rigged but not deployed outside the door, sitting in the doorway, ready to jump on their low-and-slow approach.

Even as he's guiding the movement of the helicopter, Davin is trying to communicate with the man in the water using hand signals. He's giving an enthusiastic thumbs-up, saying, "Don't worry, we're going to get you." What's strange is that the man continues to wave frantically as though he can't see the signal.

Fleming brings the ship to a hover, still expecting the PJ to ride the hoist down. But Davin and Doc are timing the waves. When he thinks the PJ should go, the flight engineer pats him on the back. Doc pauses until he thinks the time is right, and jumps. His object is to hit the crest of a wave passing ten feet beneath the helicopter, not the trough forty feet below.

As he's going down, Doc's mind is racing. "The

guy's going to be in pretty bad shape. If there's one guy, there'll be others swimming over to me. I've got to get him on the hoist, take him up, and get right back in the water."

The instant Doc goes out the door, Davin hits the interphone. "PJ's in the water."

Fleming's momentary reaction is confusion. That's not how he briefed it. That quickly turns to anger when it sinks in that his instructions have been ignored. What comes out is a stream of Gaelic. The words don't particularly matter to the crew; the tone conveys their meaning. In spades.

When Doc jumps, he's wearing his dry suit, fins, a snorkel, and a survival belt that includes fluorescent green sea dye packed in what looks like oversized tea bags. The dye is supposed to be rigged so that when the PJ pulls a lanyard, it deploys. In this case it begins pouring into the water as soon as he hits. That's not a problem; in fact, it's a big help to Davin. The sea dye drifts in a big V like a boat driving through the water. Follow it to the narrowest, brightest point, and that's where Doc is.

For Doc, the jump is near perfect. He seems to catch the side of a wave and actually slide down it toward Alex. But in the front of the helicopter Fleming senses that something is definitely wrong. The ship is staying ten feet above the surface, but he's being guided into a trough between two waves. There's no question in his mind that Doc didn't land on a crest ten feet beneath the HH-60. He landed on the backside of a passing wave, almost at the bottom of a trough—ten feet beneath the ship. Fleming is concentrating so hard on adjusting power and listening to Davin, he almost doesn't hear Chris Baur. "Ed! Ed! Take it up." Baur is looking straight ahead through the windshield at a forty-foot wall of water coming right at them, a good ten feet higher than the previous six waves. A rotor blade tip hitting the wave would be like smacking into concrete. Fleming looks up, applies power and lifts the HH-60 up, letting the wave pass underneath them.

What they're trying to do is keep the helicopter a constant height above the surface of the water, which is varying by thirty to forty feet. It means Fleming has to continuously yo-yo the ship. Down this low he can't rely on the radar altimeter; its accuracy is plus or minus two feet. That's an acceptable two percent error if you're at 100 feet; at ten feet it's a terminally unacceptable twenty percent error.

In order to maintain the hover precisely where Davin wants him to be, Fleming needs to be able to make precise moves in three dimensions. If he's instructed to move five feet to the left, he needs to figure out just how far that is. When they're picking someone off a mountain, it's easy. He's got a rock on the right and a tree on the left that don't move. By triangulating, he can figure how far five feet is. He can't possibly pick a moving whitecap and use it as a marker. It won't work. What he's using is debris floating nearby—a box, a wooden pallet, a sneaker. Yes, they're also moving, but they're moving in relationship to each other, so it works.

Seconds after Doc jumps, Davin's left hand manipulates the control to lower the penetrator while in his right he holds a loop of the cable, carefully feeding it out. He's expecting it to get grabbed by the crest of a wave, pulled away from beneath the helicopter, then pop out of the wave and swing back. He's just got to make sure it's not swinging where Doc's head happens to be, so he's still giving the pilots instructions to adjust their position, left or right, forward or back.

While Doc doesn't hit the crest of a wave going by, he does get a lucky break. Falling into the backside of the wave, he swims hard and fast down its face— almost body surfing—and ends up directly behind Alex, who is inexplicably still waving and shouting. When he jumped, Doc was braced for the shock of 37 degree water. It took a second to realize that it hadn't happened, the water is warm and he's actually beginning to sweat profusely in the long johns he's wearing under the dry suit. This is good news, because it means he can spend more time in the water waiting for the additional survivors he expects to come swimming to him.

Coming up behind Alex, he taps him on his right shoulder and asks, "Do you speak English?" Alex whips around and immediately grabs the PJ, who he outweighs by fifty or sixty pounds, and inexplicably answers, "No, I don't."

Aboard Jolly 08
2:50 P.M. local time (12:50 P.M. EST)

At almost the same instant that Rich Davin in Jolly 14 spots Alex, John Krulder in 08 sees him too, and yells that there's a guy in the water waving his arms. Both helos immediately turn toward the survivor, but it was apparent to Buschor and Sengstacken that the lead ship was going to make the pickup. They watch Doc jump into the water, then turn and begin looking for the other survivors they figure must be nearby. And then the flight engineer spots a second survivor wav-

ing about 100 or 150 yards away. Krulder hits the
radio to Jolly 14. "We've got something in the water
we're going to check out. Maybe another person." The
only person who can hear him and acknowledge is
Chris Baur. Fleming and Davin have set the interphone so they only hear each other.

Seated on the left side of the cockpit, Sengstacken
can see people in the water, and at least one of them is
waving. Moore's already in his wet suit, hood, and
gloves. As he moves toward the door that Krulder has
thrown open, he puts on his mask and fins, prepares to
adjust his snorkel. Still wearing the headset, he hears
one of the pilots call, "One minute out. You ready to
drop?" The ennui that had set in is gone. In its place,
adrenaline is pumping by the quart.

"PJ going off headset." Moore pushes the headset to
the back of the cabin and positions himself in the open
door, ready to deploy. Every muscle and nerve in his
body are just waiting for Krulder's signal to go. His
hands are on the edge of the door and he's in a crouch,
like a spring fully compressed, waiting for the release.
Moore can now clearly see the victim. He squats a bit
lower, about to lunge out and away from the hovering
helicopter, when John Krulder's fist shoots out in front
of his face.

It's the signal to STOP! Something is wrong. Don't
do anything. Don't jump. Don't move. Don't even
breathe heavy. It's an incontrovertible order. But it's
an order that makes no sense to the PJ. "Why is he
stopping me from jumping on this guy?"

With the noise, the only way they can communicate
is with hand signals, and Moore is having a difficult
time seeing them because his mask is getting foggy
and he's too sweaty to unfog it. Krulder's hand stays

in front of the PJ's face, then points him back to the other side of the cabin, even giving him a little shove in that direction. Moore moves as quickly as he can with swim fins on, finds his headset and puts it on.

"What's this all about?"

"You're not jumping in there!"

"Why?"

"There's sharks down there."

Finding sharks in the Gulf Stream in December, 1,200 miles east of New Jersey, with dead or dying men in the water, doesn't surprise Dr. George W. Burgess, director of the International Shark Attack File at the Florida Museum of Natural History, University of Florida. It would surprise Burgess if sharks *didn't* show up under these circumstances. It's the way life is cycled and recycled in the ocean, he says, where virtually nothing goes to waste. Every organism that dies eventually will be consumed by another. That holds for bacteria breaking down the smallest life-forms to sharks ripping apart the carcass of the largest whale. Humans who perish in the ocean inevitably become part of that food chain.

Initially, Burgess ticks off four species that could have homed in on the survivors of the *Salvador Allende*. Blues and makos, which are common open ocean sharks but are primarily fish eaters, oceanic white tips, and tiger sharks. Upon reflection he adds one more species: silky sharks.

The spot where the ship went down is on the periphery of the range of the oceanic white tip, characterized by huge dorsal and pectoral fins that make them easily identifiable, and possessed of a savage reputation which was enhanced during World War II when it's believed they, along with tigers, decimated the crew of the USS *Indianapolis*, which had been torpedoed while en route from Tinian to Guam, having just delivered the components for the Hiroshima atomic bomb. The vessel took two hits and sank within twelve minutes. Only 316 of the 1,196 men in the crew survived several days of shark attacks before being rescued. Two weeks later the war was over.

The fearsome tiger shark, which worldwide accounts for more fatal attacks on humans than even the great white, would certainly be attracted to people thrashing about in the warm Gulf Stream waters. A tiger shark will eat *anything*. It is the quintessential opportunistic feeder, consuming a wide variety of marine life as well as carrion and inedible objects. The stomachs of tiger sharks have revealed an incredible mix of floating and bottom junk, including chunks of coal, wood, leather, fabrics, plastic bags, burlap sacks, small barrels, cans, and pieces of metal. One shark was found with an anchor in its gut.

All sharks' senses are especially attuned to anomalies in their environment—strange sounds and scents draw them in. Even though these particular species lead singular lives, the number of individuals drawn to the same attractant gives rise to the impression that they feed in large schools. From great distances sharks can detect the sounds or vibrations associated with a sinking ship. As they come closer, their olfactory senses come into play. Swimming forward causes water to be forced into the nasal sacs behind their nostrils. Signals are sent from there, to the olfactory bulbs, which constitute the largest part of a shark's brain. Analyzing the water it's swimming in never stops. The result is that sharks can zero in on the tiniest concentration of blood or other bodily fluids in the water. On some sharks the sense of smell is so well-developed that they can detect blood or food in concentrations of only one part per ten billion parts of seawater. If conditions are right, a shark can detect prey up to more than half a mile away.

Once they close in on a target, their keen sense of sight kicks in and they move in to attack. If the target is obscured by cloudy water, for example, the shark's sixth sense, an ability to detect microelectromagnetic fields generated in the muscles of prey, leads them to food.

Shipwreck victims, alive or dead, release bodily fluids into the water. While it's generally thought that chances of fending off a shark attack are better if there's a group of people working together, the scent cone downstream of a group will inevitably be stronger than that released by a single individual. The shark's olfactory bulbs can quantify the scents, guiding the animal to their most intense source. If Alex was not downstream of his dead or dying shipmates, then the cone formed by the scents they were releasing into the water didn't envelop him. The sharks homing in on the source of that scene cone would most likely not target him. That may explain why Alex Taranov was not ripped to pieces, while his shipmates a hundred yards away were. That docsn't mean that given the large number of sharks rushing into the area, one of them wouldn't happen upon him. It's almost a certainty that when his leg was brushed by something feeling like sandpaper, it was a shark. Being intelligent animals, sharks are wary of attacking a target until they ascertain whether the target can fight back, inflicting injury. "Bump and run" or "bump and bite" are typical of their approach to an object in the water. It's conceivable when Alex was bumped, he spontaneously kicked out, driving the shark away. (Kicking back at an attacking shark, and attempting to gouge its eyes, are recommended as defenses that often work.) Since the animal was already picking up a much stronger olfactory signal from the group of bodies nearby, it made a decision to move on.

After reading the descriptions of the shark attacks provided by Davin, Moore, and Buschor of Jolly 08, Dr. Burgess came to the conclusion that all of the victims were dead by the time Taranov was being rescued. He doesn't rule out the possibility that they had been attacked while still alive prior to this time.

With Jolly 14
Approximately 1,200 miles east of New Jersey

Putting a bear hug on your would-be rescuer is generally not a good thing to do, but it's a normal reaction and Doc is ready for it. What he's quickly trying to figure out is if Alex is about to give up and sink, or is he just happy to see him? He's not terribly worried about getting pushed under, because he's wearing an inflatable life jacket with a Scuba buoyancy compensator. All he has to do is yank the lanyard and he'll pop to the surface.

His concern right now is to get Alex out of the water as quickly as possible. Alex doesn't look good, and there's something strange about the fact that he's not quite looking at Doc while he is explaining that they're going to put him on a chair and pull him up to the helicopter. Despite Alex saying he doesn't speak

English, it's apparent that he does understand enough for the two to communicate. Doc asks if he can swim to the cable. The response is inconclusive, but it's only about twenty feet, so Doc begins towing Taranov to the penetrator, which is already on the surface, kept there by a buoyant flotation collar. In seconds Doc sees a problem: despite Davin's best efforts to control it while the helicopter yo-yos, there's excess cable in the water. It's scary. What he really needs to keep the cable away as he tries to put Alex on the penetrator is a third hand—or a second PJ. While they normally carry two Pararescuemen in each helicopter, concern over space limitations in the cabin dictated that Doc and Mike Moore would fly alone. One way or another, Doc's going to have to cope with the cable and waves on his own.

The penetrator has three paddle seats that fold down. The PJ is supposed to position the survivor so he's seated on one of the paddles. Then he passes a safety strap around his back, underneath his arms, hooking it to the penetrator. The survivor is now on a seat and seat-belted in place for what should be an uneventful ride up. In rough seas, however, all bets are off. Putting a man on a penetrator is like trying to help him sit on a beach ball. Just when you get him right where he's supposed to be, it pops out on the other side.

Meantime, Davin is doing a running commentary for the pilots. "He's working with the survivor. He's got the survivor. He's hooking him onto the penetrator; hold your hover. Five right, five down." They need to keep the helicopter as centered as possible over the person. If he's not directly beneath them and they pull power on the cable, the survivor can become a human pendulum.

The combination of heavy seas and rotor wash from the hovering helicopter is taking its toll on both Doc and Alex. With every breath they're inhaling water. It's nearly impossible to speak, hear, and breathe. The only reason Doc can still see is that he's wearing his mask. If it weren't so serious, it would be comical. Here's a Pararescueman from Long Island trying to communicate with a seaman from the Ukraine as saltwater is sprayed into their faces while two jet engines hovering overhead generate jackhammerlike noise in full stereo surround-sound. It's fortunate that most of their communication can be accomplished with body language, because getting Alex onto the penetrator is proving to be more difficult than expected. Each time Doc gets Alex sitting on one of the paddles, a wave breaks over them, knocking him off. Time after time they're both pushed underwater, gulping saltwater while trying to catch a breath of air. It's physically demanding work for Doc. He's still fending off slack cable in the water, while trying to muscle Alex back onto one of the paddles. Alex is unable to help; after thirty-two hours in the water, he has no physical strength left. Finally, while holding Alex to the penetrator, Doc manages to keep the cable at bay and at the same time give Davin the thumbs-up signal to begin the lift.

The combination of turbulence and concern over getting hit by an unusually large wave is making it difficult for the pilots to keep Jolly 14 in the precise hover that Davin needs in order to avoid the pendulum effect. Davin compensates by taking advantage of the fact that water is much more forgiving than land. He puts a little tension on the cable—not enough to lift Alex out of the water but enough to troll him to the correct position under the HH-60 before he begins the lift.

Slowly, the hoist starts to turn and Alex begins to feel himself being lifted out of the water. His chest is clear, then his waist, then his thighs. He knows he's just seconds away from being out of the ocean for good. But just as his legs are about to break free from the wave going past, he slips off the paddle. The cable is still going up, and without anything to sit on, Alex drops like the condemned man at a hanging when the trapdoor is sprung. In the helicopter above them Davin is expecting to see Doc pull himself onto one of the paddles and ride up with Alex. What he sees instead—and feels through the cable—is Alex dangling from the penetrator, legs flailing in the water, held there only by the safety strap under his arms. The flight engineer has to make an instantaneous decision. Should he slack off and drop Alex back into the water, or continue the lift with Alex suspended from his armpits, leaving Doc to wait in the water until he can offload Alex, guide the pilots back into position over the PJ, and drop the penetrator to him?

Looking up, Doc immediately knows what Davin is trying to decide, and he's not surprised to see Alex continue upward. He would have made the same choice. Without having Alex or the cable to worry about, it's easy enough for him to kick back and wait his turn. He has no reason to be concerned. Even in rough seas, he's floating comfortably over the swells, with mask, flipppers, survival vest, dive knife, radio, chem lights, and green sea dye still marking his spot in the ocean. This is a gig he's been doing for twenty years. Besides, he's still expecting to see other survivors in the area. And as Jolly 14 moves away, its slowly rising prize dangling beneath it, James Dougherty does a slow 360 in the warm water, hoping to see another survivor of the *Salvador Allende* swimming toward him.

Carefully tending to the hoist, Davin continues his play-by-play for the pilots. "He's halfway up, he's three-quarters of the way up, he's approaching the bottom of the door. Be prepared to give me slack up front." As Alex's head rises above the level of the floor, Davin kneels and waits until Alex is above him before he stops the hoist. He reaches out, grabs Taranov around the midsection, spins him around so he's facing out—he doesn't want Alex to be able to grab him—and shouts for the pilot to give him slack in the cable.

On the center console between the pilots is a switch that moves the cable in extreme slow motion. Baur reaches back with his right hand and toggles the switch while at the same time Davin pulls Taranov down and in. He quickly unstraps him from the penetrator and gives Alex a healthy shove on the slick, wet floor, sending him sliding toward the far corner of the cabin. Taking care of the survivor will have to wait until he gets his PJ back.

From the water, Doc watches 14 slide away from him, sees Davin wrestling Alex into the cabin. It strikes him that throughout the rescue ordeal Alex had remained calm and professional, amazing considering what he'd been through. Doc Dougherty guesses that the helicopter is perhaps fifty yards away from him; it'll take them a few minutes to return. That's when he realizes the water is very clear, no oil slick at all, so he takes a moment to dive a few feet under the surface where the noise of the HH-60 is blocked out for the first time in more than eight hours. Surfacing, he slowly turns until he sees Jolly 08 in a low hover off in the distance, but can't tell what they're doing. He begins considering possible scenarios. Perhaps for some reason it might make sense for 08 to pick him up. Or maybe Buschor's helicopter is picking up survivors. Maybe they've got some seriously injured people in the helicopter that Mike Moore is already working on. Doc thinks they might want him to stay in the water and perform triage. He can put the more seriously injured on 08's penetrator, so John Krulder can hoist them up, allowing Moore to stay and concentrate on providing medical care. Then Doc can send the less seriously hurt up to 14 and Rich Davin, who can just stash them on the blankets until the PJ is clear to return to the helicopter and begin treating them.

Still unaware of the shark attack taking place a hundred yards away, Fleming brings Jolly 14 around in a tight circle, concentrating on listening to Davin's instructions, which will help him maneuver the ship until it's almost directly over the PJ in the water. Just flying the HH-60 in sixty-knot winds is a Herculean task; flying it blind—neither pilot is able to see directly beneath the helicopter—with pinpoint precision to keep the hoist directly over Doc, moving in three dimensions in response to Davin's call, is almost impossible. Almost. That's one of Ed Fleming's guys in the water below. Ed Fleming is determined to make sure they get him out.

FIFTEEN

Aboard Jolly 08

John Krulder's seen a lot of gore during his time flying rescue, but nothing like this. The helicopter is hovering no more than ten feet above one of the *Salvador Allende* crewmen, and as Krulder and Moore watch, three sharks are tearing him apart.

What gets to Krulder is the expression on the man's face. Terror. It forces him to confront the fact that he had been alive moments ago, and now he's not. With his stomach turning, Krulder thinks, I don't want to play any more; let's go home. But he knows they have to keep searching.

Looking through the plastic floor bubble, Graham Buschor feels frustration and disappointment because there's nothing they can do. It goes through his mind in a few milliseconds. Then he hits the radio switch, calling Jolly 14. "Get them out as soon as you can. There's sharks in the water. We've got sharks over here." Looking down again, he sees the sharks tearing into another body, completely ignoring the tornadolike downdraft from the helicopter right above them. Buschor sees stripes on their backs and concludes they're tiger sharks, up to eight feet long.

In the back, Mike Moore has put his gunner's belt back on, which keeps him tied inside the helicopter. With the side door still open, he gets down on the floor and slides his head out to get a better look. "I see this guy in the water going up and down. Originally, when I first looked at him, I could've sworn he was looking at me. And then all of a sudden I see this silver flash in the water. Clearly you could see it was a pretty large shark. And then as soon as he hit the guy, he would just keep going, and as soon as he went by, another one would come from another direction and hit him. They just kept hitting him. And I realized about the third hit that his legs were basically gone."

As Moore crawls back from the door he suddenly comprehends that John Krulder had just saved his life. He'd been totally focused on preparing to jump and couldn't see clearly through the fogged mask. Nevertheless, he's considering going down on the hoist and trying to retrieve the man's body when it dawns on him that Doc is still in the water. "Hey guys, we need to get over there and cover him."

Aboard Jolly 14

Alex Taranov is thirsty, exhausted, and confused. When Rich Davin shoved him back into the far corner of the cabin, Alex couldn't understand why the flight engineer was being so abrupt. He actually thinks Davin is angry with him. So saying nothing, he sits in the corner and covers himself with a blanket. At this point the only person in the helicopter who knows about the sharks is Chris Baur, and since he knows Fleming and Davin are in close communication as they maneuver to pluck Doc out of the ocean, he opts to say nothing at the moment. Even if they knew about them, they couldn't do anything to get Doc out of the water faster than they were already.

If they had known about the sharks a few minutes earlier, there's no way Davin would have brought the penetrator up without Doc on it. They've got a comprehensive hand signal language, and the flight engineer would have signaled "Shark!" to Doc, who says he would have ridden the hoist up with Alex, "Even if I had to hang onto the bottom of it."

As soon as Fleming has the HH-60 where Davin wants it, he drops the cable with the penetrator. Doc has no problem grabbing it. He sits on one of the paddles, and without unhooking one end of the safety strap as he had to do with Alex, he pulls it over his head and under his arms, gives the flight engineer the thumbs-up, and is hauled clear of the water almost instantly. He pulls his face mask down around his neck, checks to see that his snorkel is tucked into his belt, and enjoys the ride.

"He's coming up. He's in the door. Cleared for forward flight." Davin's objective is to let the pilots get out of the hover as quickly as possible, since it's not only difficult to hold over the ocean, but is the most vulnerable position for the helicopter to be in.

Aboard Jolly 08

Seeing Doc safely hauled back into Jolly 14, they can now turn their attention back to the people in the water. Moving down the debris line looking for survivors, Krulder finds himself getting nauseated. Moore, a highly trained paramedic, is forcing himself to remain almost clinical about the situation to keep from becoming emotionally overwhelmed. "The sharks weren't hitting them all. Some of them had already been hit and left. You could see they were carcasses. It appeared they would eat the carcass until all the intestines were gone, and they would leave it. We'd find a raft with three torsos tethered to it, and the legs and midsection would be gone." It's a characteristic shark attack on men wearing flotation devices. The animals have difficulty pulling the upper torso under the surface, so in their feeding frenzy they initially target the body parts within easy reach.

Before Krulder had seen what they thought was a man waving, Moore had been preparing to videotape Doc effecting the rescue. Now someone suggests that he tape the shark attack, and for a moment he thinks about doing it, but decides that morally he can't. "No, I don't want to document this. Let it rest in peace."

Seeing the bodies in the water reminded Buschor of his own experience trying to survive in the ocean. Before that happened to him, he says they'd go on searches, find bodies, and wonder how they died. "They had all this survival equipment, they get all this survival training. Well, I found out very quickly how you can die. A combination of exposure and exhaustion. It's a miracle that we survived that. And it's a miracle that Alexander Taranov survived. All the bodies we found, it was heartbreaking. We found three, four guys all tied to one another, one, two, three, four, right in a row. Tied to a life raft, and you know what killed them? The exposure killed them. Just being out there at night in the cold water, they're exhausted, it got to them, you slip underneath and you drown. You just can't maintain that any more. And then the sharks feeding on the bodies. It was heartbreaking. I'd been in the Merchant Marine, you see kids seventeen years old all the way to guys in their sixties. It's tough, y'know, it's really tough."

As Jolly 08 continues down the line they spot a partially inflated raft with the remains of three people tied to it by the tether lines that would enable them to get back into the raft if they were tossed out. Sharks had already disemboweled the three. Moving on, they find more victims, singly and in groups, and see the sharks hitting anything and everything in the area that's floating—boxes, boards, flotsam of all kinds.

In the rear of the helicopter Moore keeps his thoughts to himself. He's certain that some of the seamen were eaten alive. If one survivor is alive, logic tells him others would also be alive. The frenzied sharks didn't just attack the ones that were dead. Everyone in that scent cone got eaten.

Analysis gives way to emotions, even with a PJ who's seen it all. "It was a sad situation, really sad. I don't think we found one body other than Alex that wasn't affected by a shark attack. It was really weird. It was an Alfred Hitchcock movie, like it totally ended up being something different than what you expected.

"When you get a briefing that morning, they spotted them all alive. You go into this location to pick 'em up, and you get out there and there's only one survivor. And the rest of them . . .

"So we know the time span of the shark attack had to be relatively close [to when we got there], because we saw the shark attacks in action. How many of them were alive at that point? You question was it an hour ago? Two hours ago? If we would've gone straight out there they would've all been rescued."

In the copilot's seat Gene Sengstacken is what-iffing the situation. "We could've been an hour off of maybe saving that guy. They lost every one of those people [that had been spotted the night before]. I don't know how they did that. They lost every sighting by the time we got out there. . . ." and his voice trails off into silence.

John Krulder sums up the situation more succinctly for the crew aboard Jolly 08. "It's a buffet line down there." The flippancy of the comment, quintessential gallows humor, belies how much seeing the carnage has affected him. He won't sleep well for many weeks, and will know precisely what it is that's keeping him awake.

Aboard Jolly 14

Thinking that he's going to be going back in to pick up more survivors, Doc crawls over to Alex without removing his swim fins. For the moment he's elated. "Now we hit it; we hit pay dirt. We're here, we're gonna be making pickups." It'll be half an hour before the realization sets in that Alex is the only survivor and Doc can devote his full attention to him.

Initially, Alex doesn't understand what's going on, especially since the first thing Doc attempts to do is use a large scissors to cut his clothes off. He tries to push Doc away, then offers to undress himself. He tries, but falls back, exhausted.

"Okay, relax," Doc tells him as he cuts off his clothing with Davin's help. It turns out that Alex is a living endorsement for the wool industry. He's wearing wool pants, wool socks, wool sweaters, all of which apparently really do retain their ability to keep the wearer warm even when wet. Once they've got him completely naked and can see no visible injuries, they stuff Alex into a sleeping bag that's been warmed with chemical heat packs, and jam one of the Canadian wool toques on his head. Remarkably, the only physical complaint Alex has is his eyes, which have been severely irritated by the saltwater. It suddenly becomes clear to Davin why Alex continued waving when the helicopter was directly over him: he couldn't see. Doc rinses them out, then places ice packs over them.

Next he takes Alex's blood pressure and pulse. Everything is fine. Logically, a man who's been in the water for thirty-two hours is going to be dehydrated, so the next step is give him an IV with glucose. Doc takes out the setup and begins to prep Alex's arm, but he pulls it away, clearly indicating, "I don't want it. I don't need it." Not wanting to upset his patient, the PJ puts the equipment away and gives Alex the water he's been asking for. After a couple of swigs Alex gags, then spits up. But he immediately tries again, and this time it stays down, as does the slice of bread they give him.

Moments later Doc and Davin are stunned when Alex indicates a need to urinate. It makes no sense. He should be dehydrated to the max. It's then that they learn of the two cans of 7UP, which Doc will henceforth call the beverage of choice for shipwreck survivors. "He couldn't have asked for anything better except maybe Gatorade or fresh water. Cola has caf-

feine in it, and that would dehydrate him. And it wasn't
a diet drink, so it had plenty of sugar for energy."

Neither of the crewmen can believe how healthy
Alex is. Davin tries several times to ask if he fell out of
a lifeboat or a raft, because he's convinced that he'd
been eating and drinking during the ordeal, and had
only been in the water a few hours after the boat or raft
went down, but it's too complicated a question for sign
language, and Alex's English is not good enough to
understand what he's being asked. He does manage to
convey that he wants to sleep, and in seconds he does.

With Doc and Alex safely aboard, Jolly 14 joins up
with 08 and they continue down the debris line, finding more bodies tied to rafts and ravaged by sharks.
When it's apparent that there are no live survivors in
the immediate area, Ed Fleming orders a rendezvous
with the Air Force tanker to top off. Now that the ceiling's moved higher, they can refuel above a thousand
feet, within legal limits for the AF crew, and then
return to searching the debris field.

There's a bit of a problem as Jolly 14 attempts to
plug the drogue off the left wing. On previous refuelings in bumpy air a number of the spokes had been
punched out and the canvas cover was badly torn. This
time Fleming hits it, but the probe pushes completely
through the drogue, which starts whipping it around.
On headsets Doc hears, "Miss!" Given his dislike for
the whole air-refueling process, the one word is
enough to get his attention. He stops attending to Alex
and waits. Fleming calmly backs out of the drogue
without doing any damage to their probe, then moves
in, hits it solidly and gets an indication that they've got
a good wet contact. "Contact!" Doc breathes a sigh of
relief as the helicopter quickly makes a controlled

movement up and to the left, then he returns to his
patient.

Doc's lack of love for the air-refueling process got
its start in PJ school when one of the instructors told a
story about picking up a patient, and on the way back
the patient saw everyone putting on parachutes.
"Don't worry," he told the immobile patient, "we do
this all the time." Then the drogue began dumping gas
before they hit it, resulting in gas all over the windshield and the smell of fuel permeating the interior of
the helicopter. To make matters worse, the patient
looked out the window, and there was the drogue, right
next to the helicopter. Knowing he was the only one
onboard not wearing a parachute, the patient was
looking wide-eyed at this thing that appeared as large
as a wrecking ball coming right at them. After that, the
instructor told the class, it was a challenge to keep the
patient calm and his blood pressure somewhat less
than stratospheric. Real or apocryphal, it's a story Doc
remembers whenever a refueling doesn't go quite perfectly.

Refueling phobias aside, Doc continues treating
Alex by the book. Every five minutes he wakes him in
order to take his vital signs. It's the PJ equivalent of the
hospital nurse who wakes up the patient to give him a
sleeping pill. When it becomes apparent that Alex is in
surprisingly good health, and that he's getting seriously
annoyed about being awakened, Doc decides he can
take his vital signs at fifteen-minute intervals. Even this
doesn't satisfy his patient, who looks at Doc as if to
ask, "Why are you bothering me?"

Doc tries to explain. "I have to do it 'cause God forbid you die on the way back . . ." He doesn't complete
the thought, because whether Alex understands it or

not, he seems satisfied. Now all there is for Doc to do
is to continue to flush Alex's eyes with fresh water and
keep ice packs on them.

As Fleming and Baur continue flying Jolly 14 down
the debris line looking for other survivors, they get a
call from the Air Force tanker above them.

"Jolly 14, this is Air Force Rescue 85. We're outta
here."

Apparently without realizing it, the young captain
flying that plane has said just about the most incendi-
ary thing he could possibly say to a pair of land-based
helicopters 900 miles from terra firma. To the HH-60s,
that C-130 tanker is the difference between life and
death. Even if they didn't have an ounce of gas available for the helicopters, they've still got rafts and supplies to drop to them if the worst should happen.
Protocol for tankers is, "You don't leave till your
replacement arrives and you're sure he can pass fuel."
And their replacement, one of the 106th's own C-130s,
is still a half hour away.

From the rear of Jolly 14, Rich Davin says, "Who's
he talkin' to? He's not talking to us?" Davin turns to
Doc. "Bullshit. He's not goin' anyplace."

Now Davin is on the radio. "No, you're not leaving
us out here. You're our stable platform, you're our
fuel. If we can't link up with that next tanker, for any
reason, weather or anything else, if he comes out and
he's got a bad hose, can't get his hose out, we got a
problem."

Lieutenant Colonel Ed Fleming hasn't yet weighed
in on the radio. What he's thinking is that these are a
couple of young pilots who've had too much time on
their hands in the cockpit between refuelings, and
they've spent it reading the several hundred pages of

well-intentioned planning documents they were
handed at their morning brief. Somewhere in those
documents there's a rotation chart showing the schedule for each of the C-130 tankers—when they brief,
take off, arrive on-scene, and return to base. Fleming
figures they've read "AFR 852 returns to base at 1230
local time," and that's what they're doing. There's
nothing in the written orders about sticking around till
their replacement arrives.

Ed Fleming's been doing this sort of thing for a
couple of dozen years, and his maxim is, "The plan is
not the reality; the map is not the territory." The Air
Force pilots figure they're just following orders. Graham Buschor, who's personally experienced the consequences of a tanker unable to give them fuel and
barely lived to tell the tale, is characteristically chari-
table. "There's a gazillion different personalities in the
world. There's people that can't do anything unless
they're told step by step how to do it. And there's other
people that're a little more creative. Everybody has
their own perspective on how to do things."

Throughout the argument, Fleming's been flying
Jolly 14 while Chris Baur and Davin handle radio
communications with the 130. After listening for a
moment, the copilot triggers his intercom switch and
tells Fleming the Air Force guys insist they're bingo,
they've got no more fuel to give, and they're short
themselves. Fleming's retort is unhesitating, and
uncharacteristically spoken in the King's English, not
Gaelic: "Bullshit!"

Baur tries reasoning with the tanker crew. Listens
for a moment, then keys the interphone: "Well, they
say that they need this fuel reserve and that fuel
reserve."

And again from the boss: "Bullshit."

Fleming tells Baur to take control, and the lieutenant colonel himself gets on the radio. He too listens
for a few seconds, then cuts in, "Bullshit! You're staying here until our 130 arrives on-scene." In theory, an
aircraft commander is the master of his domain. Rank
isn't a consideration in the cockpit; the pilot of that
C-130 rules his aircraft like the captain of a ship.
That's the theory, but this far from land, over a very
nasty part of the Atlantic Ocean, Ed Fleming invokes a
higher power: common sense.

The contretemps take place on the radio frequency
that's being monitored by both helicopters and all the
C-130s involved in the mission. One hundred fifty
miles away in King 74, Major Kevin Metz has heard
the whole thing. He too guesses the tanker pilots have
a flight plan and don't want to deviate from it. It
includes landing at Shearwater with more than adequate reserves in their tanks. He takes it as a sign of
inexperience. "Sometimes you want to keep another
10,000 pounds [of fuel] onboard for Mom and Dad
and the kids, and sometimes you can't do that."

Apparently, Professor Fleming's very short but
intense course in Rescue Reality 101 has given the
Patrick pilots a sudden understanding that this is one
of those times when they *can't* do it. They not only
agree to stay until King 74 arrives on-scene, they say
they've recalculated bingo and can stick around for a
while. A half hour later the swap out of tankers takes
place without further discussion.

Even so, Chris Baur dials in a high frequency radio
channel he often used when he was flying for the
Coast Guard and calls Yanky 03 to respond. As they'd
arranged at the early morning briefing, the Marines are

monitoring the channel. Baur says, "We need you back out here. Now." The Marines, who are twenty minutes out of Shearwater on their way back in for fuel, roger the call and push their plane a little faster. Calling ahead, Pilot Jon Omey arranges for a hot refuel of 80,000 pounds, telling the base they'll come in to grab some box lunches and immediately turn around and head back out to sea. To Omey and his crew, *Semper Fi* is more than just a catchy rallying cry.

SIXTEEN

Aboard Jolly 14
4:00 P.M. local time (3:00 P.M. EST)

When the 106th's tanker arrives on-scene, the aircraft commander, Lieutenant Colonel Phil Rogers, urges Fleming to continue searching for just a few more hours. They'd found Alex, maybe there are others who are still alive. But in the three hours since they picked up Alex Taranov, the PaveHawks have been crisscrossing their way down the debris field without a single live sighting. Now Ed Fleming is wrestling with one of the most difficult decisions of the day: when to call it quits?

The HH-60 pilots, Fleming, Baur, Buschor, and Sengstacken, have been strapped into the seats of Igor Sikorsky's $10 million torture chamber for upward of eight hours. It's going to be at least a six-hour trip back to Shearwater, and they can't be certain of the weather.

Fleming's sciatica has been acting up for a while, causing shooting pains in his left leg. Add to that the fact that he has to relieve himself in the worst way, but his attempts to utilize the iced tea bottle he's been given are hit and miss. Chris Baur hasn't even tried to use a bottle. He just seems to have remarkable bladder control. The guys in the back have had an easier time of it, and several Ziploc bags filled with urine are stacked against the rear bulkhead near the sliding door.

Finally, reluctantly, Fleming says it's time to go. In the back, as Doc checks Alex's pulse, he wakes up. "Are there others?" he asks, pointing to himself.

"No," Doc says. "No others that we've found. A ship picked up one man, but that's all."

The news is understandably depressing, and Alex is quiet for a while. Then he asks, "Where are we going?"

"We're going to Halifax," the PJ answers.

"Is that America?"

"No, it's Canada."

Doc tucks Alex back into the sleeping bag into which he's put all the chemical heating pads he'd planned to use if they'd picked up fourteen people. Between the pads and the wool blankets and the sleeping bag, Alex should be not only warmed up, but medium rare by the time they land at Shearwater.

Although he's disappointed at not having picked up more people, Ed Fleming isn't unhappy about heading for the barn. This is the longest mission he's ever flown. The forty-seven-year-old pilot has done all eight of the air refuelings thus far, and both the physical and mental strain are beginning to show.

With one more refueling imminent, Fleming finally gives in to the messages his body's been sending. "Chris, I really need a break." He's been reluctant to have Baur handle any of the refuelings because, while the younger pilot's done them before this mission, he hasn't completed his qualification requirements yet.

Nevertheless, he thinks Baur is a very skilled pilot, "a very confident young guy."

Turning over the controls just prior to the refueling, Fleming says, "Chris, if you bend this probe, I'm going to be cussing at you all the way to the water." And then an afterthought, "Probably in Gaelic, and you're not going to like it."

While the severe turbulence they'd experienced earlier has diminished, they're still not flying in the gentle zephyrs of a warm spring day, and Fleming is paying close attention, planning on talking his copilot through the maneuver step by step. They set up for the drogue off the left wing of the unit's C-130, and as the Herc passes them to take the lead position, they can see that the basket has taken a beating, leaving only half of it intact.

Getting clearance for a wet contact, Baur moves the HH-60's probe toward the bouncing basket. On his first attempt he misses the contact point in the center of the drogue and pokes the probe between the spokes, moving much too close for comfort to the huge plane. When flying as an instructor, Fleming always has one hand near the collective, the other near the cyclic, so if it's not going the way he wants, he can quickly input the controls and at least make it recoverable. When Baur runs the probe through the basket, Fleming takes over without a fuss and backs it out of the broken spokes with a tug on the cyclic.

It's almost always easier for the pilot in the right seat to hit the basket because the probe is directly in front of him. When the copilot attempts it, he's got to adjust for the angle of view from the left seat, not a big thing, but added to the variable winds and the vortices coming off the C-130, it keeps him on his toes. Flem-

ing's had years instructing younger pilots, and he's
refined the technique to what he knows works. "A critical thing is to provide positive feedback, even if
somebody's about ready to plunge you into the side.
You don't want to get that person tense, so you're
always kind of massaging the conversation. 'Yeah,
you're looking okay, but next time I'd like you to do
this, and I want you to watch out for the three o'clock
position on the drogue [where] there's some spokes
missing. But actually, it looked real good. I want you
to ease in this time.'

"Even though what happened was borderline, you
need to project with your language a little positive
[feedback], but at the same time you need to present
the information that he needs to execute the contact."
Baur takes another run at the drogue, but misses,
requiring him to set up for a third attempt. In the rear
of the helicopter Doc Dougherty is paying rapt attention to the process. Discovering that he was in the
ocean with man-eating sharks may actually be slightly
less troubling for him to deal with than having to sit
through a dicey aerial refueling over which he has no
control. To Doc's relief, Baur tags the drogue solidly
on his third attempt, and they top off their tanks without any untoward incidents.

CFB Greenwood
2:00 P.M. (1:00 P.M. EST)

With the exception of navigator Gilles Bourgoin, who
has opted out, all the members of Rescue 306's crew
are seated in a circle in one of the squadron conference
rooms. The meeting's been called by the base psychol-

ogist to give them an opportunity to talk about the mission and how they feel about it. These sessions were instituted by the Canadian Air Force when it became apparent that their crews needed a formalized procedure to talk through highly emotional experiences.

The psychologist's primary task is to enforce the rule that no finger-pointing is allowed, as well as to make it clear that the entire session is off-the-record; nothing that's said is to leave the room. It's an opportunity to get it all off their chests. The aircraft commander, Jonathan Forrest, welcomes the process, acknowledging, "It was obvious that some of us were pretty hard affected by what happened."

What Forrest comes away with is confirmation that they did everything they could do, that they're not responsible for what happens to the people they tried to help. As the aircraft commander, he feels he has the most to gain and the most to lose on a mission like this. The fact that his crew was highly complimentary and not critical of his performance is a relief. Just the fact that the crew even thought about the difficulties faced by the pilots feels good. The debriefing is the first time Forrest and copilot Kevin Dort have a chance to speak about the frustration of not being able to see the instruments well enough to know their speed or confirm the plane's attitude. And it's the first time SARtech Andre Hotton even knew of the problem.

The crew comes to an agreement that there were conditions out at sea that were beyond their control. All of them were frustrated, because after that first successful daylight drop to the lifeboat and the radio conversation with the survivors, everything began to spiral downhill. And the next day everyone they'd spotted had disappeared. "You're emotionally drained and you're physically drained," Forrest says. "When we left, it was like you couldn't feel any lower or more helpless. You have to leave; if you don't leave, you're not gonna survive, yourself. And what have we accomplished? The lifeboat thing was very small by then, because we were leaving them. When we first happened on-scene, we've got them a radio, we have equipment to them, somebody's gonna be here. There's vessels. When we got on-scene, there was gonna be a vessel there before we left. The logical side of me said, 'No bloody way.' Obviously, the emotional side of me said, 'I sure as hell hope so.' Right?"

The bottom line on the session? "We all came out of it satisfied, not having any guilt, [knowing] that we'd done more than was required of us. That's what came out of the debriefing, realizing that it was beyond-the-call-of-duty type stuff that was happening. We did more than what was expected or asked of us. If you can't be happy with that, what can you be happy with? Basically, Mother Nature rules. That's my saying. I'll live and die by it."

Aboard Jolly 14
5:45 P.M. local time (3:45 P.M. EST)

As twilight begins to close in on the returning helicopters, the weather continues to cooperate. In the lexicon of the aviators, it had gotten soft. The wind is still blowing hard, and the seas below are still very high, but compared to what they've been through in the last twelve hours, the winds are mild and the turbulence minimal. It isn't meant to stay that way.

Flying toward the setting sun, they can see a wall of black ahead of them. Fleming says it's like traveling through Kansas, and all of a sudden you look ahead of you on the highway and it's black, and everybody fleeing toward you in the opposite lane of traffic has their lights and wipers on. They've got roughly 300 miles to Halifax, and it's suddenly become apparent that they're going to have to fight for every one of them.

This is the same storm they passed through on their way out to find the survivors, and it was the roughest flying any of them could remember. The difference is that on the way out, they were fresh. Now they've been through the ringer and are worn-out. Ed Fleming's forty-seven-year-old body is telling him loud and clear that he's playing a young man's game—and losing. He's having a difficult time hearing people talking to him on the radio. It's like a bad phone connection, only worse. Not only can't he hear very well, but he can't see the body language of the person he's trying to communicate with. At home or in an office, that may not be critical. But at the tail end of a long mission, not understanding what your flight engineer is telling you is problematic, so you have to ask him to repeat it, once, twice, maybe three times to be sure.

Aboard Jolly 08
5:47 P.M. local time (3:47 P.M. EST)

Flying in formation behind Jolly 14, Buschor watches as Fleming's ship hits a black wall of clouds and disappears. Seconds later he's in it too, bouncing all over the sky with head winds slamming into them. It's disheartening. Buschor is thinking they went all that way and only picked up one guy, now they're trying to get home and are being pummeled by the weather. He backs off from the lead ship, increases separation, and gets them dialed in on the distance measuring equipment and radar. Then he takes 08 down, trying to get out of the storm by going underneath it. Since the rotor blade deicers on Jolly 08 aren't working, down is the only safe direction for them to go. Without knowing precisely how high up the storm goes, it would be too risky to try and climb through it hoping to find clear air before the ice buildup knocks them out of the sky. Now he begins to think about what the head winds are doing to their fuel burn.

Their last refueling, the ninth, should have put enough gas in the tanks to get them back to Halifax with fuel to spare. A full load of 4,500 pounds can easily take them the final 300 miles when their burn rate is a normal 900 to 1,200 pounds an hour. But it's become apparent the words "normal" and "*Salvador Allende* mission" are destined never to occur in the same thought.

Buschor's flight engineer, John Krulder, is already dealing with the fuel situation. The last thing he wants to hear is that they've just hit a fifty-knot head wind that's knocked their ground speed down to a crawl. A few turns on his whiz wheel and Krulder knows that plans for a few cold beers with an early dinner have just been put on hold. Krulder asks the pilots, "Hey, what's the closest spit of land?"

Buschor, getting a sick feeling in the pit of his stomach because he knows why the question is being asked, says, "Saint John's."

"What the GPS there? How far out are we?"

"An hour."

Here it comes. Buschor and Sengstacken brace themselves.

"Well, guess what? We only have forty-five minutes of fuel left. Maybe fifty."

Krulder gets on the radio and contacts Rich Davin in Jolly 14, to double-check his calculations. Davin says, "Yeah, I got about the same thing." The two flight engineers contact the navigator in King 74, give him their numbers, and wait to see what he says. Moments later Major Dennis Diggett calls them back. Unfortunately, they're right. They've gone from having a half hour's worth of fuel to spare to being a half hour short of making it to Shearwater. Everyone knows what that means: they've got to plug the tanker one more time, only this one will be on night vision goggles, somewhere inside the storm—if they can find a soft spot that will work. If they can't—the word "ditch" comes quickly to mind.

Krulder is only half kidding when he hits his interphone button and starts yelling at Buschor. "This is all your fault, you little troll," a reference to Graham's diminutive stature. "You did it again. It's gonna happen again, you sonuvabitch. The only reason I'm flying with you is 'cause lightning doesn't strike twice."

Professing a confidence he doesn't really feel, Buschor says, "Don't worry. I've been here. We'll make it through this."

In the back, Mike Moore is doing his own quiet what-iffing and he doesn't like the answers he's coming up with. The reason for sending two helicopters on a mission like this is that if one gets in trouble and goes in, the other is in a position to effect a rescue.

Since Jolly 14 has working deicers, its survivability is greater than 08's. *If they can refuel.* If they can't, both HH-60s are in trouble.

Up front, Buschor begins to consider their options. Can they get to Sable Island? Can they make it to Gorilla Rig, the oil platform they passed on their way out. Then the technical problems begin racing through his head.

"Well, right now the visibility we're at is zero-zero." They can't see five feet ahead of their windshield, and they can't see anything above or below them. Buschor continues working the problem. "So the way we're gonna get to Sable Island is to progressively bring it down, bring it down, bring it down." He and Sengstacken talk about how they might do this safely, and they come up with the notion of painting the island on radar, then driving in lower and lower until they can see the shoreline and are able to land. There are no navigation aids on the island, but there's a light tower with a rotating beacon that can be helpful in clear weather, but hidden in the clouds it's nothing but a hazard for a blind helicopter. The other problem is that they're not sure they even have enough fuel to make it to Sable Island. And the oil rig is even farther away. It's time to discuss the problem with the boss.

Aboard Jolly 14
6:00 P.M. (4:00 P.M. EST)

While Jolly 08 is getting beaten up in the thin layer of air between the ever-lowering ceiling and the whitecaps below, Ed Fleming and his crew are up above, getting the living crap kicked out of them. Fleming's physical condition has continued to deteriorate. He'd had it, and he needs Chris Baur to spell him on the controls. His orders are to keep the ship at 1,000 feet. Inexplicably, Baur keeps bringing 14 down to 300 or 400 feet, causing Fleming to say, "No, I said a thousand feet," take control, bring it back up to 1,000 feet, and give it back to Baur. Moments later they're descending down to 300 feet again.

The third time it happens, Fleming is ready to go nuts. "What're you looking at?" he asks the younger pilot. Baur points to the barometric altimeter. Instantly, Fleming understands what's gone wrong. They've flown through so many different barometric pressure zones that the standard altimeter is useless. He points to the radar altimeter, saying, "Look at that. Fly on that."

Even then the altitude problem isn't resolved because the turbulence is increasingly violent, at one point knocking Baur back into his seat so hard that his helmet picks up indentations from the radio rack behind him. Holding a thousand feet proves to be impossible. Just staying between 800 and 1,200 feet above the water is difficult enough. Thoughts of Jolly 110, the helicopter that Buschor was copiloting when they ditched in a storm very similar to this one, are impossible to keep from coming to mind. Not that Fleming believes he's going to ride the HH-60 into the ocean, but he realizes that they're going to have to do some very difficult things to survive. From the moment they entered the storm he knew they might have to turn around and backtrack out of it, refueling in clearer air farther out to sea. It's something Fleming has done on several prior missions, and it's a decidedly better solution than ditching the helicopter. But it means extending the mission by hours, and they're already flying on the ragged edge of total exhaustion. None of the occasions he's backed out of a storm before came after thirteen hours of flying time.

Aboard Jolly 08

Independently of Fleming, Graham Buschor has arrived at the same solution: if they can't find a soft spot, they need to turn around and go back to where they know the air is more conducive to refueling. The fact that they've been in the soup for forty minutes and are now about sixty miles into the storm doesn't bother him because if they turn around, the fifty-knot head wind that they're presently fighting will turn into a fifty-knot tailwind that will shoot them out of the storm like a rocket. There's one thing about which Buschor is certain: it doesn't matter how many hours he has to fly, it doesn't matter if they have to go to Virginia to get around the storm. He's not going into the water again.

Aboard Jolly 14

Until they hit this storm Ed Fleming has been adamant that the two helicopters stay together. He has serious concerns that if they get too far apart in this weather, they'll never find each other again. But without working deicers, Jolly 08 can't climb through the clouds, joining 14 in the search for clear air in which to refuel. Even though *their* deicers are operating well, no one in Fleming's helo knows how high the storm clouds go, how high they'll have to go to get out of them.

For Rich Davin the pucker factor has kicked in big-time. His mind is going a million miles an hour, trying to remember from past experiences the way this kind of situation has been handled. The only good news is that they're not in immediate need of fuel. They just know they can't make it to land without refueling one more time. The bad news list is a lot longer. Not only are the two helicopters no longer near each other, their unit's C-130, King 74, isn't able to keep them in sight. The Herc crew is tracking the HH-60s on radar, but they're all acutely aware that if something untoward were to occur, the PJs, rafts, RAMZ package, and other life support gear on the plane will be a long time coming. That falls into the what-if category, and in the scheme of things is not an immediate concern.

The question of the moment is, "Where?" Where will they find air clear enough to make refueling on night vision goggles possible? After fourteen hours of flying, gassing up on NVGs is not an exercise any of them are looking forward to, but it's a lot better than the alternative.

Just as all four of Jolly 14's crew are throwing their two cents into the mix, the bad news list gets a bit longer. King 74 calls to say they've been climbing to see how high up the storm goes, and they're passing through 12,000 feet and still in it. Absolute maximum altitude for the HH-60s is 13,000 feet, and at that height they're supposed to be on supplemental oxygen. Going above the storm is clearly not an option. Their only hope now is that King 74 or the Marines who've come back out in Yanky 03 find a hole inside the storm, or that they punch through the other side of it into clear air.

While each of them is concerned, no one is really

talking about it. For years Fleming's picked up on the fact that when things in an aircraft are going well, and it's quiet, the crew is able to discuss anything—personal or professional. But when they're "really in the garbage, you're just working. Nobody is going, 'Jeez, I'm really worried about this or that.' You're working." It doesn't mean you're not concerned, it's just not something you discuss *while you're in it*. Truth be told, Fleming is having serious concerns. "It's not driving a car down the road. And if a gearbox goes on a helicopter and you're out over the ocean at night, there's no survivability. It's going to be very, very difficult. Some people might survive, but you're going to lose people." Ditching in the ocean is constantly on his mind. In the back, Doc is thinking about the temperature of the water beneath them. They've long since departed the area of the Gulf Stream and the warm water he fished Alex out of. If they go in now, their chances of survival would not be good.

Ditching in the ocean is something Ed Fleming's thought about even before the accident with Jolly 110 made the procedure a reality for everyone in the 106th. "You always 'what if?' What's going to happen if you lose a tail rotor gearbox? If you lose control and you end up corkscrewing yourself into the water? How do you get out of something that corkscrews itself into the water in thirty-foot seas?"

Fleming's reverie is interrupted by the first bit of really good news they've had in a while. Jon Omey has flown Yanky 03 ahead of the Jollys, doing a weather recon. The Marines report that there's just about another 100 miles of storm to go through, and then they'll be in the clear all the way back to Shearwater. On the heels of that report, King 74 calls to say they've found a clear spot at about 5,000 feet that's large enough for them to refuel in.

Now the problem is getting up there without picking up a heavy load of ice. It's something over which they have no control. They have to go up to refuel. If they stay below the clouds, they're going to run out of gas. If they go up, they might get into real trouble with the ice, but they also might make it, in which case their problems are almost over.

Fortunately, the latter is the case. Both helicopters get up through the storm without serious icing, and they're both able to rendezvous with the tanker. Next step is to prepare for refueling using NVGs, something none of the pilots is looking forward to. Normally they configure for NVG refueling while they're still on the ground. Now they have to spend the next fifteen minutes getting ready. The goggles need to be focused, caps removed, and then mounted on their flight helmets. The lights inside the HH-60s have to be reconfigured because even the slightest amount of light in the cockpit will diminish the effectiveness of the goggles. Thankfully, after all this technological foreplay, the refueling of the two helicopters comes off without a hitch—or a ditch.

The flight back to Shearwater from that point on is almost anticlimactic. Both Jollys go back down beneath the cloud deck and head in. Their first indication that they've almost made it are the lights of Halifax masked by haze and fog. Then they can begin to see through it, picking out the silhouettes of buildings, and finally they cross over the beach.

In the rear of Jolly 14, Doc is telling Alex that there's a huge crowd of reporters and television cameras waiting for him. Communicating with the

Russian-speaking sailor is difficult, but Doc knows the message has gotten across when Alex suddenly seems to panic. "But I'm naked!"

Choking back laughter, Doc tells him not to worry, since he won't be getting out of the sleeping bag. There's no way he'll be allowed to walk. "You're going to be in the sleeping bag when we put you on a stretcher, then we're going to put you right into an ambulance and take you to the hospital."

Alex asks if someone has called his wife to tell her that he's been saved, and then suddenly he begins to cry. The realization was sinking in that his friends were lost, including Sergey, whom he'd known for eighteen years. It's a realization that both helicopter crews are experiencing in their own way, at the same time. They went out to save twenty-eight people. They came back with one. "Bittersweet" is too clichéd to describe what they're feeling.

CFB Shearwater
8:40 P.M. local time (7:40 P.M. EST)

Both helicopters touch down on the runway and begin to taxi toward the operations building. Over the radio, Jolly 08 is told to turn off and park near one of the hangars, while the other helicopter, carrying the survivor, is led right up onto the tarmac in front of the media horde. Fleming is too tired to recognize and do something about the injustice of splitting them up in the last moments of the mission. Buschor and his crew are irate, but there's no timely way to correct the situation. So Jolly 08 pulls up to a hangar, the engines are shut down, and the crew virtually falls out onto the ramp. The moment requires a conscious decision for the pilots: do they lie down on the ground and try and work out the kinks that have taken root over the last 15.2 hours? Or do they run to the rest room and relieve themselves?

In front of the waiting media, the Jolly 14 crew is going to be faced with pretty much the same decision. Doc Dougherty is as anxious as the others to use the facilities, but the rule is that he can't surrender his patient to anyone less medically qualified than he is. In this case it means only a medical doctor will do. An ordinary ambulance attendant doesn't come close. Doc begins searching for the doctor he's told would be there, completely overlooking the short, blond-haired woman who has wheeled the gurney up to the door of the helicopter. Not seeing a doctor, Dougherty is thinking that he's going to have to ride the ambulance to the hospital with Alex, a trip he'd just as soon skip. Wondering aloud where the doctor is, Doc asks the woman, "Who are you?" In what Rich Davin describes as their "brain dead" condition, he's completely missed the fact that she's wearing a bright yellow vest with fluorescent red lettering that says DOCTOR. Quickly, he briefs her on Alex's condition, reading off his vital signs, which he'd written on the helicopter's window in grease pencil.

Davin, meantime, is dealing with a problem of another sort. They'd neatly stacked the plastic bags filled with urine against the door. When it opened, the bags fall onto the concrete just as the rotor blades stop turning and the swarm of media people come running up to the aircraft. "What's that?" one observant journalist asks, pointing to the bags of yellow fluid.

Thinking quickly, Davin says, "Hydraulic fluid."

"I thought hydraulic fluid was red," the journalist responds.

"This is *used* hydraulic fluid," the flight engineer knowingly says.

As Alex is transferred to the gurney—in his sleeping bag—Davin notices that neither of the two pilots has moved. Then, slowly, Chris Baur begins to climb out the left door. Ed Fleming doesn't move until Lieutenant Colonel John Flanagan from the 106th comes up and helps him out, then supports him while he tries to straighten up. Looking around at the onrushing throng, Fleming has only one thing on his mind: where's the bathroom? Baur and Davin are already ahead of him. As dozens of strobe lights flash in their faces, Doc Dougherty helps roll Alex to the waiting ambulance. When he puts him inside, Alex grabs Doc's hand and holds it. There are tears in Alex's eyes. Thanks to CNN, it's a shot seen 'round the world.

Rocky Point, Long Island
7:40 P.M. EST

True to her word, Barbara Dougherty has continued the household routine during the *Salvador Allende* mission, carrying on as though nothing unusual was happening. With four kids who are only seven, five, four and two, it's best not to alter the bedtime routine, so she doesn't. That is until the phone rings and an excited voice shouts, "Quick, put on CNN." She slams the phone down and rushes to the television, flipping through the channels until the CNN logo pops up in the corner of the screen, with the added line LIVE FROM SHEARWATER, NOVA SCOTIA. There, with a smile on his face, is her husband, James "Doc" Dougherty, shaking hands with a portly man lying on a gurney, wearing a Canadian Air Force wool toque on his head. She watches Doc help slide the gurney into the waiting ambulance, and the picture cuts back to the CNN studios. There's not much drama in video of a PJ racing to the rest room.

As soon as the kids are in bed, Barbara hits the phone. There are parents and in-laws to call in Florida, siblings in Colorado, other PJs' wives nearby. The calm, cool, in-control demeanor has vanished. This mission was a real one. She won't remember the missed vasectomy appointment for at least two days.

At the Halifax Holiday Inn
Much, much later that same night

After peeling off their mustang suits, showering, and calling home, the helicopter crews find their way to the hotel bar. They're looking for the Marines, who have somehow managed to get driven to the wrong Holiday Inn. True to their motto of *Semper Fidelis*— Always Faithful—they determine where the helicopter flight crews are and waste no time getting there. There's a rumor going around that the helicopter guys are buying.

And finally . . .

Alex Taranov is taken to Dartmouth General Hospital, where he spends two days in intensive care, then another twelve days recovering from his ordeal. At first he suffers from constant dizziness, is unable to maintain his balance, and has double vision. Nevertheless, he asks for help writing a letter of thanks to Doc Dougherty. He dictates it in Russian.

My dear kind James!

I am struggling to find the words to express my gratitude for your brave, selfless actions, risking your own life to save mine. It is very difficult to say what I feel.

I must tell you first of all that you did not only save my life, you also saved my wife, Larisa, and my daughters, Lena and Ludmilla. Without your courage, they would be alone, a widow and two orphans.

For the rest of my life, I shall always feel a bond of kinship with you, akin to what one feels for one's parents or one's own family.

I was so disappointed that you were unable to make a return trip to Halifax so that I could offer my thanks in person. Had you done so, then the moment you landed, I would have filled your helicopter with fresh flowers!

I salute your bravery and your generosity, and I earnestly hope that I have conveyed at least some of the inexpressible gratitude I shall always feel for you.

Sincerely,
Alexander Taranov

Ten days after he arrived in the hospital, Alex wakes up to discover that normal vision has returned and he's able to walk unaided. Although his doctors think it best that he remains hospitalized, Alex wants to be home in the Ukraine in time for Christmas, so on December 22 he's discharged, and flies to Newark

International aboard an Air Nova jet, looking more like a businessman in his new dark suit, white shirt, and tie, than a shipwreck survivor. Quickly processing through U.S. Immigration at Newark Airport, Alex emerges into the arrival area to see a slender young man in an Air Force uniform waiting. "I just take a look at the label on his uniform—it has name 'Jim.' I asked him, 'Are you James Dougherty?' He says, 'Yes.' " At that, Alex drops his suitcase, grabs Doc in a bear hug, and lifts him off the ground, turning around and around and around with absolute joy. Moments later he's introduced to Rich Davin and Chris Baur, as well as half a dozen other support people from the 106th. Ed Fleming, unfortunately, was unable to be there. Alex is also overjoyed to see Victor Maydan, a BLASCO superintendent with whom he'd worked years before and who was responsible for his promotion from motorman to marine engineer. The company had sent Maydan to the U.S. to accompany Alex home.

After two days of debriefing by Ukrainian authorities interspersed with several good meals accompanied by "a couple shots of vodka—for my health," Alex flies back to Odessa. His wife and oldest daughter are waiting for him at the airport. As soon as he sees them, he triumphantly shouts in Russian, "I've won my war with the ocean."

EPILOGUE

The search for survivors of the M/V *Salvador Allende* continued until Wednesday morning, December 14, approximately three and a half days after Alex Taranov was located. No additional survivors were found. Lieutenant Bill Kelly and the others working the case on Governors Island looked at weather, water temperature, survival curves (length of time in water against water temperature and what PIWs were wearing), on-scene reports including shark predation, and the debriefing of the two survivors, before reaching a consensus to halt the operation, always an emotion-laden decision. Their recommendation is passed up the chain of command, and the actual decision to suspend the search is made by the vice admiral. Kelly was spared the onerous task of notifying next of kin in this case; it was handled by the Ukrainian Consulate. By the time the Atlantic Command Center called off the search and rescue operation, forty merchant ships from nineteen different countries had responded to the AMVER summons, making it the largest rescue effort in the history of the mutual aid pact.

Alexander Taranov received permission to remain in the United States for three years following the commencement of legal proceedings in New York and Houston. Vowing never again to go to sea, he spent three years in Texas as a ship mechanic—but only on ships tied firmly to the dock. His wife and two daughters joined him in Houston, but though the children adjusted well, his wife had difficulty learning English and missed her family. After a year they returned to the Ukraine. In 1999, Alex received $20,962.62 in a settlement. The visa obtained for him by his lawyers permitted him to stay and work in the U.S. for three years. But a year later he decided to return to Ukraine, and abandoning his plans to open an auto repair garage, he enrolled in three months of special education and training classes at the Odessa Marine Academy. With his Marine Officer papers current, he returned to sea as second engineer on the M/V *Sundance II,* a 750-foot Greek-owned bulk carrier.

Lieutenant Colonel Ed Fleming retired in 1999 as a full colonel from his post as Vice Commander of the 109th Airlift Wing of the New York Air National Guard. The unit, based at Stratton Field near Schenectady, flies both traditional landing gear as well as ski-equipped C-130s on missions in support of U.S. scientists working in the Arctic and Antarctic. Colonel Fleming was the principal consultant to the National Science Foundation when the need arose to send medical equipment and medicine to a woman doctor near the South Pole who had discovered a lump in her breast but was unable to be evacuated during the Antarctic winter, when temperatures were 85 degrees below zero Centigrade. When she finally was brought out, it was on one of Ed Fleming's airplanes. Fleming completed his dissertation, titled "Human Factors Error in a Cue and Symbol Saturated Environment," and has been awarded a Ph.D. from Walden University.

Captain Graham Buschor has been promoted to major, and continues to be a full-time HH-60 pilot with the 106th. He's also been designated the unit's safety officer, and has been sent as far away as Alaska to investigate helicopter accidents. Buschor's sense of humor remains delightfully intact.

James "Doc" Dougherty continues as a part-time PJ and full-time correctional officer. Alex has visited Doc at home several times, always bringing a supply of vodka and tomatoes—sort of a two-handed Ukrainian Bloody Mary. Doc talks regularly with Alex, who has never missed sending a birthday card to the man who saved his life.

Mike Moore took early retirement from his job as Director of Emergency Medical Services at Fort Monmouth, New Jersey, in order to devote full time to his first love, being a pararescue jumper. He's still cooking on unit deployments, and annoying Graham Buschor at every opportunity.

Rich Davin remains a flight engineer with the 106th. He and PJ **Tim Malloy** have started a business manufacturing and selling safety kits for boaters, jet skiers, sailors, and others to wear while they're on the water. The kits include a signaling mirror, chemical light, whistle, and colored balloons to help rescuers find the wearer should he be lost at sea, day or night. They're also developing a lightweight pack containing an inflatable life preserver. (For more information: *www.surviveit.com*)

John Krulder remains an HH-60 flight engineer with the 106th whose enthusiasm, according to one of the unit's veteran pilots, "is still unmatched by any other crew member at the 106th—or anywhere else."

Captain Chris Baur was promoted to major, and with the help of Ed Fleming, was assigned to C-130 pilot school. He now flies fixed wing aircraft for the 106th and continues to fly passenger jets for Continental Airlines. After leaving the U.S. Customs Service, he and a friend started their own private investigation agency, which they continue to operate part-time.

Major Gene Sengstacken continues to fly HH-60s for the 106th and helicopters for the Suffolk County Police Department.

Colonel David Hill has retired from the Air National Guard.

Lieutenant Colonel Robert Landsiedel still commands the 102nd Rescue Squadron of the New York Air National Guard.

Lieutenant Bill Kelly is now a U.S. Coast Guard lieutenant commander, based in Boston. He's the only member of the RCC New York team that worked the *Salvador Allende* rescue still in the Coast Guard.

Jonathan Forrest left the Canadian Air Force a year after the *Salvador Allende* rescue mission. He now flies passenger aircraft for Air Nova, a division of Air Canada. He was elected chairman of the local pilots union at the most difficult time in the history of Canadian commercial aviation: during the merger of the two mainline Canadian carriers, as well as a separate merger of the five regional carriers. He and his wife Michelle have two daughters. They still live near Peggy's Cove, Nova Scotia.

Captain Kevin Dort is now an aircraft commander, still flying C-130 rescue missions with the 413th Transport and Rescue Squadron, 14 Wing, CFB Greenwood, Nova Scotia.

SARtech Team Leader Sergeant Ron O'Reilly lives on Vancouver Island, where he's assigned to 19 Wing Comox and flies rescue missions over the northern Pacific Ocean as well as northwestern Canada. He's president of the Para Rescue Association of Canada.

Sergeant Andre Hotton is still a SARtech with the 413th Transport and Rescue Squadron, 14 Wing, CFB Greenwood, Nova Scotia, and has been promoted to team leader.

Captain Gilles Bourgoin, the navigator on Rescue 306, is now an air controller stationed at the RCC in Victoria, British Columbia, on Vancouver Island.

Captain Jon Omey left the Marines because he wanted to spend more time with his family at their home in Reno, rather than commuting to Marine Reserve air bases in New York and Texas. He now lives in Reno full-time, where he flies jets for Federal Express. He's also joined the Nevada Air National Guard and is flying C-130 aircraft older than he is.

The helicopter flight crews were honored for setting distance and endurance records in the HH-60, and received the American Helicopter Society's Captain William H. Kossler Award for Bravery. Although the 106th Rescue Wing received congratulatory calls and messages from the Secretary of the Air Force as well as from higher headquarters, none of the helicopter crew members who literally put their lives on the line has been recognized with an adequate award for heroism. A meritorious service medal they each received at a public ceremony at Suffolk, from the Director of the Air National Guard, Major General Donald Sheppard, was rescinded in the expectation of them receiving a higher honor. It never happened. Lieutenant Colonel Ed Fleming attempted to put the crews of Jolly 14 and Jolly 08 in for the Distinguished Flying Cross, the Air Force's highest honor for heroism that can be awarded in peacetime, but it fell through the bureaucratic cracks. The DFC would have made a significant difference for Dougherty, Davin, Moore, Krulder and their families, since noncommissioned officers who receive it can also be given a fifteen percent increase in their pension upon retirement. Both Jolly crews did receive the New York State Medal for Valor, the state's highest award, and in 1996, Dougherty was awarded the first Air National Guard Medal for Heroism at a ceremony in Washington, D.C.

Despite unofficial recommendations from the noncommissioned officers who flew aboard Rescue 306, the Canadian Air Force never recognized with an appropriate award the skill, bravery, and beyond-the-call-of-duty dedication of the aircraft commander, Captain Jonathan Forrest, and his copilot, Captain Kevin Dort.

GLOSSARY

AC—Aircraft commander. The pilot. In a C-130 the AC is in the left seat. In an HH-60 the AC is in the right seat.

ACC—Atlantic Command Center, also referred to as RCC New York.

AMVER—The Automated Mutual assistance Vessel Rescue program. A voluntary association of military and civilian ships ranging from tugboats to supertankers, operated by the U.S. Coast Guard. When an AMVER ship sails, it files its float plan with the AMVER computer. If a mayday occurs, the RCC can query the computer and determine what ships are within 50, 100, or 200 miles of the stricken vessel.

AOR—area of responsibility. The western North Atlantic is divided into a Canadian and a U.S. area of responsibility.

ballast—in the *Salvador Allende*, seawater taken into the bow bulb and other tanks that could be shifted front to back and back to front in order to level the ship after cargo has been loaded.

C-130—Lockheed-built four-engine turboprop cargo aircraft that has been used by military forces all over the world in a variety of configurations since the late 1950s. The C-130s used by the 106th have an internal fuel tank in the cargo hold which can be removed. The U.S. Marine Corps version flown on this mission is the KC-130, primarily a refueling tanker.

C-140P—Canadian Air Force designation for the Aurora; similar to the U.S. Navy P-3 Orion. Aircraft designed to fly for up to sixteen hours, originally used to locate enemy submarines underwater.

call sign—designation of a specific ship or aircraft for use in radio communications. The *Salvador Allende* was UWAG. The Marine refueler was Yanky 03. All U.S. Air Force rescue-configured C-130s are designated "King" plus a number. While actually on a rescue mission, the radio designation in both the U.S. and Canadian Air Forces temporarily changes to "Rescue" plus a number.

CAMSLANT—Communications Area Master Station Atlantic. The military radio station in Alexandria, Virginia, through which radio transmissions from military aircraft were relayed to RCC New York.

CASP—Computer Assisted Search Program. Computer program that tells RCC personnel which way a certain type of object will drift and how fast it will move, in a specific area of the ocean. The information is useful until they can get an SLDMB inserted, which will then provide real-time data rather than computer-projected positions based on data gathered through past research. Both the American and Canadian RCCs have this type of program.

CBC—Canadian Broadcasting Corporation.

CFB—Canadian Forces Base, as in CFB Greenwood.

dry suit—A type of full body suit, including boots and gloves, worn in extremely cold water. Several layers of specialized fabric insulate the diver, without allowing water inside the suit. A good dry suit can cost upward of $2,000, compared to $200 for a wet suit.

E-City—Elizabeth City, North Carolina. U.S. Coast Guard Air Station where C-130 SAR aircraft are based.

ELT—Emergency Locator Transmitter. Device aboard airplanes that sends out a radio signal when triggered. ELTs can be triggered manually or by a sudden deceleration, as in a crash. They can also be triggered by a hard landing in a small plane, resulting in a false alarm being transmitted.

EPIRB or **121.5 MHz Beacon**—Emergency Position Indicating Radio Beacon. A device that, when triggered, transmits its position to passing aircraft or satellites. EPIRBs can be manually triggered or set to begin transmitting if immersed in water, as when a ship sinks. The EPIRB will float free of the ship and automatically begin transmitting its location.

FLIR—Forward Looking Infrared Radar.

HH-60—Sikorsky helicopter designated PaveHawk by the U.S. Air Force. Originally built as a transport for the Army, the helicopter has gone through various permutations in the Air Force, the last couple being the addition of internal fuel tanks and an air-refueling capability through a probe mounted on the right front of the aircraft.

Hercules—The C-130 aircraft built by Lockheed.

INMARSAT—Begun in 1982 primarily to provide communication for commercial, distress, and safety applications for ships at sea, the name is an acronym for International Maritime Satellite Organization. Most vessels have an INMARSAT number, which can be accessed through the civilian telephone system in most countries.

Jolly—Radio designation for the HH-60G helicopter flown by the 106th.

Jolly Green Giant—Nickname for the H-3 helicopter used for rescue during the Vietnam War.

knot—unit of speed equal to one nautical mile per hour, equivalent to 1.15 statute miles per hour.

lat/long—abbreviation for latitude and longitude.

mayday—(from the French *m'aidez*) the international distress signal used by ships and aircraft.

M/V—Merchant Vessel, as in M/V *Salvador Allende*.

Met office—Meteorology office at an air base.

nautical mile—unit of distance equivalent to 1.15 statute miles. Ten nautical miles = 11.5 statute miles.

nav—shorthand for "navigator" onboard an aircraft.

NVG—Night Vision Goggles. Light intensification system used by SAR personnel on U.S. and Canadian aircraft for night searches. With NVGs, a dim flashlight can be seen ten miles away.

OSC—on-scene commander. Preferably, a Coast Guard cutter, but in the early days of this mission, duties were assigned to an aircraft in the search area.

PaveHawk—Air Force designation of the HH-60G helicopter flown by the 106th.

PIW—Persons in the water.

PJ—U.S. Air Force Pararescue Jumper. PJs are trained in all aspects of search and rescue, are capable of performing minor surgery, and are fully combat trained. They're trained to operate in all types of environments, from the Arctic to underwater.

POB—Persons onboard.

port—the left side of a ship when facing the bow.

RCC—Rescue Coordination Center.

RCC New York—Rescue Coordination Center located on Governors Island in New York Harbor. Also referred to as ACC—the Atlantic Command Center.

rogue wave—Gargantuan, freak wave, often more than 100 feet from bottom of the trough to top of the crest, characterized by a steep forward face preceded and followed by a deep trough, often described by mariners who survive the encounter as "holes in the sea." For years it had been thought that rogue waves were the result of a confluence of wave crests, a kind of 2+2=10 situation. However, the latest theory advanced by applied mathematicians and oceanographers, is that ocean currents or large fields of random eddies and vortices can sporadically concentrate a steady ocean swell to create unusually large waves, even in a relatively calm sea. The likelihood of a rogue or freak wave occurring is even greater when the direction of travel of ordinary waves is in opposition to a significant current, such as the Gulf Stream, or the Agulhas Current, which flows southward along the eastern side of South Africa and routinely runs into storm waves surging north up from Antarctica. Yet another factor in the formation of these waves has to do with seabed topography. The African continental shelf is shaped in such a way that it funnels the Agulhas

Current directly into the storm waves, resulting in immense, steep-fronted waves. RCC Halifax has an astonishing infrared videotape taken from a search plane that shows a rogue wave slamming head-on into a huge tanker, forcing her bow down. By the time the wave completely passes by, the ship has vanished.

SAR—search and rescue.

SARtech—Canadian Air Force sergeant whose specialty throughout his career is search and rescue.

SKAD—survival kit air droppable or deployable. The Canadian SAR standard SKAD has four bundles, connected to each other by 280 feet of floating yellow polypropylene line. The end bundles are ten-man life rafts; the center bundles contain medical equipment, clothing and blankets, a radio, and other useful supplies.

SLAR—Side Looking Aperture Radar found on Coast Guard C-130 SAR planes.

SLDMB—Self-Locating Datum Marker Buoy. A cylindrical device about three feet tall which is dropped from SAR aircraft near a life raft, lifeboat, or stricken ship. It drifts along with the object in the water, and continually transmits its position to passing satellites. Another type of marker buoy transmits a radio signal that can be picked up by aircraft in the area but not by satellites. Some SLDMBs also transmit the water temperature. By tracking the position of the buoy with each new satellite pass,

RCCs can determine which way the current and wind in an area will move wreckage, lifeboats, or survivors.

starboard—the right side of a ship when facing the bow.

Stokes litter—wire basket with a frame contoured to give support to the occupant and to keep the frame between the patient and objects that could cause injury. Once a patient is properly placed on a Stokes litter, he can be hoisted into the helicopter, treated while en route to a hospital, and taken to the EM without transferring him from the original litter.

TACAN—transmitter/receiver device on an aircraft that allows another aircraft to see a digital readout indicating the distance separating the two. In the *Salvador Allende* rescue, both helicopters programmed TACAN codes so they could instantly tell how far apart they were, even in zero visibility.

UMIB—Urgent Marine Information Bulletin. Type of broadcast originated at an RCC which is sent on radio frequencies generally monitored by all ships at sea. Typically, it's an announcement of a mayday, its location, and a request for assistance.

UTC—see "Zulu."

wet suit—neoprene suit worn by divers that traps a layer of water between the skin and the inside of the suit. The water is warmed to body temperature, and helps keep the diver warm. There is an initial shock between the time a diver jumps into ice cold water and the time the water inside the suit warms up.

Zodiac—brand name (which has almost become generic, like Kleenex) of a type of inflatable boat that has extraordinary stability due, in part, to a very low center of gravity. The Zodiac used by PJs can be folded into a box suitable for deployment into the ocean by parachute, inflated from a CO_2 tank, with a 35 HP outboard motor attached. The tough job is being the PJ who has to crank the starter cord a dozen or so times to clear the water from the engine.

Zulu (short for "Zulu time")—used in the military and in navigation generally as a term for Universal Coordinated Time (UCT), sometimes called Universal Time Coordinated (UTC) or Coordinated Universal Time (but abbreviated UTC), and formerly called Greenwich Mean Time. In military shorthand the letter Z follows a time expressed in Greenwich Time, as in 0730Z. Greenwich Time, now called Universal Coordinated Time, is the time at longitude 0 degrees 0 minutes—the prime meridian or longitudinal line that separates East from West in the world geographical coordinate system. This line of longitude is based on the location of the British Naval Observatory in Greenwich, England, near London. "Zulu" is the radio transmission articulation for the letter Z. The highly technical, official U.S. government definition of UTC can be found at: *http://www.its.bldrdoc.gov/fs-1037/dir-009/_1277.htm*

In the *Salvador Allende* rescue, in order for the New York RCC, Halifax RCC, and a ship in the mid-Atlantic to avoid confusion about the time a ship might arrive at a particular location, they quoted it in Zulu time. Each location could then extrapolate what that meant in their own time zone. Midnight—0000 hours Zulu, was 7:00 P.M. EST in New York and 8:00 P.M. in Halifax; 0500Z is midnight in New York and 1:00 A.M. in Halifax.

HER NAME, TITANIC
The Untold Story of the Sinking and Finding of the Unsinkable Ship
by Charles Pellegrino

On the evening of April 14, 1912, the awesome ocean liner *Titanic* struck an iceberg and vanished into the sea.

Seventy-three years later, a dedicated group of scientists set sail in search of the sunken behemoth—an incredible mission that uncovered shocking secrets buried two miles below the ocean's surface.

Author Charles Pellegrino combines two enthralling modern adventures in one— re-creating the terrible night the *Titanic* went down as well as providing a first-hand account of the remarkable expedition that found her final resting place.

0-380-70892-2/$6.50 US/$8.50 Can